SONG
for an
UNSUNG HERO

SONG

for an

UNSUNG HERO

BY ERIK LUND

Song for an Unsung Hero

Library of Congress Control Number: 2009900830
ISBN: 978-0-615-27447-8

Printed in the United States by J.S. McCarthy Printers,
Augusta, Maine, using Certified Wind Power.

For

Ben, Ted and Kristin

and for

Theia and Cosmo

TABLE OF

CONTENTS

INTRODUCTION

The legal right for woman to record her opinion wherever opinions count is the tool for whose ownership we ask.... Let woman's sphere be bound only by her capacity.... I believe the world grows better because I believe in the eternal order there is always a movement, swift or slow, toward what is right and just.

> —Lucy Stone (1818-1893), abolitionist and orator, founder of the *Woman's Journal*, the foremost women's suffrage publication of its era

DIANE LUND WAS A WOMAN WHOSE FUNDAMENTAL BELIEFS were informed by what is right and just. A very private person, she didn't allow her own reticence to interfere with that pursuit. In a time before discrimination against women presented a legal issue, she was one of the forerunners who presented the face of woman and the case for equality for women. Her life and her work, for legislation, for fairness, in academia and the governing body of law for the legal profession, served to move our society toward where it is today.

Today it's hard to recall the extent to which discrimination against women in education, opportunity, professions and employment existed in the United States of the 1950s as a part of the fabric of our society. There were no constraints against discrimination because of sex. Public school teachers who married at a time when they were fertile could be dismissed at will. Women employees who became pregnant could be fired because they were pregnant, regardless of their talents, experience and achievements, without legal recourse. Male-dominated unions didn't include protection of women's interests in their collective bargaining agendas. For that matter, there were very few women in the trades at all because they'd been denied access to the vocational education and training that was critical to employment in industry.

A decade earlier, during World War II, a significant number of women had received that training and education because of a shortage of men in the workforce – they were away fighting for our country. The experience raised many women's consciousness to understand that they were as adept and as skilled in the trades as men were. Rosie the Riveter had performed a man's job in fabricating planes, tanks and warships. In the absence of men away on the front lines of war, women had filled their roles in industry with no noticeable loss of talent or commercial production.

But when the war was over and the men came home, the women were discharged from their jobs – men's jobs – and were expected to return to their proper sphere, procreation, tending the home fires, keeping house for the men and raising their children. By and large they did so, but not without reservations, and not without a clear understanding that they were as capable of performing physically difficult and intellectually challenging tasks in industry and management as men were. This fact was, however, irrelevant. Men believed – and it was generally accepted among both men and women – that the household role was the appropriate one to which women should be consigned.

In a real sense women were raised in bondage to this concept. To challenge it, to go beyond its bounds, was not acceptable. To seek to be equal was too aggressive and raised darker suspicions as well.

But while women discharged from their wartime jobs acceded to society's pressures to conform to the norm yet again, many of their daughters did not. Raised on their mothers' stories of accomplishment during the war years, daughters began to form a new wave of feminism, a generation sure of itself, its skills and its capacity to meet the standards of performance required of anyone, male or female, in the vocations, the professions and the arts. This generation would change the public perception of women's roles.

Many women were instrumental in causing this massive shift in our culture. Some were highly visible and outspoken. They were the stars, the spokeswomen who ignited public debate and controversy over women's roles, but they couldn't have succeeded in their quest without the quiet ones who proved them right and succeeded themselves, both in changing the law to bring equality for women and in demonstrating that women were worthy of the change.

They were the unsung heroes.

Diane Lund was one of those heroes, an important figure in the development of laws mandating equal status for young women students in the public schools and prohibiting discrimination against women in the workplace. Women who became masons, carpenters, electricians, plumbers, welders, mechanics, machinists and steelworkers are in her debt. She blazed important trails for women in the academic and legal world, becoming the first woman professor on the regular law school faculties of Northeastern University, and then Harvard, and the first woman chair of the Massachusetts Board of Bar Overseers, the governing board for lawyers.

She didn't come to Harvard's faculty for reasons of status, prestige or power – those concepts were alien to who she was – but because it was important that women, and women law students in particular, see that a woman not only could succeed but could be accepted at the highest level of male-dominated academia. Once there, her advocacy caused the ranks of women admitted to its law school to swell, and qualified women to be appointed to its faculty.

As a member and chair of public committees and boards Diane persuasively presented women's perspectives and personified women in their new assumption of positions of authority and respect. She was the first woman to chair the state's Board of Bar Overseers, the governing body for all lawyers, and, as a member of its Judicial Nominating Commission, was instrumental in the appointment of the first wave of women judges in Massachusetts.

She was never satisfied – or able – to accept unfairness in any of its forms. She was a welcome sight to panhandlers because she always had a pocketful of loose dollar bills.

She believed there was nothing she could not do and nothing that *women* could not do.

In the 1976 bicentennial year, she and her eleven-year-old daughter Kristin marched with other members of N.O.W. in the Patriots' Day parade in Lexington, singing the anthem exploited women millworkers had sung as they walked out on strike from the Lowell mills in 1878:

As we come marching, marching, we bring the greater days,
For the rising of the women means the rising of the race.
No more the drudge and idler – ten that toil where one reposes,
But a sharing of life's glories … bread and roses, bread and roses.

The message wasn't mere symbolism. In Diane's view, a sharing was not only logical but critical to a fair organization of society. Why should exigency be the trigger to participating in life's glories? Why shouldn't women be allowed to apply their varied talents to the greater good and still tend to the needs of their families and children? Why not a sharing? Why not bread and roses?

There was a price to be paid for the way she lived her life, and she paid it. The lessons learned at Harvard were hard, as were other lessons in discrimination learned both earlier and later on. She absorbed those lessons in private, without complaint. Nonetheless she persisted, and persisted with grace.

Most people have to confront the ordinary tasks of life – making a living, raising children, putting food on the table. What distinguishes a few is that they rise above everyday ordinariness and are not consumed by it. They keep their ideals, their desires and their vision, and act upon them. They put themselves personally on the line and leave behind a legacy for others.

Diane Lund was one of those people.

There are lessons to be learned from an examination of her life, even as the pendulum swings back against women. The divergent views in our culture about women's role in it not only haven't gone away, they appear to have engendered increasingly bitter and emotional debates. The forces at work are complex and the experiences of an important figure in the battles which brought women to their present state of legal equality need to be understood.

This book describes Diane Lund's life from a unique and personal perspective, because I was her husband, lover and best friend, and the portrait of her life wouldn't be complete without an understanding of the relationship we had. The book, however, is intended to be more than a memoir. I set about this work with great seriousness, both because of the extraordinary person she was and because of the importance of the issues she confronted. Many aspects of her life were separate from our life together, and I had only a surface knowledge of them at the time. I've researched contemporaneous material and interviewed countless people who shared those other areas of her life and who, like me, thought of her as their best friend. In the process, I learned a great deal about the woman I loved, aspects of her that I never knew. I am enormously grateful to the many people who have helped me because, in the end, this book is a love story.

Erik Lund, 2009

PROLOGUE

I SANG TO DIANE AS SHE LAY DYING, MUCH TOO SOON, THE SONGS I once had sung to woo her. She was barely twenty in that long-ago time, with sparkling eyes, an upturned nose, a sudden unexpected bounce in her walk when she was happy, quiet when she was not. Through our whole life together, a life now about to end, she'd heard me play this same guitar, stopping what she was doing to listen to the song and smile….

> … for I have loved you so long,
> Delighting in thy company.
> Greensleeves was all my joy …
> And who but my Lady Greensleeves?

Did she hear me now?

She was quiet, her breathing slowly subsiding as she rested on the rented hospital bed in our home, involuntarily and ignominiously attached to tubes. Some of those tubes had given her the sustenance and medication that had extended her life a few more weeks, a few more days, while the metastasized cancer did the last of its deadly work.

A couple of hours earlier, she had opened her eyes, however briefly, and we'd looked at each other while I held her hand. I thought she could hear me.

> …Don't you think, dearest Diane, that you'd better agree,
> To make love while the nightingale sings in the trees?
> To make love while the nightingale sings in the trees?

We had had a dream.

Here in the Maine farmhouse we and our closest friends had bought and rebuilt, we'd live out our lives together, drastically slowing the pressured pace of life and simplifying its daily tasks. We'd watch the deer distant in the fields, the wild turkeys as they marched confidently and regally by, herding their young, the occasional fox raising its kits under our barn and the migrating birds as they stopped by each spring to sample our feeders. We'd grow flowers and grapes and harvest the apple trees. When the fierce northwest wind blew in off the Kennebec River from Richmond in fall and winter, we'd sit inside by the glowing warmth of the woodstove and, in spring and summer, sit on the flagstoned patio in the lee of the ell of the farmhouse, listening to the water run off a stone that jutted from the patio's surrounding stone wall into the little fishpond we'd built. We'd take long walks, some along the river on the path that had been there for over two hundred years, others inland up to now-abandoned roads in the hills of this part of Maine. The bright orange, red, yellow and brown leaves of maples, birches and oaks would carpet our way in the fall. We'd ski those trails in winter and the woodstove would warm us on our return.

Four months before the reconstruction of the house was complete, Diane was found to have colon cancer, was operated on and afterwards knew that she was going to die. We explored and discussed extraordinary measures, experimental, unproven drug programs in other parts of the country that promised no cure, but did promise pain. We would have had to move away from our home and family. She said no.

Miraculously, two months later, she rallied to become herself again, and we moved into our new home in September, on schedule, ready to live at least a small part of our dream, hoping for a miracle.

But there was to be no miracle.

She wasn't diminished by the news. Whatever happens, she said, *we're* going to have fun! And we did. She was full of plans and projects and – as in her whole life – moving forward with her work, and with our fun. Her concerns in this last year of her life, as in all other years, would be for others, not for herself. She was concerned about me and what I would do when she was no longer with me.

Sometimes, in sadness, she cried, and I cried with her, but I only remember her being frightened one time. Late one night as we were preparing to go to sleep, she turned to me, eyes wide, and said, "Erik, I think we've made a terrible mistake...." I held her then, for a long time, until she slowly uncurled and drifted off to sleep. Those words have echoed in my memory and won't go away, although I never heard them again. I had always wanted her to feel safe, and now she no longer did. The helpless finality of it was unfathomable.

We had planted hundreds of daffodils in a glorious arc through the grassy field reaching from the farmhouse down toward the river, a seemingly infinite variety of daffodils. And we'd see them spring up, the first flowers of April and May. Spring came, as it must, the daffodils bloomed and the birds came. The chickadees and sparrows who had weathered the winter were joined first by robins, then juncos, red-winged blackbirds, killdeer, goldfinches, droves of swallows sitting on power lines, swooping and feasting on the first flying insects of spring; then rufous-sided towhees, flickers, cedar waxwings, brown-headed cowbirds, rose-breasted grosbeaks, bluebirds, phoebes, bluejays, orioles, far off an occasional wood thrush and, close at hand, bob-o-links trilling their liquid waterfall of notes. Overhead, majestic eagles and enormous turkey vultures soared, wings widespread, casting shadows on traces of lingering snow.

In the middle of all the teeming life of spring, on May 13, 1995, with friends and family all around, Diane died as she had wanted, at peace, and in her own home. We who were there were devastated. Many others who were not there now lived in a world diminished by her loss.

CHAPTER ONE

ORIGINS

S HE WAS BORN DIANE VALERIE THEIS IN GLENDALE, CALIFORNIA, on July 15, 1938, and grew up in North Hollywood, in the San Fernando Valley. Her parents had modest means. They were midwesterners who'd come of age during the Great Depression and had emigrated to southern California to find work and a good place to raise and educate the two children they would have. They encouraged others to share that experience and join them. They and their friends and relatives in Los Angeles were a family, a close-knit group that looked after each other to the ends of their lives. Neither her parents, George and Meryl Theis, nor any close friend or member of their families, had a university degree until Diane, not quite twenty years old, completed Stanford in three years, graduating Phi Beta Kappa. Next came Harvard Law School. There, she would graduate magna cum laude, thirteenth in a graduating class of 482, all but a half dozen of them men.

High-spirited and precocious, Diane was raised in the San Fernando Valley when it was still safe for young girls to ride their bicycles through the heart of Los Angeles to Griffith Park. She knew her own mind, and had a strong sense of what was right and just. She came by these attributes honestly, since they were a reflection of the lives led by her parents, and their parents before them.

George Theis was the son of immigrant German Catholics who had settled in northern Minnesota, intending – and failing – to make a go of farming. His parents, Frank Theis and Anna Renk, were born in Germany in 1861 and 1866, and lived in the neighboring towns of Konitz and Schoenfeldt in Prussia, where they knew each other. They came to the United States in 1883 on the same boat, together with their siblings and other German immigrants. Their families settled in largely German-speaking communities in Minnesota. Frank and Anna were married in Winona in 1886. Over the next twenty years, they would have fourteen children, so many they ran out of new names for them. (As good Catholics, they had to bear the names of German saints.) George, August, Edward and Frank were favorite ones, and they appeared in various combinations and sequences among their ten male children. Diane's father, George, was the eleventh child, born in 1902. Frank lived to 71 and Anna to 86.

Anna was a meticulous housekeeper. When they had guests, she followed close behind them to pick up any debris they might have brought inside. Eventually, when they could afford one, the Theis home boasted a gleaming new bathtub, but it was for show, not to be used by the family. A corrugated metal washtub was good enough for Anna's children.

In the midst of child-bearing and child-rearing, Anna also managed the family finances, such as they were. Frank Theis first worked on the railroad, laying track, then as an odd-job logger and in the sawmill and the foundry in Winona. In 1909, when George was seven, Frank decided to take up farming and rented, on shares, the first of four different farms on which he would barely eke out a living. Two years later, he rented his second farm, in Minnesota City, and in 1914, a farm in Gilmore Valley where they had an apple orchard and raised corn and wheat. Finally, in 1917, they bought a 240-acre farm on Garvin Heights, in the upper Gilmore Valley, which they would hold for ten years. Frank and five of his sons had earned the down payment the previous year by baling hay. George remembered baling 150 tons of hay that year.

Meryl Willey, Diane's mother, came from a family where hard work and good works ran hand in hand. Her parents, Wesley Willey and Beatrice Boyd, and her maternal grandparents, Leroy Brotherton and Alice Boyd, had homesteaded in North Dakota in 1899 and 1900. They were part of one of the last homesteading migrations in the United States. Fifteen or so Iowa farming families loaded their worldly goods into rented boxcars and made the trek to the North Dakota plains, looking for better land.

Alice Boyd had been born in Bremer County, Iowa Territory, the daughter of Henry and Lucinda Boyd, who were of Irish descent and had come to Iowa from Kentucky. Alice had given birth to Beatrice in 1882 without benefit of clergy. Her daughter was rumored to be the fruit of a brief liaison with a traveling salesman when Alice was twenty-six. Alice, who lived to be 83, was a strong-minded woman, and never told anyone who Beatrice's father was. It was a rough and ready time, Iowa was still the frontier, and no particular stigma appears to have attached, either to Alice or to Beatrice.

Alice and Leroy Brotherton married in 1885, when Beatrice was three. Leroy had emigrated from England and been married once before. By 1899, when she and Leroy hired a boxcar and joined the emigrant train, Alice had lived in Iowa for forty-three years, long enough. Beatrice was seventeen and two Brotherton sons, Grover and Clyde, were then thirteen and eleven. They and their few worldly possessions were accompanied to North Dakota by Beatrice's 25-year-old boyfriend, Wesley Willey.

Wesley had likewise come from a hardscrabble pioneering heritage. His father, William, had fought with the Iowa Volunteers in the Civil War and had been wounded in the siege of Vicksburg in 1863. Twice married after the war, William fathered eighteen children, six of whom died in infancy. Wesley was the third of the six children of the first marriage, to Marion Butler, who died in 1879. Three years later, William married Cynthia Adams. Wesley, nine years old, left home not long after his father remarried. William died in 1924 at the age of 83.

Placed on a siding, the railroad car was home to the Brothertons, Beatrice and Wesley for a short time while Leroy and Wesley broke sod and built a hut to shelter the family. Soon after, they built a cabin from lumber they'd hauled by horse and wagon from thirty miles away. Their homestead was midway between two small towns, Rock Lake and Calvin, each nine miles away.

On August 9, 1900, not long after the Brothertons were settled on their homestead, Beatrice and Wesley Willey were married. They filed claim for a homestead in Devil Lake, Lansing Township, just west of the Brotherton homestead. There, after several more trips to haul lumber, they built the wooden cabin that was to be their home for the next seventeen years. Diane's mother, Meryl, was one of eight children born to Beatrice and Wesley. The first, Carl, was born in 1902. Meryl, born in 1905, was the third.* The family included two other girls, Alice, born in 1909 and Aldah, born in 1912. The one-room school the children attended (later expanded to two rooms)

The homestead in North Dakota. Standing, l. to r.: An unidentified friend, Wesley, Grover, and Clyde; seated in front is Leroy with baby Carl Willey. Beatrice and Alice are in the wagon.

---

* In order, they were Carl, Boyd, Meryl, Forrest, Alice, Aldah, Clenyce and Don.

was the pride of the community. It had a pot-bellied stove for heat and the students brought potatoes to heat on the coals so they could have baked potatoes for lunch.

Diane's maternal grandparents,
Wesley and Beatrice Willey.

"When the weather was real bad, my father would take us to school," related Meryl. "Otherwise we had a pony – his name was Dick – and a little house on top of four wheels so we were protected from the wind and the cold. When it was cold we had blankets. When it wasn't, we didn't. There was a barn at the school where the horses stayed after we unhitched them and we always took along hay for the horses. There was very little good weather in the winter when we went to school and it was three miles…."

The school was also the center of social activities. Community Christmas parties were held there. Since there was no outside entertainment, the community provided their own. Many people could play the piano or an organ or a fiddle, or they could sing and sometimes dance a jig for their neighbors. Their life was centered on community, school and church, and on the common effort to survive in an environment which was often hostile.

Wesley was successful in this rural context and was one of the first in the community to own a car, a Model T Ford. In 1917, shortly after their youngest child was born, Wesley and Beatrice decided to move to Calvin, a more settled community, where their children could receive a broader education than they had in the two-room schoolhouse. Wesley's own schooling had been occasional and irregular, something he regretted, and he didn't want his children to have the same experience. He believed in the importance of education and took to heart that part of North Dakota's state constitution which spelled out its importance:

> A high degree of intelligence, patriotism, integrity and morality on the part of every voter in a government by the people being necessary in order to insure the continuance of that government and the prosperity and happiness of the people, the legislative assembly shall make provision for the establishment and maintenance if a system of public schools which shall be open to all children of the state of North Dakota and free from sectarian control. [Constitution of North Dakota, Art. VIII, Sec.1]

That ideal was more achievable in Calvin. There, not only did the boys attend carpentry classes and the girls domestic science classes, but they both had classes in English, mathematics and history.

Living in Calvin also made it possible to join the Presbyterian Church. They were an observant family, but the only church near their homestead had been a small "Dunkard" meetinghouse. The Dunkards were a devout but somber sect who kneeled in church when they prayed and always wore dark clothes, with women's dresses ankle length. Dunkard women wore no jewelry; they wore white net prayer bonnets underneath a black bonnet tied with ribbons under the chin. Martha and Leroy Brotherton belonged to this congregation, but Wesley and Beatrice Willey weren't comfortable in this type of worship. Beatrice had a strong streak of independence, a trait she passed on to her descendants. While religion had played a strong part in her upbringing in Iowa, her church there had been one that was open to and oriented toward the larger community. The Willey children became regular churchgoers when they moved to Calvin, and the principles preached in the Presbyterian Church were an important fabric in their life.

In Calvin, Wesley sold and maintained cars, farm machinery and associated equipment. The weather was favorable and times were good for North Dakota farmers. He bought on credit and sold on credit. But in the mid 1920s North Dakota was hit by drought, crop failures and the onset of the Great Depression. Savings were lost as the banks closed. Almost all the farmers in the area lost their farms. Deeply in debt, they were unable to pay their obligations to Wesley Willey and he became bankrupt. However, he never felt that bankruptcy was the right way to deal with the obligations he had incurred. For the rest of his working life, he set aside money from his earnings to pay his creditors what he had owed them. He imbued his children and grandchildren, by example, with the same standards of responsibility, obligation and morality he himself had observed.

The Willey children, except for the youngest, Don, were on their own financially by the mid-1920s. Meryl had gone to State Teachers College in Valley City, North Dakota, and over the next few years worked as a schoolteacher in several North Dakota communities, where she boarded with local families. Money was scarce and entertainment hard to come by. One day the husband of a couple with whom she was boarding bought and brought home a radio without consulting his wife. "She was so angry at his having wasted good money on something so useless," wrote Meryl later, "that she didn't speak to him for three days and wouldn't listen

Meryl Adeen Willey
State Teachers College – 1927

to it for two months. It was the first radio I was to hear in someone's house. It was a delightful and entertaining way to spend the evenings."

Meryl contributed a portion of her salary to help pay for the education of her younger brother Forrest, thought of as the brightest in the family. Forrest justified his family's confidence in him and went on to become a highly respected and beloved Minnesota high school principal and school superintendent who cared deeply for his students. Tragically, toward the end of his career, he was killed by one of those students, a disturbed young man who he was trying to persuade to give up the handgun he was brandishing.

Meryl's educational and teaching experiences in the 1920s were mixed, in part because of cultural and institutional expectations and demands made on women teachers, and in part because of the bias against an independent woman in a man's world. Both things were hard to accept for a woman who had grown up in a household where her contributions and her mother's contributions were considered equal to those of the men, and where each individual's independence in the household was honored. Teachers (she would write in a memoir) were told they "should be a fit example outside of school." They had to "measure up to the best." It naturally followed that it was, for them, "impossible to attend dances and card parties" and still be regarded as "fit enough" to be teachers. Women teachers were "supposed to represent certain ideals in the community" and – it goes without saying – they were expected to be virginal.

Then there was the hypocrisy. When she applied to school boards for teaching positions, she came to understand – to her dismay – that the single most important factor on her applications was not her education or her experience, but her photograph. "They judged entirely from that – from looking at the photograph." In one school in which she taught, the principal "pestered me. After school, he would chase me around and I didn't want to have any kind of an affair with someone I had to spend so much time with…."

While Meryl recognized the practical drawbacks of the career she'd chosen, she and other women teachers she worked with did not necessarily subscribe to the moral standards of the day applied to teachers. They regarded those standards as "theory," and they would live their lives as they saw fit. When Meryl and her lifelong friend, Blanche Duncan, a young woman who taught in a neighboring community school, were befriended by the Swansons, a sociable family in Blaben, North Dakota, they found, happily, that the Swanson house was filled with young men and women on the weekends. "We used to go to some very fine dances and dance all night long. I had a boyfriend from Hope and Blanche had a boyfriend, and right from the beginning I spent almost every weekend at the Swansons' house. They would come out and get me and then our boyfriends would come there to pick us up and we'd go dancing and to shows…." The era of the silent movie was just ending, and Meryl and her friends drove over a hundred miles to see, and hear, the first full-length "talkie," "Mammy," starring Al Jolson.

Meryl taught in one-room schoolhouses and in community schools from the time she was seventeen. Some of the students early on were as old as she was and, as she was a slight young woman, many of them were much bigger than she. She learned that to maintain discipline she needed the help of the young men in her school. "Wayne was seventeen, almost as old as I was, and he would kind of want to hold my hand and things like that which he should not have been doing. He was always hanging around me, and he was big. So I had to keep him on my side – otherwise I couldn't control the class…."

She taught reading, writing, arithmetic, spelling, grammar, geography, United States history, nature study – and elements of agriculture ("because that was the main industry"). How to teach, and what to teach, was left to Meryl's own judgment. Since the schools were small, the various age groups were mixed together, and she had to set up different groups in different sections of a room so that each group could do work appropriate to their age. One of the subjects she was required to teach was temperance, but since North Dakota prohibited alcoholic beverages, there was very little opportunity to develop intemperate habits. Meryl herself was a lifelong teetotaler.

Devastated by the disastrous impact of the Depression on the car and machinery business in Calvin, Wesley and Beatrice moved to Browns Valley, Minnesota, in 1928, close to the North Dakota line. Ever resourceful, Wesley learned shoe repair and opened a shoe store and shoe repair shop. By this time, the big bands had begun to tour the country, and an overnight stop for them between Minneapolis and points west was Browns Valley, where there was a large dance hall. Guy Lombardo and his band, among others, played in Browns Valley. Meryl came home to visit her parents more often. It was at a dance there when she was twenty-two and in her fifth year of teaching that Meryl met George Theis.

A small and wiry man, surprisingly strong for his size, George was out looking for work and a steady wage. Jobs in Minnesota were scarce, especially for a young man with little formal education who, with his father and brothers, had worked a series of

The one Theis tractor was always breaking down, and the sons became expert, like it or not, in the art of diagnosing and repairing motors with whatever materials were at hand. It was a hard life. One day, one of the sons, Frank, went out with a horse and plow to a far field and failed to return for dinner. When two of the other sons went looking for him, they found the plow and the horse, still tethered to the plow, but no Frank. He'd left, not to return for three years. After he reappeared, no one ever learned where he'd been, nor did they ask.

unproductive and unprofitable farms. The Theis sons were supposed to stay on at the Gilmore Valley farm and make it productive, but except for Albert and Leo, who eventually took over the farm, they rebelled at this task.

In 1925, George and his brother Eddie bought a used car and set out on their own, looking elsewhere for work and adventure. Ultimately they ended up in California, but first their travels took them to parts of Minnesota and North Dakota where, stopping overnight, they would take in a country dance. One of those dances was in Browns Valley. George met Meryl and they hit it off, so he and his brother stayed a couple of days longer than planned. When they left, he and Meryl promised to write.

The Theis brothers turned westward. Their car broke down on the prairie, twenty miles from any town, but not far from the railroad line. Having figured out what part they needed, Eddie hopped a slow-moving freight train heading back where they'd come from, while George stayed to guard the car. Several hours later, having caught another freight, Eddie returned with the part. They repaired the car and were on their way again.

When the car gave up the ghost entirely, the brothers were stranded with no transportation, a few clothes and very little money. They rode the rails west and south toward the Mexican border, working odd jobs. Eventually they worked their way north again into Southern California, in time to join illegal migrant Mexicans in working the crop harvests.

The migrant workers were paid virtually nothing for their labors, something which struck George as unfair, given how hard they worked. He began organizing a union. Not surprisingly, George's job ended shortly thereafter, when he was persuaded by the owner's hired guards to leave the territory quickly and head further north. (As he said later, "It was an easy decision to make.") Their next stop was Los Angeles, where he and Eddie found steady jobs working at the Santa Monica Swimming Club, a health club and marina just west of the city. Eddie was the restaurant's chef; George, an attendant. The work was steady and the pay was good.

California was still in its infancy as a land of opportunity, a place where fortunes would be made by capturing water and supplying it to a semi-arid desert, but the lure of fame and fortune wasn't what brought George. He came for work and hoped to make a decent life. After four years of correspondence and a couple of visits back home, George wrote to Meryl in 1931 to ask if she wouldn't like to come out and join him in Los Angeles so they could get married. This wasn't the first time he'd suggested marriage:

> After he started wanting me to marry him, I'd say – I was a little snip, then – "Well, if I don't meet somebody else that I like better, well then we'll see about it." Actually I'd always wanted to go to California. I wanted to get out of the snow, out of shoveling coal into furnaces at those schools, out of

washing up in ice water. After teaching at Ashley, I went to Oakes and stayed there for two years. By that time I'd saved enough money that I could come to California.

Besides, at age twenty-six, she was already reckoned an old maid by the standards of the day, and she was having none of that. This time she accepted with alacrity. Meryl wrote back, told George she would marry him and she'd get in touch when she got there.

Meryl was in no hurry. As long as she was going anyway, she intended to see some of the country whose geography she'd been teaching. She and Blanche pooled their savings and left North Dakota by bus, traveling a meandering route that took them up to Oregon and Washington, and only eventually south toward Los Angeles, where she and George became reacquainted.

When Meryl and George decided it was time to marry, they made plans to go to Santa Monica City Hall, where the ceremony would be performed, with Blanche and Eddie the witnesses. Even then, there was no rush. On the way to City Hall they looked out the window of the streetcar (Los Angeles had public transportation then) and saw that a brand-new silent movie starring John Gilbert, known as the "Great Lover of the Silver Screen," was showing. They stepped off the streetcar, bought tickets and spent the afternoon.

George and Meryl (at left) on their honeymoon with Blanche and Eddie.

They could always get married another day, and they did, on December 9, 1931. George and Meryl were happy to have Eddie and Blanche share their honeymoon, if a few days riding burros among the cactuses and bright desert sunshine of Ensenada can be called a honeymoon. Times were good.

Blanche decided to return to the Northwest to settle, but Meryl thought Southern California too fine a place to leave, and she wanted to share it. Soon she was writing her siblings urging them to join her and George. It wasn't long before she was followed by her sister, Aldah, and years later, by their younger brothers, Don and Clen.

The Great Depression eventually reached California, and jobs and money became scarce. Aldah, who had met and would marry Andy Meyers, another transplanted midwesterner, lived in a rented single family house with George and Meryl. After Aldah and Andy married, all but George, who had been fortunate to have kept his job at the Santa Monica Swimming Club, went out during the day to look for work, pooling what money they could earn. Meryl was not qualified to teach in the California schools and although she thought of taking courses in order to get her teaching certificate there, there simply wasn't enough money to do it. During the worst of it, Meryl went back to Minnesota and George moved in with a cousin in Los Angeles to save on rent. Andy and Aldah stayed on in the house and paid the rent.

The swimming club's members included a number of movie moguls. One of them took a particular liking to George and asked him if he would like a better-paying job at Columbia Pictures. He accepted without hesitation and would stay at Columbia working on movie sets and locations for the next thirty years.

Bright, gregarious and cheerful, George learned quickly and liked to work. Those traits brought him steady employment as a jack-of-all-trades at Columbia. He could do virtually everything that needed to be done on a movie set. At various times he was an electrician, a mechanic, a best boy and a grip. Everyone liked him and welcomed him, except for the union chiefs. The union was a closed shop and new members were generally limited to sons of its existing members. For most of his years with Columbia, despite performing union work the whole time, George was not a member, but eventually he became one and thus a beneficiary of the very generous pension plan the union negotiated with the movie industry.

By 1935, things were looking up again economically. George and Meryl's first daughter, Noreen, was born late that year, and Diane was born two and a half years later. Still renting a house in Los Angeles, the family now had to move because they needed more room for the girls. In 1938, they bought their first house, on Satsuma Avenue in North Hollywood, which was then a sparsely populated part of the San Fernando Valley filled with orange and lemon groves.

In another three years the country would be at war, the country's young men, including Clen and Don, would be in the military, the California defense plants would be humming and more jobs would be available than men to fill them. In 1943, Wesley and Beatrice Willey left the midwest and joined their children in California. With their arrival, George and Meryl sold their first house and bought another one on Satsuma, a one-story wooden frame home with a small porch. Wesley and Beatrice lived in a smaller house in the rear of the lot.

Wesley, now over sixty-seven, wanted to participate in the war effort. Besides, he hadn't finished repaying his debts and thought he needed to work. Not long after they arrived, Meryl drove her father to the Lockheed aircraft plant to see if they could find work for him. To her surprise, she found that Lockheed wanted them both. Wesley worked in the tool repair shop, while Meryl became a welder working on a huge spot-welding machine assembling wings for B-17's and later for B-29's. Beatrice cared for Noreen and Diane while Meryl was at work. Meryl had never before done any similar work and found the challenge was to her liking – but her job ended with the war as the men came home from the service looking for the jobs the women had held. When Wesley died, Diane was seven years old. She remembered her grandfather well and knew her grandmother even better, as Beatrice lived another twenty years after Wesley's death.

After the war, George decided to add a second floor to the house for the girls' bedroom so that their first-floor bedroom could be used as a den. He drew the building plans and did the work himself. When completed, the upstairs bedroom consisted of one very large room with two windows looking into the backyard, its own bathroom and a large walk-in closet. For the girls it was palatial, their own private "very special place."

In March 1954, after Noreen had graduated and Diane was a junior in high school, George and Meryl bought their third home in North Hollywood, on Corteen Place, a rural, quiet, tree-shaded, idyllic spot. George built a family room in the rear and remodeled a guest house in the backyard for Beatrice's use. When her daughters were grown and out of the house, Meryl returned to teaching as a first-grade teacher in a small private school, where she enjoyed total independence in running her classroom. She had been active in the community and in the school PTAs so long as her daughters attended the public schools, and continued to be active in the Presbyterian Church and its activities. Being able to teach again was a return to her roots that made up for the disappointment of losing her job at Lockheed, and she continued to teach until George retired.

In 1964, a voracious Los Angeles re-zoned Corteen Place for apartments. A developer paid George and Meryl an astonishing sum for their lot and moved their house and guest house to another street. George retired in 1967, and he and Meryl moved eastward to Friendly Valley, California, a retirement community that was one of the first of its kind. There they would live for nearly thirty years, the longest time by far that they had stayed in one place.

CHAPTER TWO

GROWING UP IN NORTH HOLLYWOOD

IANE'S UPBRINGING WAS STRICT, AND FAMILY EXPECTATIONS were high. Much of her extracurricular life revolved around the North Hollywood Presbyterian Church, whose core beliefs and teachings concerning the obligations and mission of its members to better the lives of others would have a profound influence on her. Apart from church teaching, George and Meryl Theis had a strong sense of right and wrong, which they instilled in their children. These were lifelong lessons.

It was an innocent time, and Diane was free from an early age both to roam with her friends throughout Los Angeles and to explore the world of ideas. She read voraciously. (Meryl was not pleased when she found her young daughter engrossed in *Forever Amber*, a risqué, bluish novel she had taken out from the library.) She was ambitious for herself and for her friends, formed her own judgments and – although the youngest of them – was the unquestioned leader of the gang of six teenage girls who became close friends in junior high school.

In the early 1940s, North Hollywood had a small town feel to it. The San Fernando Valley was sparsely populated, except for ubiquitous orange and lemon groves. Hobos walked along the railroad tracks that ran through the Valley beyond a gravel crossroad at the west end of Satsuma Avenue. They'd come to houses on Satsuma looking for food and offering to work. Meryl never sent them away hungry. Diane, her older sister Noreen and their friends sometimes played along the tracks and encountered the hobos. They were wary of them but their presence was not considered a matter for great concern.

Just beyond another gravel crossroad to the east on Satsuma Avenue, a high white picket fence enclosed two caged and de-clawed movie lions whose roars could be heard through the neighborhood. Not your usual neighbors, even in Los Angeles. Uncle Don would take his nieces to peer through the cracks in the fence at the lions in their cages, telling them that "one of these days" he was going to wrestle one of the lions. Being very young, they believed him, and thought him very brave. Don had a penchant for fanciful stories, and so, perhaps, did Diane. When I heard the story many years later, Don had indeed wrestled one of the lions in his cage.

Midwest farm culture stayed with the Theis family. Once a week Meryl would go with her daughters to a small neighborhood grocery store to buy raw milk. When they could no longer buy raw milk – it had been deemed not safe to drink – Meryl had to buy pasteurized milk. Diane and Noreen were so used to raw milk at that point that it took them a long time to get used to the different taste.

Refrigerators were rare. Instead, an iceman came in his truck to deliver blocks of ice to the iceboxes in the neighborhood. All the neighborhood children looked forward to his coming in the hot days of summer. They would run to the open rear of his truck while he was carrying a block into a house and scoop up small broken pieces of ice to put in their mouths. The iceman's popularity was second only to that of the Good Humor Man, whose arrival was announced by the musical tinkle of his ice cream truck coming down the street. A nickel would buy an ice cream cone, a dime a double scoop.

Until the start of World War II, the Fourth of July was a big event. In the evening when it grew dark, neighbors would gather, sitting on their lawn chairs on a corner of the sidewalk, to watch spectacular fireworks displays that lit up the sky in brilliant bursts of color, rockets exploding high in the air into intricate patterns drifting slowly down in a windless summer sky. When the war started, there were no more fireworks displays, only searchlights scanning the dark for enemy planes.

The war brought tension and apprehension to what had been an untroubled existence. Japanese-Americans were being interned because of their origins. Diane and Noreen knew from their parents that they were of half-German descent, and they'd heard George's stories about pretending to be Austrian during the First World War. They worried that friends or teachers would find out the truth and report them. Air-raid drills at school, where students had to leave their classrooms to sit on hallway floors, backs against the wall, were frightening to young children. Neighborhood blackout drills required covering windows to keep in any glimpse of light.

The war also brought lessons in frugality. Food and gas were rationed, and everyone had a ration coupon book. Oleomargarine had appeared as a less expensive butter substitute, but was both rationed and regulated. White in color, it came in a clear plastic bag with a large red pill in the middle of it. One of the girls' tasks to aid the war effort was to squeeze the margarine bag until the red pill dissolved and the white margarine turned buttery yellow.* It took a great deal of squeezing.

George planted a Victory Garden in a vacant lot beyond the backyard fence, grew corn, vegetables and berries, and raised chickens, rabbits and geese on a mini-midwest farm in the environs of Los Angeles. He was not unusual in doing so – it was the patriotic thing to do. The girls collected eggs daily, and George sold them to fellow workers at Columbia. Some eggs went into an incubator to hatch – an exciting event for the girls. Feed for the chickens came in bags infused with colorful patterns and designs. Meryl made nightgowns and other clothing for her daughters out of them.

The girls named the chickens and were upset when George and Meryl decided to have one for dinner. Their farm-raised parents and grandparents were not moved, and turned a deaf ear: "Off with its head!" George would say, taking an axe and putting action to words in the backyard. Once the headless chicken stopped running around, grandmother Beatrice plucked the feathers off the bird, George gutted it and Meryl cooked it.

Uncles Don and Clen joined the army. Don was ordered to New Guinea, Clen to the South Pacific. In his V-mail letters home, Don said he'd bring them back a talking bird or a baby kangaroo or a koala bear, whichever Noreen and Diane wanted most. They spent days agonizing over the decision. The bird didn't sound like much fun, the kangaroo would grow too big, but the koala bear would be just right, so they wrote Uncle Don and told him they had decided in favor of the koala bear. Clen wrote to say he'd been given a horse, which he had named Diane because the horse had a mane the same color as Diane's hair. They expected Don to bring back the koala bear and Clen the horse for them to ride, but it was not to be. They were glad to see their uncles again, but disappointed to learn there was no koala bear and no horse.

The uncles were always an important part of the family. On Christmas Eve, Don would dress in a Santa Claus suit, pound on the front door and enter bellowing, "Merry Christmas, everyone! Ho, ho, ho!" Diane and Noreen were believers and would get on his lap to tell him what they wanted for Christmas. That is, until the year Diane asked him why he was wearing Uncle Don's army boots. Christmas was not the same after that.

North Hollywood's main street, Lankersheim Boulevard, was lined on both sides with small shops, markets, banks and two movie theaters, the Valley and the El Portal. Meryl, Diane and Noreen would often walk from Satsuma to Lankersheim to the

---

* By government regulation, margarine producers could not sell yellow-colored margarine because – it was said – people would be fooled into thinking it was butter. Margarine and its coloring had to be sold separately and consumers had to add their own color to the pasty-colored product.

George and Meryl with baby Diane and sister Noreen.

Diane and Noreen in 1944.

Diane was an avid reader all her life.

Rear, l. to r.: Don and Rita Willey, Rita's sister Helen, Aldah and Andy Meyers, George and Meryl, Beatrice, and Clen Willey with Diane on his lap. In front are Valerie Meyers, Noreen, and Drew Meyers. (c. 1948)

A family vacation around 1950. Noreen, Valerie, and Diane are in front at the right.

movies and to the local shops. There were interesting places like Mr. Phillips' shoe store, where they could stand on the platform of a machine in the center of the store, put their feet in a slot at the bottom of the machine and peer down through a screen at the greenish-looking bones of their feet. They did it over and over. No one warned them about the radiation.

The girls were avid fans of Roy Rogers and Dale Evans (and especially of Roy's horse, Trigger), and watched their serialized movies at the El Portal. In their own backyard, wearing cowboy hats and shooting toy guns, they rode the lower branches of a fig tree pretending to be Roy and Dale. They argued about who would be who. One day, Diane fell off her branch, landed on her back and had the wind knocked out of her. Noreen thought she was dead, and ran to get Beatrice. When Diane got her wind back, they remounted their "horses" immediately.

They looked forward each week to the arrival of John, a roustabout who brought his two horses, Comet and Dixie, to the neighborhood for children to ride around the block. Diane and Noreen both saved up 25 cents each week, the cost of the ride.

Since there were no buses in the Los Angeles of the 1940s, streetcars were the means of public transportation. On special occasions, Meryl would take the girls by streetcar to go shopping downtown, a ride that ended in a long tunnel and an underground terminal. Sometimes the three would ride the streetcar to Hollywood to have lunch at the Piggly-Wiggly restaurant on Hollywood Boulevard. Then it was off to a bookstore where each picked out a book of her choice, usually a Nancy Drew mystery, sometimes Anne of Green Gables or a Black Stallion book. Next they would see a movie. Choosing what movie to see wasn't easy because there were so many movie theaters on Hollywood Boulevard: Pantages, the Egyptian, Grauman's Chinese (where the stars' footprints and handprints were pressed into fresh concrete) and others.

The family clan took driving vacations together up and down California, to the beaches, the mountains and the desert, and to most of the western states, stopping to stay in National Parks like Zion and Bryce in Utah, Yellowstone in Wyoming, Sequoia and Yosemite in California, Mt. Rainier in Washington (the girls went barefoot in the snow) and Crater Lake in Oregon. The trips were usually riotous and unrestrained, often marked by the men's practical jokes on Noreen, Diane and their younger cousin, Valerie Meyers.

The practical jokes took many forms. The uncles knew Noreen detested peanut butter, and for years they contrived (successfully) to inject peanut butter into chocolates and other treats she loved to eat, and under sticks of gum. On one trip to a wooded campsite where the girls had to sleep outside on picnic tables for lack of beds in the cabins, Don, Andy and George waited until they were asleep, then began prowling around the tables and under them making growling and snuffling noises like bears. There were rustling noises from the trees overhead and a whump, as if something big had fallen from a tree. The girls made a dash for the cabins, where they received little sympathy – but the mosquitoes were fierce that night and they ended up sleeping in the car with the windows rolled up.

The family's penchant for teasing and pranks wasn't a one-way street. While on a family vacation in the early 1950s after Diane had learned to drive, George had parked his beautiful new red-and-white Ford some distance from their rented cabin. ("Never, never, *never* leave the keys in the car," he cautioned. "Always take them with you!") On returning from a horseback ride with Valerie, Diane saw the keys still in the ignition. She got off her horse, started the engine and drove the car around to the back, hidden from view behind another cabin, and said nothing. George was speechless when he found his car gone, and almost as speechless when he found that his very responsible daughter was indeed responsible.

When George expressed an opinion, he had an impact. Meryl had fixed a cheesecake dessert for the family for fifteen years, but the girls didn't like it much and finally asked her why she made it. "Well, because it's your father's favorite!" she said. "Not necessarily…" said George, and they never had cheesecake again.

George was a solid figure in Diane's life, but not a dominating figure in the family. He was a car mechanic, a plumber, a painter, a landscaper and a gardener, very like his jack-of-all-trades roles on Columbia Studios movie sets and locations. He could fix anything. His marriage with Meryl was a good one, but they had different roles in the family. George had wonderful stories to tell about his upbringing, his odyssey coming to California and his life working for Columbia, and Meryl ran the family's affairs. George was always there, but he was quiet about views that he might have held concerning their daughters' upbringing.

Lankersheim Elementary School was within walking distance, less than a mile away, and Diane and Noreen walked the four blocks from an early age along Magnolia Boulevard at the south end of Satsuma Avenue. As a teacher, Meryl recognized Diane's potential and determined to do everything she could to foster it. She was pleased when the teachers at Lankersheim, whose kindergarten Diane entered in 1943, likewise recognized her potential early on and she was skipped a grade. Meryl's ambitions for Diane probably paralleled her own ambitions as a young woman which had never been realized. Later, they'd conflict with her desire to keep Diane close so she could share in her achievements, but in the end she acceded to Diane's decisions as to how she wanted to lead her own life. It was not easy for Meryl to let go.

The Art Linkletter show was a hugely popular and nationally broadcast children's radio program of the time. It had its origins in a man-in-the-street interview between Linkletter and his five-year-old son Jack. ("Kids say the darnedest things!" was Linkletter's byword.) Listener response was overwhelming and Linkletter began doing more and more candid interviews with children until he at last created his "House Party" program, on which he let local schools pick the participants, smart and extroverted five- to ten-year-olds who were articulate and frank, and not yet old enough to be cynical. "Send me the kids you'd most like to get out of the classroom for a few hours," he told teachers. Diane was one of the kids chosen for the show.

Hollywood was a land of instant stardom and riches for bright and photogenic children, and Meryl was ambitious for both her daughters. Noreen was a beautiful blonde child; Diane, already vivacious and articulate, had Shirley Temple brunette ringlets and a sparkling smile. Meryl enrolled them both in the Children's Screen Guild in Hollywood. At the Guild (located on "The Crossroads of the World," a cobblestone cul-de-sac) children could take lessons in anything that pertained to entertainment, dance, voice and drama. Outstanding students received casting calls for movies with children's roles.

When Diane received a casting call from Walt Disney Studios in 1946 for "Song of the South," it was a major event in the Theis family. Auditions were held in the Hollywood Bowl. Five girls, one of them Diane, were given screen tests. Meryl accompanied Diane to the audition and the screen test. In the end, the studio's decision was between Diane

Diane with her grandmother Beatrice.

and Luanna Patten to star opposite Bobby Driscoll. Luanna, one and a half weeks older than Diane, had been a professional model since the age of three, already had had a couple of small roles and had an agent who knew how to lobby for the part. She was the choice.*

Diane did not like to be second best in anything, and many years and accomplishments later, she still talked wistfully about losing out to Luanna Patten. One can only speculate what Diane's life would have been like had she won the role, but it can hardly be doubted that with her mother's ambition driving her on to Hollywood success, Diane's course might well have been very different.

Meryl recovered nicely from the blow, however, and moved on. Her daughter was not to be a movie star, but she would be a star nevertheless. Meryl kept a close eye on her daughter's achievements and environment, from school matters to the choice of young men she dated, and she did what she could to influence the outcomes. She

---

* "Song of the South" was later reviled because of its portrayal of Uncle Remus, a lovable Uncle Tom character whose homey narrations to white children of the adventures of Br'er Rabbit and Br'er Fox were illustrated in Technicolor on-screen cartoons.

When they were older, Noreen would bask in the sun in a bathing suit on a beach towel on her Aunt Aldah's front lawn, attracting male attention and making her studious younger sister feel like a geek. Noreen always had boyfriends around, sometimes to her mother's dismay. Meryl had a pair of long-necked giraffe figurines with their necks intertwined and she dubbed them "Noreen," a reference to the giraffes necking. Diane enjoyed letting her friends know about the nickname.

became president of the Lankersheim PTA and was for twelve years a Sunday School teacher at North Hollywood Presbyterian Church. She gave six years to scouting, hosting and guiding her daughter's Horizon Girls den, and she was president of the North Hollywood Junior High PTA.

Sibling rivalry between the sisters was inevitable. From an early age, Noreen, a stunning blonde, was the beauty in the family, while Diane was the brains, the child shown off to family and friends. Noreen, the elder by three years, was acutely conscious of the competition early on. In 1941, Noreen had been visiting grandparents Wesley and Beatrice Willey in Oakes, North Dakota, for a few weeks when Diane and Meryl arrived by car to join them. Meryl sent three-year-old Diane up to the front door by herself to announce their arrival. Noreen answered the door and on seeing Diane immediately closed it. When Beatrice asked who was there, Noreen answered, "Nobody."

Life changed radically for Diane when she entered North Hollywood Junior High. By this time, the gang of six had been formed. Donna Lawson was Diane's oldest friend – they had met in the first grade and would be best friends for life. Charlotte Kaup met Diane and Donna in the fifth grade. Gretchen Vannice joined them from a different elementary school. Betty Jo Baker came with her family from the East Coast. Virginia Marvelli was a friend whose mother gave piano lessons, which all of them took. It was an eclectic group with very different personalities, and there were jealousies among them. No matter how smart or talented one of the group was, Diane always seemed to be just a little smarter. The jealousies remained largely unspoken, however, because Diane never did or said anything to indicate that she thought she was better than the rest of them in any degree. Perhaps this accounts for the fact that Diane, although the youngest, was the leader of the gang.

What they did and when they did it revolved around her. She had tremendous energy and initiative and was full of mischief. She organized neighborhood scavenger hunts, going door to door knocking on strangers' doors after dark. On Halloween they all wore costumes and went trick-or-treating in the neighborhood (even after they were in high school). At Christmas they went caroling. Diane "would have one outrageous idea after another," Charlotte recalls. "She always needed to be doing something, and the group would do anything she suggested. 'Let's do this!' she would say, and we'd go do it." One night, for a lark, they went to a séance at the House of the Living Dead in Hollywood, where a psychic was doing readings from people in the audience. She came to Charlotte and said she had a message from her dead grandmother – and then she named her! They were astounded but couldn't stop giggling.

They studied together, agonized over boys and clothes, endlessly discussed important issues ranging from civil rights to Jack the Ripper, and took bicycling day trips to Griffith Park to see the planetarium and to Forest Lawn to see the art. Under Meryl's supervision, they went horseback riding or on hiking trips in Griffith Park.

Theater and music were important to them. They attended the Civic Light Opera every year (each purchased one ticket and donated that ticket to an annual birthday pool). They went to the Biltmore Theater and the Huntington Hartford Theatre to see *The Teahouse of the August Moon* and *The Caine Mutiny Court Martial*. After the *Caine Mutiny* performance, they walked across the street to the Brown Derby to have dinner and met the stars, Lloyd Nolan and John Hodiak, who autographed their programs. They saw virtually every musical production that came through Los Angeles. Theirs were the cheapest seats in the top balcony, the worst seats in the house, but that didn't deter them.

Nor were they deterred by other considerations. They rode the streetcars to Chinatown, Olvera Street, Farmer's Market, the Hollywood Bowl and the Greek Theater. After learning that there was a back way into the Greek Theater, Diane led them up to the spot and found it. They all sneaked in to find seats up in the back, but the ushers spotted them and marched them in humiliation down past what seemed like endless rows of the paying audience and out the door.

They wore three-inch heels for the first time at junior high graduation. Diane was thirteen, two months short of fourteen. The others were fifteen. After graduation, still dressed up, they rode the streetcar to Olvera Street, where they flirted with the soldiers and sailors. When they decided to go home at 11 p.m., they couldn't remember the route. The others were shy and a little frightened but Diane unhesitatingly went up to strangers and came back with the directions.

The gang had a strong sense of commitment. They all went to church and joined church youth organizations. They belonged to Horizon Girls (the Girl Scouts' senior Campfire Girls organization). Horizon Girls was a philanthropic organization that raised money for its good works. They persuaded the ventriloquist Edgar Bergen to bring his famous "dummy" Charlie McCarthy, and put on a benefit for them. Selling tickets door to door, they and other members filled the theater, over a thousand seats. The club hosted a fashion show in the spring, with Diane as the emcee and Gretchen, Virginia and Betty Jo as models. Diane would become its president when she was a junior in high school.

While the Presbyterian Church's religious teaching did not stay with her, as such, the church's advocacy of involvement in social action did. The Presbyterians had a

The Horizon Club hosted Edgar Bergen and Charlie McCarthy, seated at center. Diane is sitting beside Bergen, Betty Jo is beside Charlie McCarthy, and Charlotte is seated on the floor at far left.

strong commitment to missionary work, both at home and abroad, and advocated for a world in which all ages, races, genders, creeds and abilities were recognized, accepted, valued and celebrated. The church urged its members to address issues of oppression and injustice, and it asked its congregation to bear witness around such issues as social welfare, community organizing and child advocacy. Diane took to heart the notion that persons of ability and good will have a duty – a mission – to remedy oppression and injustice.

The church's summer retreat was Forest Home, a woods camp located 100 miles from Los Angeles in the San Bernardino Mountains above Redlands. It was a long trip in the church's old and slow bus on rural two-lane roads through orange and lemon groves. Soon after they arrived they were asked to pledge themselves to Jesus Christ during a nighttime ceremony. Gathering in a huge outdoor amphitheater, a burning bonfire in its center, each one had his or her pledge written on a small piece of paper wrapped around a stick called a "faggot." The minister asked them to answer for their sins and they all stood up. Led by the minister, they congregated around the bonfire, threw the faggots in, and were thus forsworn as missionaries, or preachers to lepers or teachers of the poor in Africa.

The moral and ethical principles taught at Forest Home were serious, and unfairness was a matter of constant discussion. Forest Home was also a magnet for other reasons. It not only provided a forum for social advocacy, it also provided much-wanted male presence. Sometimes the two interests coincided. When a young minister was fired because he was deemed too radical, Diane and Donna were deeply affected. "It was said he lost his faith and was driving a cab," says Donna. "We thought that was romantic – and decidedly unfair!"

Later, when Diane, Donna and Charlotte took summer jobs at Forest Home, the reality of young people working together at a summer camp provided a different kind of guidance. Their focus was securely on the boys and on summer romances. There was yin and yang about this because they found they needed to fend off advances from the young ministers. There was no lack of those advances, nor of discussions about hypocrisy. Fortunately there were other opportunities.

While they were all attractive girls, they were not the cheerleaders, nor the most popular at North Hollywood High School. They were the smart ones, the ones who wanted to do things, to think about and discuss issues and ideas and to be leaders in matters of service to the school and the community. Diane and Betty Jo worked in the school library, where they discovered Kenneth Roberts, Alan Paton, Ernest Hemingway, Thomas Costain and Samuel Shellabarger. Diane, Betty Jo and Gretchen were members of Jourdaines, a social club sponsored by the YWCA.

Diane became president of Las Doncellas and a member of Las Amitas, both teen public service groups. She received the Good Citizenship award in a contest sponsored by the D.A.R., and was later elected president of Las Madrinas, an all-girl honor society. Grades were part of its criteria but equally important was how good a citizen she was and how many school service activities she was involved in. Gretchen was its vice president. Virginia, Betty Jo and Charlotte were also members.* The organization's objective was "to work to help the school in every way possible." Its members assisted in the process of student registration, course choices and scheduling, welcomed visitors and ushered at school events.

Boys, needless to say, were important. When Diane persuaded Betty Jo to join her in taking advanced math classes, something virtually unheard of at the time for high school girls, the real reason they took those classes (they handled the work easily) was that was where the boys were. One of the boys had a 1938 Packard. Ten kids could pile into it and drive to Bob's Big Boy, a drive-in hamburger heaven which was the place to go, and to be seen.

Meryl tried to channel Diane's social life into activities connected with the Presbyterian Church because she regarded it as a safe haven for her daughter. And so it was until she met Neil at Forest Home. Neil was handsome and tall – six feet two

---

* By this time Donna's family had moved into a different school district in Los Angeles.

to Diane's five feet seven – and came from a good family in the San Fernando Valley. But he was four years older, had a fiery temper and drove a low-slung, hopped-up convertible with a muffler cut-out that attracted a great deal of attention. While Meryl distrusted every boy who dated her daughter, she was beside herself when Diane at fifteen began regularly dating someone much older, even though he was a Presbyterian. Meryl's eggs were all in the Diane basket – she was the one whose achievements would do the family proud – and Neil posed a threat to that ambition. Diane and her mother had huge arguments. Meryl was certain Diane would get pregnant and that would be an end to her dreams. On one memorable occasion when Neil came by, Meryl forbade her to go. Diane drove off with him nevertheless as Meryl, shouting after them, chased the convertible down the street.

When Diane told Neil she intended to date other boys, he insisted she could not. Telling Diane there was something she could not do was never a sound tactic, as her mother already knew. She began dating others, and one night when she and a date drove up Mulholland Drive to find a parking place, Neil followed them there. After they stopped, Neil strode up to their car and began beating on the locked driver's-side door next to Diane's terrified date. When Neil put his fist through the window, Diane opened the passenger-side door, got out and confronted him. She told him to go home or he would never see her again. He did. Despite this incident, she continued to see Neil, even after she had gone off to Stanford and met another young man who became important in her life, but was equally possessive.

North Hollywood High School was a triumph for Diane in all ways. She was becoming her own person, independent of her mother's wishes. She'd inspired and guided her friends, and given them the confidence to move ahead and make something of their own lives. Betty Jo would have been daunted by the prospect of advanced math classes had it not been for Diane's example and encouragement. She steered Charlotte into academic classes. When Charlotte had great difficulty with geometry and geology, Diane met with her before school in the library and went through the lessons with her. All six had confidence that they were going somewhere and were bound for big things.

Where Diane was going was Stanford University. Admission had not been a problem. She had achieved the highest score on the SAT tests of any high school senior west of the

"My life," says Betty Jo, "was never the same after I met Diane. I wanted to grow up to be like her. While there is a little of each of the six of us that is some part of the others, there is a large part of all of us which is Diane."

"I probably would not have gone to college but for her," says Charlotte. "As it was, thanks to her, I went to Occidental – a very good school."

Even today, Charlotte and Betty Jo believe Diane shaped their lives.

Mississippi. Being able to pay for that superb education was something else. On April 25, 1955, Stanford wrote to inform her that "the Committee has awarded you a Mabel Wilson Richards Honors Scholarship of $1000 for the academic year 1955-56." The scholarship would be renewable each year on maintenance of at least a 3.0 average, and would pay a major portion of her tuition.

She still needed to supplement her parents' modest means. Despite virtually no interest in the subject, she entered the Betty Crocker Homemaker contest, which awarded cash prizes on the results of a written examination. A test-taker without peer, she was one of twenty-nine Los Angeles winners. In May, at the annual Bank of America Achievement Awards ceremony for high school seniors,* Diane received the award for science and mathematics. The honor carried with it a $250 scholarship.

One important event remained before Diane left North Hollywood to be on her own for the first time. On August 5, 1955, just after she had turned seventeen, Diane was maid of honor when Noreen married Carl Hunter. A few weeks later, in September 1955, George and Meryl drove her to the Stanford campus. No one knew what to expect, least of all Diane.

Diane as a senior at North Hollywood High School, 1955.

---

* "To honor those seniors whose records as students indicate most promise of future success and service to society," not only through grades but because they have "demonstrated qualities of leadership, character, personality, regard for others and a sense of civic responsibility."

CHAPTER THREE

THE STANFORD EXPERIENCE

THE SEEDS PLANTED BY THE Presbyterian call to serve the public good bloomed when Diane arrived at Stanford and met another extraordinary young woman, Sue Borshell. Sue was sixteen, Diane barely seventeen, the two of them the youngest women in the freshman class. Both now free for the first time from family convention, they explored together the intellectual world of unfettered ideas, ideas freely discussed long into the night.

Stanford seemed an ideal forum. Its reputation and intellectual atmosphere attracted the top echelon of students west of the Mississippi. Its spacious campus, thousands of acres given by the railroad baron Leland Stanford in the late 1880s, lent a physical component to its students' new sense of freedom. Renowned landscape architect Frederick Olmsted had laid out the core of Stanford's gift – long, low two- and three-story buildings connected by arcades and Spanish arches – around a spacious double quadrangle lined with imposing live oaks and eucalyptus trees. Charles Coolidge, a prominent Boston architect whose firm was heir to the tradition of H.H. Richardson, drew the detailed building plans.

The campus centerpiece is the soaring Hoover Tower, where ex-President Herbert Hoover worked in his later years while living on the Stanford campus. Hoover was once a construction engineer by profession and the tower was familiarly known to Stanford students as "Hoover's Last Erection."

Built of sandstone quarried south of San Jose, transported to the site by a special spur railroad line built by Stanford, the buildings echoed the Spanish Mission tradition. When the university opened its doors in 1891 to 559 students, it was hailed as the most splendid example of college architecture in the country.

Stanford promised to be welcoming for women because Stanford – unlike Harvard – had admitted women to its student body from the day it opened its doors.* Its original buildings included Roble Hall, a women's dormitory in the southwest corner of the campus. When Diane entered Stanford in the fall of 1955, Roble was ivy-covered and with a red-tiled roof, and exclusively a dormitory for freshmen women.

If one assumed that Stanford would encourage women to achieve academically and professionally, and that a liberal view of women's roles would prevail, that wasn't the case in the 1950s.

Different rules applied to women than to men. Women had a 10:30 p.m. curfew, perhaps 1:30 a.m. with permission and 2:30 a.m. with special permission on rare occasions. They had to sign in and sign out of Roble. They had a strict housemother (who later married Mark Hatfield, a future governor of Oregon). The parietal rules embodied the university's view that it had an obligation to its young women's parents to watch over and protect them. Women had a dress code that required them to wear skirts or dresses to class and prohibited their wearing slacks on the university's quadrangle, not to mention (God forbid!) jeans.

The male-to-female ratio was more than four to one, and women had difficulty being taken seriously as students. There were no women role models on the faculty and no incentive for women to become interested in law, engineering or medicine or, for that matter, academia. Their advisors rarely discussed with them what professional ambitions they might have. The unspoken (and sometimes spoken) assumption was that they'd come to Stanford to find a suitable husband, and they'd been admitted to the university because they had the capacity to become suitable wives for the best and brightest young men the West had to offer. They were there for breeding purposes.

The attitudes of the men on the faculty toward their attractive female students reflected this view. Their interest in women in their classrooms was often not academic, especially (but not exclusively) in the case of those who were bachelors. Male professors (married or not) pursued social and sexual relationships with their students, and women found themselves invited on dates or to dinner by male teachers who were assessing and grading their work. They found the experience disorienting, and were unsure how to respond. No guidance was offered.

Sexism was particularly rampant in the hard sciences and the professions. One

---

* Jane Stanford, who'd planned the school with her husband, had insisted on its being coeducational from the start and later had assumed responsibility for its financial well-being for ten years after her husband's death.

gifted young woman who had enrolled in an advanced engineering course was called aside by her professor in the first week of the course. He knew why she was there, he said, "to get her *MRS.* degree." She was taking the place of a man in his course and if she didn't withdraw, he would flunk her out of it. She didn't, and he did. There were no institutional repercussions on account of his actions because there were no principles governing his conduct and no forum to which women could appeal. The professor's conduct was a fact of life. Women who invaded male-only domain had no recourse but to accept the reality of male views of their expected station in life. In this instance, the student had had dreams of a career in engineering. Dispirited, she left Stanford and never returned to her dream.

Diane and her roommates encountered sexist attitudes that would be unthinkable today. One, a valedictorian in her Kansas City high school, settled on philosophy as her major. A requirement was a term paper that would synthesize and comment on various strains of philosophical thought. She succeeded in producing a splendid work, both thoughtful and analytical. Shortly after the paper had been handed in, the professor asked her to stay behind after class. Basking in the glow of what she knew to be a first-rate piece of work, she expected to be complimented. Instead the professor accused her of plagiarism. No student, he said – and certainly no girl – could have produced such original work. Shy by nature, she insisted through her tears that the work was entirely hers. He was unable to prove otherwise and had to accept it, however grudgingly. She was scarred, and the experience is still vivid for her today.

Another decided to go on to do graduate work in political science, and applied for a Woodrow Wilson Fellowship. Stanford had two three-member panels – all male – to interview applicants and evaluate their work for the purpose of making recommendations. A professor on one of the panels was fond of saying publicly that he saw no point in women going on to graduate school because further education "would be of no use to them in running a vacuum cleaner." He routinely rejected women applicants. By chance, this young woman was interviewed by the other panel, and received her fellowship. She later earned a master's degree and a Ph.D. in political science and went on to a successful career with the State Department in Washington.*

A third classmate, a biology major with a brilliant record, was guided into a career as a medical laboratory technician. In time, she became the director of the medical lab in a major San Jose hospital, but, in a later era, she would have been a physician.†

The attitudes that held women back in the 1950s were not confined to the academic and professional worlds – the prejudices were part of our national culture. One reality

---

* Her attorney daughter is today a member of the Office of Legal Counsel in the Department of Justice and raising a daughter of her own.
† Today, putting on her laboratory director's hat, she remarks ruefully that she misses the high performance standards that characterized lab technicians when she was younger – the women who forty years ago would have become lab technicians have become doctors.

of that culture was that there were few professional opportunities open to women, regardless of their talents and academic achievements. Their families expected that their daughters would marry when they graduated and then begin raising families – and indeed, having a strong relationship with a man was important for women at Stanford. Most of them expected – and were expected – to have a steady boyfriend and to marry that boyfriend. A large percentage of women in Diane's class married immediately after graduation.

Diane and her roommates weren't excluded from these expectations. One roommate's mother told her that if she went on to get her Ph.D., she'd never get married. Diane's mother, while ambitious for her, thought she'd marry and settle down close to home. The mother of the woman who pursued a career in the State Department never gave up hope that she would choose to be a high school teacher. On learning that her daughter was considering law school, she was appalled. Her son told her that the only women who were successful lawyers were "battle-axes" and not at all feminine. Her parents wouldn't give her the money she needed to take the Law School Aptitude Test.

There were exceptions. Sue Borshell's mother had long held radical political views*and wanted her daughter to become a fiery human rights activist lawyer. However, despite scoring in the 96th percentile on the Law School Aptitude Test, Sue rejected the law as her career. She had wanted all her life to become a teacher and that's what she became, following her own star and not the star set out for her by others.

Perhaps their decisions reflected the rebelliousness of youth; or perhaps they were decisions made by a generation of women who, for the first time, felt empowered to shape their lives as they saw fit and not as others saw fit for them. It's interesting that despite their experiences, neither Diane nor her close friends resented then, or even much later, the sexist attitudes they encountered at Stanford. They internalized the cultural attitudes of the times and that internalization stayed with them. They were not the generation that organized and rebelled against male domination. That generation would come next. Instead, their memories of Stanford are generally positive and they hold themselves fortunate to have been admitted to such a highly selective institution. It represented a major opportunity few women had then, and something for which they've been grateful.

Sexism was not a burning issue for Diane and Sue when they entered the university. What the two of them first discovered in each other was not intellectual – it was the immediate excitement of being part of the "new talent" on campus, objects of focused male interest at a time in their lives when male attention was at a premium. They enjoyed being attractive young women on a campus where they were outnumbered by men four to one. They and their third suite-mate had been the nerds in high school, the valedictorians, not the "popular girls" that the football players dated. At Stanford, they reinvented

---

* She was arrested several times in the Seattle Vietnam War protests – and came to the Republican Convention in New York City in 2004 hoping, at the age of 88, to be arrested again.

themselves, heeding their mothers' advice to "dumb down" so the men wouldn't be scared off by their brainpower.

Stanford did two things to encourage social contact among its freshmen. It published and distributed the "Frosh Book," a roster with photos of the entering freshman class, and it sponsored mixers. The pool of new talent was not just female, and women as well as men pored over the photos. In their third-floor suite in Roble, the three girls and their new friends tried to decide who was the cutest boy. There was no consensus. Their introduction to Stanford was an intense period of "endless parties" in which the men from one freshman dorm would come to meet the women in another.

Sue viewed Diane as both brilliant and "stunningly beautiful," a virtual social butterfly. Diane was five feet seven inches tall, had auburn hair cut short, which framed a mischievous face with sparkling eyes, and wore clothes that flattered a taut, trim and slim figure. Perhaps most important, she exuded a playfulness that men seemed to find irresistible. Within five minutes of arriving at a party, she would be surrounded by men while she stood demurely, hands folded, smiling, blinking her eyes and saying sweetly to the boys, "Go ahead, snow me…." She acted like someone in a Doris Day movie, "but it worked so well! The rest of us were jealous beyond belief."*

It was a heady time. So many handsome young men, so little time. They needed a strategy, an idea which appealed to Diane's sense of organization. "Suki [Sue] had a brainstorm," she said. "We would start a file on the boys, since they were what we were interested in, and in that way we could keep everyone straight! Our file got fuller and fuller until we had to give it up…."

The file cards described the young men they met. Some turned out to be interesting, some not: "When this one called, we were always busy…. Dear old Jeff turned out to be a cad and we kissed him off…. All-American good-looking guy but a pseudo…." Others stayed on the list: "Duncan is great and Suki had a good time…." One of their cards was for Steven Breyer, later Mr. Justice Breyer of the United States Supreme Court. His card read:

> 9-23-55
> Breyer, Steven
> Dorm: Freedman 17
> Law, Democrat
> 6', Fine looking
> Brilliant – discuss politics, but not conservative.
> Serious, hard to tease – D.T.
> (x-tra special!) – S.B.

---

* Sue Borshell Leonard interview.

Steve Breyer had been one of Sue's high school classmates and they had dated occasionally. She bristled when, during his confirmation process, an article described him as the smartest person in his high school. "He wasn't," she says. "I was!"

At the bottom of the card was Diane's note: "One of the greatest guys ever! And what a beautiful mind…."

They were self-confident and high-spirited in their encounters with men, Sue especially so. They became part of Stanford's football scene. "We all went to the football games in red skirts and white blouses, clutching red pom-poms and pinning Indian feathers in our hair,"* wrote Diane. "I really felt a part of Stanford when I sat in the stands yelling and knowing that the team down there was <u>mine</u>! We beat Cal 38-0, and then we beat Southern Cal in the Coliseum!" They went together to the annual football rally where virtually the entire student body cheered as a forty-foot-high wooden structure was set afire on the dry bed of Lake LaGuinta behind Roble Hall.

In private conversations with their friends in Roble, they were outgoing and unrestrained.

They examined sexual issues candidly, without reservation. Although older by two years, their suite-mate, who'd been brought up in Kansas City, thought the two of them were much more sophisticated than she was. She still remembers free-flowing conversations about lesbianism, something about which she knew nothing. She was shocked by their candor in these conversations, and the shock never entirely dissipated.

One of Diane's early ambitions was to become a fashion designer. She had an eye for style and could translate that eye to paper effortlessly. For a time, to earn some money, she modeled for a Stanford-area dress shop. These ambitions quickly became sidelines. Her conversations with Sue Borshell about politics, religion and social justice expanded her ambitions forever – but, her doodles in the margins of her class notes and her letters would always be filled with elegant line drawings of stylish women.

Diane modeling "a knockout dress of pure silk taffeta, set off by white organdy bodice," as described in a store ad.

---

*   Stanford teams were then the "Indians" not the "Cardinals" of today.

SOCIALIST AND PACIFIST

Sue and Diane shared their most personal thoughts on religion, philosophy, men and politics, as well as sex. While Sue, concerned about prejudice, had listed on her application her religion as Unitarian, it was not. Her family, unlike Diane's, was not observant on religious matters. Nevertheless, the two of them visited various churches in the Palo Alto area during their first few weeks at Stanford to see if there were one where they'd both feel comfortable. In the end, they concluded that religion, apart from humanistic principles, wasn't something on which they had common ground, either with each other or with the denominations they visited. From that time on, except when she was home, Diane no longer attended Sunday services.

While the Presbyterians had instilled in Diane a strong sense of mission, she hadn't incorporated that sense into political views. Sue Borshell, by contrast, held radical political views derived from conversations with her mother, who was by conviction at least a socialist and very near a Communist. In 1956, Stanford was a conservative campus solidly liking Ike. When Sue appeared in its dining rooms unabashedly wearing a large Stevenson button, she was heckled and hooted at unmercifully. Eventually she decided to leave Stanford at the end of the school year, and transferred to Berkeley, where the political atmosphere was measurably more compatible. In the interim, she and Diane spent many hours parsing at length the relative merits of socialism and capitalism.

Socialism appealed to Diane's sense of fairness and social justice, and was consistent both with the teachings of her church and with the way in which her close-knit family had ridden out the Depression. While she never advocated socialism, her personal beliefs and behavior mirrored its principles until the end of her life. She never charged her clients any more than they could afford to pay, and sometimes charged not at all. She was always generous to others with money. The idea of having wealth made her uneasy.

The principles underlying pacifism were also consistent with Diane's own beliefs. War was anathema to her and coercion never a part of her life. She believed that everything worthwhile could be achieved by cooperation, and she would later reject notions of the value of the adversary system that Harvard Law School sought to instill in its students. She held that advocacy had value only if one believed in the ends of that advocacy.

Sue Borshell and Diane remained friends after

Diane's pacifism in the face of the Communist threat of the 1960s and 1970s gave rise to the only running argument I can recall our having during our years of marriage. Even under Communism, she thought, our society could move forward cooperatively to achieve its legitimate goals.

Sue transferred to Berkeley,* but their friendship didn't regain the strength and intensity that had characterized their year together as freshmen. Nevertheless, the influence of their early friendship stayed with Diane during the whole of her life. They had shared not only philosophical discussions of religion, politics and governmental systems, but many other important things, serious things – doing well in their courses – and fun things – the pursuit of handsome young men they met. For two young women on their own for the first time, the year had been exciting, eventful and formative.

DECIDING ON A CAREER IN THE LAW

Diane's ability to read quickly and to absorb information from textbooks and her classes was extraordinary. Eager to learn, she took extra courses each quarter, enjoying challenges such as having to produce original term papers. Her concentration and focus were legendary among her friends. She could simultaneously absorb and assimilate information from her texts, which she had annotated in the margins, and compose term papers, referring back and forth from her own notes to the texts she would cite, which were strewn about on her dorm-room floor. If need be, she stayed up the entire night in order to finish a paper on time. She needed no written outline. The outline was in her head.

Organization and mental discipline were keys to her earning the A's that seemed to come to her effortlessly. She could compartmentalize the various aspects of her life: a compartment for each of her courses, another for social life, another for relaxing with friends. When she was in one or another compartment, her concentration was fierce, shutting out anything extraneous. When she studied, she studied. When she partied, she partied. One result was that she never seemed pressed and always had time to do the things she wanted.

Among other things, oddly, she became a disk jockey at KZSU, Stanford's radio station, playing classical music and contemporary records such as Frank Sinatra's *In the Still of the Night*.

In June 1956, her application for admission to Stanford's Honors Program was approved and in August her full scholarship was renewed.

Diane's discipline may well have been instilled by Meryl, but Meryl was concerned that the ambitions and goals she had for her daughter were slipping away at Stanford. She'd devoted much of her life to her daughter, as tutor, guide, Girl Scout den mother, hostess and organizer, and was convinced that her work might be undone by Diane's new-found freedom. Not impressed with her daughter's self-discipline, nor with the selflessness she believed was critical to leading a worthwhile life, Meryl wrote Diane after Christmas vacation:

---

* Sue returned to Stanford a year later for her junior and senior years.

Discipline is what you lack. Get busy and make yourself do a few things you dislike doing; because you know that doing these things may make someone else happy. This is the only way you gain character – the harder the task is for you, the more you gain by doing it. Please spend the next few Wednesday evenings in the Chapel meditating on these things which give me such a troubled heart. I know you are surrounded by so much activity that you do not have a chance to really think about the spiritual things of life – and unless you will get away by yourself and really ask God to help you grow in your spiritual life as well as your mental life, you are at a standstill – or, worse, slipping. God can only speak to you in a quiet place – and without this guidance, you are lost.

There were other issues – the conflicts one might expect between a mother and her seventeen-year-old daughter:

What a relief to finally get a letter from you!!! All last Saturday afternoon – after I came home from work and found no letter – I could just see you lying in some morgue for the last two weeks – unclaimed and seemingly no one caring about your whereabouts. It would have taken only one minute of your time to write on a slip of paper "I arrived safe and sound – and am knee deep in activities.…"

Just stop and think – just what did you do the ten days you were home to show us in a small or large way that you really were glad that you were one of the family – and were fortunate to have parents whose big dream was to have a daughter well educated in the school of her choice – and able to make decisions which would bring her a lifetime of happiness? It would have been so easy to have dinner ready once in a while – to have kept your room spick and span, to at least have said thank you for all but mortgaging the house to get you money for clothes, etc., etc.

The letter closed on a softer note:

Goodnight – loads of love to a very fine girl – who we hope stays that way.… It sure was nice you got the highest marks in your corridor.…

Diane kept this letter among her papers – almost alone of her mother's letters – for forty years. The fact that she had reinvented herself at Stanford wasn't lost on her, and perhaps this reminder was needed to rein in her new persona. Or perhaps it was a reminder of what she was fighting against, and reinforced that persona.

While her mother may have thought her immature, that was not the impression she gave to her classmates. From the beginning of their freshman year, they felt she was more emotionally mature and wiser than most of her peers, despite her young age, and that she had a healthy perspective and sense of humor about the social challenges and academic rigors Stanford presented. Her approach to men at the freshman year social exchanges was one example. Another was her response to a standard, but important, assignment early on in a freshman English composition course, which was to write a how-to essay on a subject of their own choice. Most opted for a high-flown unimaginative topic such as "How to Be an Intellectual," to demonstrate to the professor the seriousness of their purpose. Diane's essay was "How to Read the *New Yorker*." It was witty, elegant and playful, and began by stressing the importance of first reading all the cartoons before getting into the articles. Few freshmen would have had the nerve to do such a thing in response to a formal assignment. The professor loved it and her classmates remember it still.

Although left-handed, Diane had invented for herself a unique and fluid way of writing totally unlike the cramped overhand style taught in elementary school. She could write quickly and legibly, using a fountain pen. In a Western Civilization exam, she answered the questions so quickly that she had enough extra time to write her own Socratic dialogue to illustrate the points she wanted to emphasize. Before going into a final exam, Diane would devise a complex mnemonic of letters to remind her of all the principles and other material she wanted to have at hand in the examination. She memorized it, then wrote it down, and the points it stood for, on her exam book at the beginning of the test period.

Intent from the outset on meeting others' expectations and then exploring and finding what limits her ability had, she was keenly aware that she was the first in her family to go to university. The idea that she might fail at something never occurred to her. She was serious about doing something worthwhile with her life; she was centered and had a sense of purpose and direction. Exactly what it was she would do was unclear at the beginning, but whatever it was, its value would lie in serving the greater community and not in personal financial gain.

She began to be interested in law as a career as a result of conversations with Sue Borshell and Jack Nessel, their classmate and close friend. Sue's mother wanted her to become a lawyer, Jack was planning on it himself, and Diane was mulling the possibility at the same time. She was also considering taking her junior year abroad at St. Andrews in Scotland, which proved to be out of reach. While Diane was playing a classical record on the turntable during one of her DJ sessions at KZSU, she wrote Sue at Berkeley:

> I may be "Stanford Sadie" next year, as I'm not going to the Highlands or the Lowlands – both St. Andrews and Bristol are full. I haven't heard from London yet, but it'll probably be the same thing…. I may go to summer school and graduate next year – get the jump on you and Jack for law school. I'm very enthused about it suddenly….

Having accumulated credits from extra courses she'd taken already and others she would take in her junior year, summer school would provide the credits she needed to graduate in three years. Having in mind the financial burden on her family, she made the decision to go ahead with summer school, still unsure about law school. One of her summer courses – International Law – caused her to become genuinely excited about a legal career, and on returning to her regular schedule in the fall, she made an appointment to see her advisor.

"Why," he asked, "would you want to go to law school? Law is a man's profession and you would just be taking a man's place in law school. You are an English major with an excellent academic record. I strongly recommend you consider something else, like becoming an English teacher…."

No one had ever suggested that her career choices were gender-related, and she'd never before encountered overt sexist attitudes directed toward herself. This was the first of many such encounters. Diane wasn't someone who gave in to anger, but to say she was taken aback by the suggestion that she should abandon an ambition because she was a woman, would be to put it mildly. Feeling insulted and demeaned, she came back to her dorm room steaming, and paced quickly and nervously about the room, so angry she couldn't sit down. If she'd ever had doubts about the wisdom of going to law school, they'd been erased. She became determined not just to go on to law school, but to go to the most prestigious one – Harvard.

She finished in the 97th percentile on the Law School Aptitude Test, and began to explore, in a typically organized way, the realities of law practice for women. Having no encouragement from her advisor and knowing no lawyers or law students to whom she could turn, she sent for and obtained a publication of the U.S. Department of Labor entitled "Employment Opportunities for Women in Legal Work." While it encouraged women to go to law school, it also made it clear they should expect their opportunities to be limited. One part read:

> The law, for centuries a profession for men, has in the past few decades opened its doors to women. The legal profession is a highly competitive one where it is not easy to gain a foothold, but where success is highly rewarded. Guidance from the legal profession is sought by the Nation and its people on complex questions relating to labor management relations, taxation, the development of natural resources, international relations and many other aspects of national life. Moreover, the law offers unique opportunities to promote justice and to help individuals protect their rights.
>
> Increasing numbers of women students give serious consideration to the legal profession in planning for a career. This bulletin is intended primarily to summarize for such students and their counselors the progress of women in the

legal field, the preparation needed and the prospective opportunities for women as practicing attorneys and in salaried positions where legal writing is required….

To women who seek salaried legal employment, excellent academic records from law schools recognized as having high standards are especially important. Many women lawyers find Government employment attractive, and various federal agencies have reported an acute shortage of young qualified lawyers. Opportunities for advancement may also be more numerous in Government service, especially for lawyers who remain in public service long enough to acquire the experience needed for responsible legal posts.

Many recent law graduates have been employed outside of the legal profession in related jobs by private industry and Government. A number of women who have succeeded in such fields as teaching, finance, writing and business administration feel that their legal training was a definite asset to their careers, even when not a job requirement….

On the whole, women's opportunities in the legal profession may grow, especially in such areas as taxation, domestic relations, probate and patent law….

Once established in the profession, a well-qualified, highly competent woman lawyer can anticipate professional success. Furthermore the individual successes of outstanding women lawyers serve to open career doors in legal fields that have been partially closed to women lawyers as a group….

The publication advised that women would be encouraged to seek Government employment, or to specialize in such areas as probate and juvenile cases, and to work on legal aid cases. It went on to say, "Women lawyers employed by law firms often have duties that involve legal research rather than client contacts and trial work in court. Experiences in legal research can be valuable for later part-time work for those who have family responsibilities but who do not wish to leave law practice entirely. Women law graduates, however, have experienced difficulties in finding employment in law firms, most of which reportedly do not interview them for employment."

Statistically, women represented 3.5% of all law graduates in 1956, and 6.5% of all lawyers and judges employed by federal, state and local governments. While the barriers to women in the legal profession were plain without having to read between the lines, the challenge was also evident. What appealed particularly to Diane were the possibilities of a career in which she could "promote justice," protect the rights of individuals and open career doors to other women. She would be a pioneer without a compass, and this too appealed to her.

It's hard to believe this is my last year at Stanford, already. Maybe I shouldn't have rushed through things the way I have, but I think I'm ready now to go on. These three years have taught me many things, and I'm grateful for them....

She applied for admission to Harvard, Stanford, Michigan and Yale and was accepted by all four. Stanford offered her a full scholarship. Michigan did the same. Harvard did not commit itself. Nevertheless the law school Diane wanted is clear from her letter home on May 7, 1988:

Your daughter is among the elite! I have been accepted at Harvard Law School!

Enclosed are scholarship forms. Get them in the mail as soon as possible. I put down that you can give me $900. It'll cost $2900, which means a $2000 scholarship? Wow!... I listed my $250 loan as outstanding. Please make me sound poor but honest – and do it fast!

On June 30 she received a telegram from Harvard that she'd been awarded a $1400 scholarship, with the additional prospect of student loans. She made her decision immediately and notified Stanford, Michigan and Yale – and Bill, the classmate she'd dated regularly for three years – that she intended to go to Harvard.

It was a complex decision and the considerations involved weren't limited to academic prestige and financial concerns. She was being pressed to accept a marriage proposal, and she wasn't prepared to say yes. Distance would make it easier to say no.

MEN IN HER LIFE

Diane had a penchant for "bad boys," men who were different from the ordinary mold and presented in some form or another a sense of risk or danger. They weren't the men her mother would have chosen for her, and the ones she brought home found her mother unwelcoming, prickly and protective. The men she favored not only fell heedlessly in love with her but became possessive, and jealous of her spending time with any other man. She regarded their possessiveness with equanimity, even if she thought she was in love – and there were times when she did. She was her own person, and she'd spend her time with whoever she liked. While she didn't crave male attention, she liked it. Even after she was married and the mother of young children, she would smile at wolf whistles that came her way from workmen on a Boston construction site as she walked by, stylishly dressed in striking clothes and wearing the high heels that made her legs look so fine.

At some point toward the end of her freshman year at Stanford, Diane prepared a list of "Boys I Have Kissed" with thirty-four names and stars beside the names to indicate the seriousness of the relationship. One star indicated they'd kissed after they "were old enough to know what was happening." Two indicated they'd "made out." The increasing intensity of the relationship was indicated by stars three through five. A more complex set of symbols indicated whether he'd said he loved her, whether she'd said she loved him, whether they'd talked about marriage and whether she really wanted to marry him. Half the names had at least one star. Only Bill and Neil had five.

Bill, known as "Slick," was tall, leather-jacketed, darkly handsome and targeted as one of the very good-looking boys in the Frosh Book. He wore his hair combed into a d.a. and drove a hot car whose rear wheels were far larger than the front ones. A football player on the freshman team, there is no doubt he had an edge to him, the "bad boy" characteristic that so attracted Diane. She'd met him, not in one of the exchanges, but in their freshman English course, and she took an immediate liking to him, even though she already had a busy dating schedule. (According to Sue, she and Diane had dates every night during their first few weeks at Stanford, and sometimes both an early date and a late date. It was a "crazy time.") Bill recalls their meeting as one in which Diane picked him out from a crowd and decided that he was going to be "it." They would date regularly, but not exclusively, for the next three years.

One of their issues – another element of risk, perhaps – was that he was from a good Catholic family in which one was expected to marry in the Church. In the 1950s, the only way a Catholic could marry a non-Catholic in the Church was if the latter took appropriate religious instruction and converted to Catholicism before the wedding. A Catholic was not permitted to participate in any Protestant church ceremony, such as a wedding, nor could a Protestant participate in any Catholic ceremony. In a moment of candor Diane was heard to remark that she simply couldn't see her children growing up and running around with crucifixes on chains around their necks. Even so, and even though she dated other men, she thought she was in love with Bill.

Not surprisingly, the possibility of Diane's marrying a Catholic posed an insurmountable obstacle in Meryl's mind, and she did what she could to derail the romance. For a Protestant from the Midwest serious about her religion – which Meryl was – consorting with a Catholic was like consorting with the devil himself, and so she viewed Bill. She had other reasons as well: in an ill-advised move, Bill had mailed Diane a pair of lace panties in an envelope that Meryl opened. Meryl went through the roof! Perhaps Diane was amused, but Bill was not. In a letter to Sue Borshell in the summer of 1956, he described Meryl's suspicious mind and asked for Sue's help to keep Meryl and his letters to Diane separated.

He also asked Sue not to give his letter to Diane, but she did. Sue also was not enthusiastic about the relationship.

In the fall of their sophomore year, Bill joined a fraternity, Zeta Psi, which seemed a likely place for him but not a place where Diane would be comfortable. The Zetes were known to be a haven for Stanford jocks, noted for their arrogance, for having wild parties and for treating women badly. (The legendary Stanford quarterback John Brodie was a Zete whose zest for life didn't stop on the football field.) Perhaps this created still another edge to their relationship that Diane enjoyed. It certainly didn't impair it.

She continued dating other men. On the same summer day that Slick left North Hollywood after a visit, Diane went off to play golf with Neil. Slick complained bitterly. On his way home, he managed to total his parents' car which, unbeknownst to them, he'd borrowed for the trip. He was all right, but it was not a happy homecoming.

That summer, Sue introduced Diane to a group of young men they called "the Chileans," who lived in a compound in the Laurel Canyon area of Los Angeles. They'd become a major part of Sue's summer social life after she'd met them by chance. Sue was staying with her father, who she characterizes as someone who could have been the prototype for Willy Loman. Divorced from her mother, he was a salesman who lived far beyond his means, owned a series of Cadillacs he couldn't afford, and was living with an attractive Swedish woman who loved horses. After they'd bought two horses and stabled them, Sue would go out to the stable to ride. There she met a charming stable boy who was Chilean, and he introduced her to a young male Chilean community.

Sons of rich and important families connected to Chile's military dictatorship, they'd been sent to the U.S. to receive an American education, which would give them social and political advantages on their return. When Diane and Sue drove to the beach to hang out with them, and to visit their compound, politics wasn't the subject of their conversations. The young men were older, foreign and exotic. They had "great parties filled with Chilean wine and dancing" where Diane and Sue were the center of attention, as there were rarely more than a few other women present.

One of them, Pedro, the son of a Chilean general, fell in love with Diane. She stayed in touch with him after she returned to Stanford, and dated him when she was home on vacation, but she viewed their relationship as fun, not serious. He had a different view. When he found that his love wasn't reciprocated, he wrote her a touching letter in which he described his feelings, said he understood she didn't share them and concluded it was best they not see each other again because he could never view her as "just another date."

In the fall of 1956, Diane met another Bill, Bill Robinson, a day student at Stanford who commuted from his home six miles away, and so was not part of the social life at the university. He was the assistant station manager at KZSU when she and a friend auditioned to become announcers or disk jockeys. The job carried no salary, but Diane wanted to do it for fun. The station's chief announcer hired her, and Bill became the studio engineer for her shows. He fell in love with her soon after she first came to work. They dated occasionally but not steadily, usually after a session at the station, taking in a movie or going bowling or simply going out on a lark.

Driving back along Skyline Drive after a midwinter trip to the San Francisco Zoo, she listened as he told her about the difficulties his family had faced and about how important his much younger brother was to him. The next Valentine's Day, he received a homemade valentine depicting a large heart divided in different sections for different parts of his life, one section being reserved for his brother. Before shipping out on his NROTC training in the summer of 1957, he came to stay a couple of days with Diane's family in North Hollywood. He remembers her saying, "I wish they would stop pressuring me – I'm only nineteen!" Given the very private person he knew she was, he thought it unusual that she'd burden him with her own problems. The statement came as a surprise because it seemed to him that she was not under pressure, she'd been making her own decisions, and she knew what she wanted to do with her life.

They had different agendas and the two agendas didn't match. She was moving on with life and expanding her horizons. He had a three-year Naval ROTC officer's commitment after graduation, and planned to go to law school after that. They were in no position to marry and both viewed the situation realistically. Another reason may have been that she'd become jaded by the interest men took in her: she wrote to Sue at Berkeley that she was growing tired of "miscellaneous characters being in love with me."

Meryl, meanwhile, was searching for a suitable husband. When Diane and one of her roommates came to stay with the Theis family over Easter vacation in 1957, Diane learned to her surprise that Meryl had arranged a date with a young Presbyterian minister. She wasn't enthused over her mother's idea of who her boyfriends should be, but she went out with him anyway, showing she was a dutiful daughter. She took defensive measures, though, making sure that the date was a double date that included her roommate and another young man. Romance had no chance on that occasion.

While taking summer courses at Stanford that same year, Diane connected with a handsome and brutally attractive Wyoming cowboy, and visited him at his parents' ranch. In a scrapbook she prepared for her parents to show her appreciation for her years at Stanford, he merited four photos, usually next to his horse, while Slick - the real contender - had not a single mention.

In the 1950s and 1960s there was a fraternity mating ritual at colleges and universities called "pinning," which referred to a fraternity

Chick Gast, the Wyoming cowboy.

member giving, and his girl accepting, his fraternity pin. The era's five-stage sequence of romance was: going steady in high school, dating and then pinning in college, getting engaged and getting married. Pinning was an expression of seriousness and a rite of passage toward marriage, and was an important goal for both men and women. Often, pinning served to remove a barrier to sexual freedom in those more rigid and unenlightened times. The couple was, after all, *almost engaged*.

Diane and Slick were not immune to the peer pressure involved and the recognition, freedom and envy that came with being pinned. In October 1957, they became pinned, an event that was formally and duly recorded (along with other pinnings) in the Stanford newspaper. She was of two minds about it. Although she was only nineteen, she was in her last year at Stanford and it was important for her, like her peers, to demonstrate that she was attractive, emotionally competent and ready for what was generally thought to be the next logical phase of her life, marriage and raising a family. Even after she'd decided on Harvard, part of her couldn't help but yearn for the more traditional and acceptable ending to her academic career, that of marriage. She may well have been still in love with Slick. The goal of marriage, however, was at odds with what she wanted to do.

It was a difficult summer for each of them. He continued to press his suit, while she tried to deflect it. In late July she wrote him a gentle "Dear John" letter which, at first, he was unwilling to accept. Finally, in late August, a week before she left for Harvard, he wrote her that he understood that she had the right to choose and that this was her choice. He wished her well and hoped that she would become "the best damn woman lawyer you can be."

A week later she would be in Cambridge, Massachusetts, registering for her classes, and she and I would meet for the first time.

CHAPTER FOUR

CAMBRIDGE & HARVARD LAW SCHOOL

BESIDES HITCHHIKING, THE CHEAPEST WAY FOR DIANE TO get from Los Angeles to Boston was by Greyhound. Two stops outside of Los Angeles, an obese, perspiring man carrying a picnic basket got on and settled in on the seat next to hers. He smelled of garlic and onions, and his basket was crammed with sandwiches similarly garnished, which he ate more or less continuously during his waking hours. From time to time he offered some to Diane who – nauseated by the confluence of aromas – had opened the window. She politely declined and kept her head turned toward the rush of fresh air. Whatever appetite she might have had for her own sandwiches had been overwhelmed. His stop was Chicago. By that time, she was unable to choose between wanting to satisfy her hunger pangs and thinking she never wanted to see food again.

Chicago was a stop she remembered gratefully, and not only because her seat-mate left the bus and she could eat again. In the Greyhound terminal, she could take a shower, and with an hour's layover, she paid for a locker and took advantage of the opportunity.

She arrived in Boston on a Thursday morning with an enormously heavy trunk weighed down by a record player, her record collection, a reading lamp, shoes, boots, warm clothes and an overcoat for the Northeast winter, and the meager remains of a cache of paperback murder mysteries. (She'd read and discarded most of them one by one on the way.) She also had two indestructible Samsonite suitcases, one so large she could barely schlepp it around. She checked the trunk and big suitcase, hefted the smaller one, and set out to find Harvard and her dorm room.

Asking directions, she managed to navigate the Boston subway system – the "T"

Langdell Hall and Library, the heart of Harvard Law School.

– and soon was climbing stairs into sunshine, open air and the confusing traffic of Harvard Square. She was ready to discover Harvard University.

For her, the word "university" meant a broad green campus with large open spaces, quadrangles, shade trees and walkways. Looking around, she saw nothing that met that description.

What met her eye instead were busy streets, storefronts, a dilapidated newspaper kiosk, a small park opposite an ancient cemetery, and an ivy-covered brick wall with brick buildings huddling behind it. She was surprised to find she was where she was supposed to be, and that the brick wall enclosed the undergraduate college. Harvard Law School was farther away out Massachusetts Avenue, across its intersections with two other busy streets and opposite a park called a "Commons," a new word for her vocabulary.

On arriving there, suitcase in hand, she learned that the law school's dormitories were male-only, and her expectation that she'd be assigned a dorm room was a delusion. A single small, cheerless brick building called Wyeth Hall, oversubscribed long since by women in the know, was Harvard's only campus accommodation for women in its graduate programs. Neither Harvard nor Stanford had thought to mention that to her. (Harvard had known for a decade that housing women law students would become an issue, but had decided to do nothing about it, noting that "if women applicants are made aware in advance that they are largely on their own in Cambridge, the problem will not be serious…."*)

Finding herself homeless was not the welcome she'd anticipated after two and a half days on a Greyhound bus with occasional rest stops and no change of clothes. And now, on the day before registration, she had no place to live. It was her problem, not Harvard's. She was given a street map of Cambridge, telephone numbers for local apartment houses and hotels, and the suggestion she check postings in nearby Harkness Commons, a building that housed the law school cafeteria. As she was ravenous, she

---

* Richards, *Pinstripes & Pearls*, p. 32, quoting 1949 Report of the Committee on the Admission of Women.

made her way there, tore into a roast beef sandwich, found notices tacked on a bulletin board, and began calling from a nearby pay phone, map in hand.

Not surprisingly, the response to her queries as to any apartment within reasonable proximity were the same – sorry, but it's been taken, and could she please remove and throw the listing away? Finally, on calling the number in a handwritten notice, she found an available apartment in a house on Inman Street off Inman Square, a twenty-minute walk toward Boston. A bit distant, but it sounded good – two rooms, cooking facilities and affordable rent. Hefting her suitcase, she told the landlady she was on her way.

Inman Square, in 1958, was a gritty part of Cambridge where dozens of male eyes followed an attractive young woman on foot. The house matched the neighborhood. Worn and dilapidated, with once-brown shingles, the two-and-a-half-story house hadn't been painted for years. Both its roofline and the floor of its small, roofed front porch sagged. The porch had a broken board. The landlady, dressed in a faded yellow-flowered housecoat and full-length dull-red apron, was gruff, but pleasant enough.

She showed Diane up creaking stairs to two rooms at the rear of the second floor. One, seven feet by ten, had a tiny closet and was barely large enough to hold a metal-frame cot with a hard two-inch mattress, a chest of drawers and a small desk and chair – except there wasn't any desk, chair or chest of drawers. There was a chest in the attic she could have, if she wanted to bring it down. The other, smaller room held an ancient gas refrigerator, a crude metal table where one person could sit to eat, a sink and an antique gas stove that looked as if it should smell of leaking gas, but didn't. The kitchen window faced out on a grassless backyard and was impenetrable because of accumulated grime on its outside. The floor and the walls had not been washed. The refrigerator, although noisy, worked.

There was no private bathroom. The narrow communal bathroom, shared with the attic apartment, was just to the left outside the door, next to the steep attic staircase. Featuring an antique metal and ceramic bathtub on stubby, lion's-paw legs, the bathroom had a yellow-stained sink over which a small flat mirror was hung, and an unreliable flush toilet that often required a plumber's helper. The dripping shower head had left another yellow stain in the tub, and the metal slide for a shower curtain above its perimeter had no curtain. The lock on the bathroom door was unreliable.

Diane paid a deposit and a month's rent in advance, in cash, and received two keys, one to the front door and one to the lock on the door to her rooms. Then she set out to explore Inman Square, to buy bedding, food and a coffee maker. She found a store that sold sheets, towels and blankets, and bought some hamburger and groceries at a convenience store, enough to stock the refrigerator. Her Betty Crocker homemaker's award was of little assistance, but fried hamburger and a boiled potato had never tasted so good. She made the bed and sat on its hard mattress to read part of a last paperback mystery she'd secreted in her purse. Registration was the next day, Friday, and classes began Monday morning. Tired, she lay down for a minute and was asleep almost immediately. She woke up next morning still dressed in her traveling clothes.

Intending to take a shower, she opened the bathroom's apparently unlocked door and met one of her neighbors from the attic apartment. Toni, a skinny nineteen-year-old bleached blonde from the Ozarks, was already in the shower, water splashing out onto the floor. Meeting a naked stranger in the shower was a surprise start to the day, and Toni's life story followed. She'd come here with Jimmy, her long-distance-truck-driver boyfriend, hoping to become a performing country-western singer. Jimmy had promised her she could get a job singing in one of the local bars. Actually, Jimmy didn't care what Toni did, exactly, so long as she stayed away from other men, was home when he came back from a road trip or the local bar, fixed him some food and was there in his bed when he wanted her.

It was a lot to absorb before a quick shower and breakfast, but an hour later, Diane was standing in line to register for classes, wondering how she'd manage to transport to Inman Street the heavy trunk and the Samsonite suitcase containing most of her clothes. A taxi was too expensive and the nearest subway stop was seven blocks from Inman Square.

"Aren't you Diane Theis?"

Surprised to hear her name, she turned to peer closely at me.

"Do I know you?"

She didn't. I'd learned about Diane the night before from my college roommate's wife, who'd just graduated from Stanford. Charlie was about to enter Harvard Business School, I was about to enter law school, we hadn't seen each other for fifteen months, and I was meeting his wife, Deborah, for the first time. Several times, she had skillfully turned a spirited conversation to the subject of an amazing and beautiful young Stanford woman named Diane Theis who was coming to Harvard Law School. The next morning, unlike many of my unshaven peers, I'd arrived at registration well-dressed, clean-shaven and early, loitering until I was sure I'd spotted her.

"No," I said, "but a friend of yours married my college roommate, and you look like the girl she described."

"Oh?" she said, eyebrows arching, "you talked about me?"

The conversation wasn't going smoothly, not the way I'd rehearsed it. She put on her glasses, briefly, to look at me again. Our conversation – and her interest in it – picked up when she saw that I was registering a car (it was uncommon for a student to own an automobile then). We agreed to have lunch. At lunch we decided to drive to the Greyhound terminal to retrieve her trunk and suitcase, and to have dinner and explore Boston that night.

Not long afterwards, Diane, wearing a loose-knit turtleneck and a skirt, was sitting neatly on the bench seat of my 1954 Chevrolet, her sneakers on the floor, feet tucked beneath her and back to the door, examining her new friend as we drove to the bus station. Hoping I was generating goodwill, I hauled her trunk and large Samsonite suitcase out to the car and, at Inman Street a short time later, up to her apartment. When the trunk was in place at the foot of her bed and she was ready to unpack, it was time for me to go back to my dorm at the law school.

My dorm rooms were on the ground floor of Hastings Hall, a Victorian, ell-shaped building with a gracious courtyard facing Massachusetts Avenue. Men were treated well at Harvard Law School, and my roommate and I hadn't had to fend for ourselves. We hadn't chosen each other, and we hadn't chosen the dormitory. As it had done for all men, Harvard had made the arrangements and furnished our spacious quarters. The large living room came with two desks and desk chairs, a wall of shelf space for books, files, records and hi-fi equipment, a large rug on the floor, a sitting area, an extra table and floor lamp, and upholstered benches in front of windows that looked out on the courtyard. The bedroom had two comfortable beds, two bureaus and a large closet. There was an anteroom where we would put a small refrigerator and hot plate to make breakfast on those mornings we chose not to take the five-minute walk to Harkness. The classroom buildings were two minutes away from the Hastings front door.

Diane and I had a late afternoon start to our evening out. It was still broad daylight when we found a parking place off Commonwealth Avenue and walked through the tree-shaded pocket parks that divide its east- and westbound traffic. While I related my truncated version of Boston's history, we crossed Arlington Street and walked on through Boston's Gardens and Commons, up Beacon Hill to Bulfinch's golden-domed State House. I assured Diane the several statues we passed were all of Paul Revere, including the famous one of George Washington on horseback. She laughed and said she didn't believe me, but she wouldn't fish out her glasses from her purse to prove me wrong. It wasn't important. What was important was we were getting to know one another.

On our way down the back of Beacon Hill from the State House, we turned into Pemberton Square toward Boston's courthouses. I pointed out the shell of the Old Howard, the once-magnificent theater-turned-burlesque house, its granite faced front and arched windows shuttered and boarded since being shut down a few years earlier for "indecency." No more Ann Corio; no more Candy Barr. I described its history, what little I knew of it. We went down Court Street into the heart of Boston's seamy combat zone of strip joints, bars, tattoo parlors, drunks, johns and prostitutes – Scollay Square. Diane linked her arm in mine.

In five years, Scollay Square would become the sterile wasteland of Government Center and City Hall Plaza, but in 1958 it was still very much alive. The Old Howard's name had been appropriated by the Old Howard Casino, a strip joint on Hanover Street. The Navy was in town and cheerful groups of bright-white-clad sailors passed by – but it was dark in the narrow confines of Cornhill and Brattle streets. We passed derelicts collapsed in doorways and skimpily dressed women wearing rouge, flamboyant hats and fish-net hose. The scene was entirely new to Diane, and she found it disturbing. She talked quietly about the helplessness of the street people and their inability to escape the lives they led.

We were still on that subject as we walked two blocks downhill past the graceful arc of the Sears Crescent, and came to the Old State House, once the seat of Colonial government and now a subway entrance. By this time, the history around us was not particularly interesting to Diane. Scollay Square was still on her mind. I'd proposed dinner at Durgin Park, so we followed Devonshire from the Old State House to Adams Square and Dock Square. I pointed at the imposing statue of Sam Adams and pronounced it yet another Paul Revere. Diane's mood finally lightened.

We dodged traffic to get across the square to Faneuil Hall. Faneuil Hall's ground floor and those of the three long, parallel marketplace buildings behind it were occupied by meat and fish markets, small souvenir shops, nondescript bars and stores with local farm produce. Diane poked through the markets, talked to the storekeepers – and wrinkled up her nose at the fish smell.

Durgin Park was a cheerfully brusque restaurant on the second floor of one of the run-down marketplace buildings. We waited in the line going up the stairs for a short time until two places opened up at one of the long communal tables covered by rude red-checked tablecloths. Bantering with the customers, equally rude waitresses worked the tables at double speed. Patrons elbow-to-elbow took their comments and insults, sent back some of their own and dug into the hearty meals they brought. Ours finished with fresh strawberry shortcake topped with ice cream. We promised our waitress we'd come back often, and left with full stomachs.

Diane was full of life and energy, as well as dinner. This was Boston! There was more to see, much more. In the fading light, we walked down to Long Wharf, where tall-masted schooners had once crowded side-by-side to discharge their cargo to the citizens of Boston. Now it was just one of the rotting wooden piers of a harbor that was no longer an important part of the city.* We walked through the financial district up State Street, and over to Jordan's, and Filene's, and Filene's Basement on Washington Street. We rode the T to Copley Square and made our way back to Commonwealth Avenue.

Along the way our conversation became serious for a time, as Diane's thoughts returned to the women and derelicts we'd seen in Scollay Square. She'd come to law school, she said, because she thought the law could provide her with the tools she'd need to enable them and others like them to escape the lives to which they'd been consigned. Making money wasn't her objective; remedying injustices was. What we'd seen tonight was only a small part of the picture.

How would her becoming a lawyer help? She didn't know, yet, but she expected

---

* Twenty-five years later, that rotting pier would become the Marriott Long Wharf hotel, one of the early anchors in the revitalization of Boston's waterfront and the Faneuil Hall Marketplace.

to find out. Lawyers could draft legislation. They could cause change, perhaps by becoming legislators themselves, perhaps by becoming judges. She couldn't see herself as a legislator, exactly, but maybe a judge. Or maybe a teacher, possibly in a law school. She had an agenda, but the mechanism for implementing it remained to be worked out. She'd return to these ideas many times in the next three years, fleshing them out as she gained a greater understanding of what was possible.

It was the kind of conversation one would expect two young people exploring their interest in each other might have. She asked me about my objectives. A trial lawyer? Like Perry Mason? Really? She seemed impressed by the idea and treated it seriously. This was gratifying on several levels. My ambition wasn't mainstream at Harvard, to say the least, but she respected it. It was what I wanted to do. And the fact that a brilliant, beautiful woman who I'd quickly become enamored of might feel this way toward my own dreams was incredibly reinforcing.

As to her own ambitions, Diane was not only serious, but without pretense, both in this conversation and the many that would follow during our life together. No one could mistake what she had in mind for herself, or for the constituency she expected to represent. I listened, respectfully, but I had a different agenda just now, and I wanted to get back to it.

What were her plans for tomorrow? She said the apartment floors and the walls needed washing and scrubbing. I said I'd be pleased to help. She'd found the old bureau in the attic that her landlady said she could use, and she needed to bring it downstairs. I volunteered. And that afternoon, she said, she'd bought an inexpensive little desk with screw-on legs, a desk chair, a table lamp and a small rug at stores near Central Square on Mass Avenue. Would I like to go with her and help transport them? I would. It wouldn't be too much of an inconvenience? It would not.

It was late when I drove Diane home to Inman Street, but she wasn't tired. It had been an exciting day, a sharp contrast to the day before. As we said goodnight, she said she was happy to have spent the day with me. She was looking forward to the weekend.

So was I.

Women at Harvard Law School

While the law school had admitted women for five years before 1958, they were few, and they weren't made to feel welcome. Discrimination was a fact of life. No laws prohibited it in hiring, and discriminatory hiring practices were not only condoned, they were open. Diane's generation of college students – the "Quiet Generation" – didn't look to challenge the status quo. It was what it was. Men's goals were to get a good education, marry, have children and be successful in business or the professions. Some of the few women who had similar professional goals also went on to graduate school and entered the professions, but their ambitions were brushed aside and considered irrelevant by men in positions of authority. The underlying assumption, always, was that women's ambitions shouldn't be accorded the same *gravitas* as those of men, because women would marry, become pregnant and retire from the workplace, intentionally giving up those ambitions. Harvard was no exception, nor were the law firms that recruited from its law school. The attitude at Ropes & Gray, Boston's leading law firm, toward hiring practices was typical of the times. Every firm should have a certain number of Jews, they thought, but not so many as to offend clients. Ropes & Gray was then about sixty lawyers (a large number for a Boston law firm at the time). That "certain number" of Jews among them was two. The firm had no women lawyers.*

Those women who found their way to law school viewed it as a logical next step after an academic record of high achievement. Despite the discrimination they faced, a law career promised to offer opportunities not available to them elsewhere. Generally having no particular agenda when they arrived other than to succeed, they were not by nature a generation of feminists – the real feminist movement began a decade later. Few women's voices protested the blatant sexism of the times. Many were simply grateful for the education and opportunities law school provided them. As a result, some were willing to deal with sexism, even if it limited their professional horizons. Others believed they could overcome the obstacles.

Diane was one of twelve women out of 520 first-year Harvard law students. Only six of the twelve would graduate. The atmosphere they encountered was outside their experience, both because of the school's harsh treatment of first-year students generally and because of its sexist treatment of women in particular. Women were an anomaly in this male bastion, a fact of which they were reminded at every turn, from the portraits staring down from the walls, to the sex of every professor and lecturer, to the reality of their tiny minority status. One described the experience in graphic terms: "We were strange to the men of Harvard Law School, we were strange to the professors…. We didn't belong there. It was as if we'd suddenly entered a man's toilet. It wasn't our place."†

When women came into the vast room of the Langdell Law Library, virtually all activity stopped momentarily as every male head raised itself from work and every male eye looked them over. The same momentary silence and rapt attention occurred when they appeared at the entrance to the Harkness dining hall.‡

Dean Erwin Griswold did nothing to dispel the women's unease. Each September

---

* When Vern Countryman, later an outstanding professor at Harvard Law School, applied to Ropes & Gray in the 1950s, he was told that, unfortunately, "that slot" had been filled by someone from the prior class. The someone was James Vorenberg, later to become Dean at Harvard Law School.

† Harrington, *Women Lawyers – Rewriting the Rules*, p. 44.

‡ Ibid, p. 98.

during the first week of classes, he gave a talk in Harvard's imposing Memorial Hall to the entering class and singled out, in sexist terms, its few women. They should keep in mind, he said, that they had a special responsibility because "you are taking the place of a man…." One woman recalls puzzling over the statement, and resenting the implication that women had a different status at the law school than men. She remembers looking around the room at the other eleven women and thinking there were very few men's places they were taking in a class of over five hundred. Surely those excluded men, if they were qualified to be admitted to Harvard, had found places in other prestigious law schools, and their careers wouldn't be blighted by their exclusion from Harvard simply because it had admitted women. *

The prior year, the entering class had included Zona Mae Fairbanks, a hard-working, energetic, feisty and insouciant young woman who'd grown up poor in a small town in Virginia. She had put herself through college at William & Mary by working for a local lawyer/judge/justice of the peace. As a lark she'd also entered a beauty contest which carried with it a cash prize, and had won. She was encouraged to apply to law school (her employer believed she already knew all she needed to know about being a lawyer) and was not only accepted but offered scholarships at all three Virginia law schools. To her surprise, she was also accepted by Harvard, but Harvard did not offer her a scholarship and deflected her inquiry about financial aid. Undeterred, she borrowed the tuition money from a local group in Virginia that decided to sponsor her. Then, answering an ad for an au pair in Cambridge, she solved the problem of room and board.

When Griswold addressed Zona's class, he sought to impress on them that they were in elite company. He read a litany of the achievements of the entering class: "Included among your number are four Rhodes Scholars, twelve Marshall Scholars, twenty-five valedictorians of their graduating class, [etc.] … and Miss Apple Pie Queen of Virginia." Griswold wasn't a gifted public speaker, so he was gratified and smiled broadly when the latter announcement was greeted by cheers, foot-stomping and wolf whistles. Zona hadn't included this information in her application and was taken by surprise. William & Mary had supplied it, thinking it might help her prospects – and perhaps it did.[1]

Each year, the dean and his wife hosted a dinner party at their home for all the first-year women. To make conversation, he'd say straight out that he'd been opposed to the admission of women, and then ask each woman why she'd come to law school, as if that were an odd choice for a woman. One woman responded, deadpan, that *she'd* come to law school to find a husband. Failing to see the irony, the dean nodded knowingly, as if his own views had been confirmed. Another said she'd come to law school because she couldn't get into secretarial school. Whether the dean laughed was not reported.

---

*   Adria Goodkin interview.

Statistically, he'd say, women practiced law for only a few years, a statement based on male folklore that reflected ignorance of the actual statistics. The implication was clear, however: women law students were "wasting the exceptional resources of Harvard's legal education."*

Whatever Griswold's own views may have been,[2] women in the class say they weren't made to feel welcome by the school or its faculty. In contrast to undergraduate schools where they were offered advisors (usually male) to help with their career choices, they found Harvard only offered advisors for men. Antonia ("Toni") Schayes, a prominent securities lawyer and wife of Professor Abe Schayes, offered informal, unofficial counseling, but that was all. Used to their undergraduate faculty taking an interest in them as students, often inviting them to their homes, women found no similar experience awaiting them at Harvard. Except in the case of professors who advised student moot court teams, faculty-sponsored gatherings which included women occurred rarely, if ever. Many women felt the faculty members they knew were flatly hostile toward them. Men at the law school may have had a similar impression because of the challenging and aggressive approach of the Socratic method of teaching,[3] but in the case of women, their very presence was resented. A number of the professors viewed them simply as intruders, and refused to call on them.†

The most notorious example of the all-male faculty's patronizing and sexist attitude toward women was Professor Bart Leach, who played a significant role in Diane's first year. Tall, lean, white-haired and sarcastic, Leach was a law school icon who'd taught Property to the first-year class for thirty years. Handsome and charming, he had an enormous ego and regarded himself as a ladies' man used to having his way. One of two faculty members to vote against the admission of women a decade earlier, Leach was also a general in the United States Air Force Reserve, a position of which he was enormously proud, perhaps because he thought it fitted his image. He viewed both himself and the law school with great seriousness. Divorced from his wife, and ultimately forced to retire from the Reserve, the law school was his life.

Leach dominated his classroom and was a harsh taskmaster. He maintained a seating chart so that he could match wits, by name, with every one of the 130 students in his section in the course of the semester, placing a checkmark opposite the name when he did. He delighted in demonstrating his own intellectual superiority. If a student didn't get it, his displeasure was often dramatic. On one occasion (which I observed), he literally pounded his head against the blackboard in frustration after an exchange with the unfortunate object of his attention. If a male student missed his class for any

---

* Harrington, *Women Lawyers – Rewriting the Rules*, pp. 45-46.
† Interestingly, although they were objects of great sexual interest and attention, women in our class, Diane among them, generally said they didn't feel discriminated against or resented by male classmates, who were friendly and treated them fairly. There were exceptions, but their attitudes were of little consequence.

reason, he made a note of it on his seating chart and called on the miscreant at the first opportunity in the next class he attended. If the student wasn't prepared, Leach would bully him unmercifully.

Women were treated differently. To call on a woman when she wasn't expecting it, he declared, would be ungentlemanly, so he set aside one day each semester – "Ladies Day" – as the only day on which he would call on women. On Ladies Day, no men needed to prepare because the entire dialogue would be with the handful of women in the class. They were required to leave their regular seats and sit together on the professor's platform, facing the men in the lecture hall, while Leach himself strutted and preened among the men, peppering the women with questions, seeking to embarrass them with hypothetical facts and cases having sexual overtones. The day's legal lesson was played for entertainment value, with the men in the hall expected to chuckle and laugh. Some did, but on the whole – at least in 1958 – the men were embarrassed by the spectacle and sympathetic toward the women.

To be put on public display, embarrassed and humiliated for the entertainment of men was an ordeal for the women. They dealt with it differently, depending on each one's personality. For one, the experience was virtually intolerable. Another thought that Leach was a sick man. Although the all-male atmosphere and the obvious bias of many of the faculty bothered her, she found it more puzzling than appalling. This was the first time in her experience that she recalled being singled out solely because of her sex. For others in the class, she recalls, it gave rise to intense anger. A half generation later, feminists would have refused to participate in Ladies Day and would have walked out if an attempt were made to compel them to do so. In 1958, it was different. However they may have felt personally, they were not prepared then to refuse to go along with the event, however sexist and demeaning, that had become a tradition in Professor Bart Leach's class.

A significant portion of his first-semester Property class concerned an arcane rule of law known as the Rule Against Perpetuities.* Leach

Later, as described by Judith Richards Hope in *Pinstripes & Pearls* [pp.97-99], Ladies Day in the mid 1960s became a sporting challenge for the first-year law school women. The cases Leach would use were the same each year, the questioning was orchestrated, the first-year women received coaching from women in the second-year class and the whole event was a lark. Perhaps Ladies Day had evolved to become pure entertainment on both sides by then, but it was nothing of the sort in 1958.

---

* Over-simplified, the rule prohibits someone disposing of real estate or other assets, whether by deed or by will, from imposing certain kinds of restrictions on the property or assets for a period of time longer than twenty years plus "lives in being" at the time of the transfer.

had written a small book on the subject, and every year he held a competition in which he invited his students to write a paper on the Rule, its rationale and its social utility. The four finalists would be rewarded by a prize and by being invited, together with a spouse or companion, to an intimate dinner hosted by Leach at his home. There he would bestow the prize on the winner – an autographed copy of his own learned book.

In the fall of 1958, Diane won the competition. She asked me to come with her. When I arrived at the dinner (the first of many Prince Phillip appearances over the next thirty-five years), Leach was taken aback at having to be gracious toward an unworthy student he'd recently chastised and written off for missing a couple of his classes.* Nevertheless he was generous in offering his excellent wine.

He seated Diane on his right and spent most of his time at dinner in private conversation with her, to the virtual exclusion of the other finalists, all men. They resented the attention he was paying her, and tried to edge into their private conversations. While he acknowledged them, and Diane sought to deflect his attention, his behavior was rude. Bart Leach felt that he and Diane had bonded.

Diane shrugged off Ladies Day, the faculty's sexist behavior, and her close encounters with Bart Leach. More troubling to her than discrimination against women was the adversary system at the core of the law school's philosophy regarding development of the law and how it should be applied. She believed then, and would always believe, that clients' best interests and society's best interests would be better served by lawyers working in cooperation, rather than confrontation. That view would guide her as a lawyer, as a legislative lobbyist for women and poor people, and as a teacher, even when she became a professor at Harvard Law School.

DIANE AND ERIK

We saw each other every day from the first day we met. We studied together, had lunch together, spoke on the phone every night, dealt with Toni and Jimmy as the need arose, and spent our weekends together. Weeknights, I often trekked to her apartment, ostensibly to study. She enjoyed the intellectual challenge of studying law, and prepared detailed outlines of her course work each evening, synthesizing what she'd learned in classes that day. We each were part of study groups within the class, and both groups benefited from her analyses. Sexism aside, Diane was engrossed by the study of law, and often said she never regretted her decision to come to Harvard. Her capacity to absorb,

---

* In Maine, where I was raised, the fall deer-hunting season was sacrosanct. I had left in early November for five days of deer hunting and missed two of Leach's three classes that week. Predictably, he called on me first thing Monday morning, and equally predictably, I was unprepared. In dramatic tones, he informed everyone that he had "grave doubts" for my future.

understand and retain information was extraordinary, as was her ability to impart to others what she'd learned and her views concerning its value, presaging a career to come. She taught me to become a serious student, which was a good thing.

Quick physically, as well as mentally, she thought of herself as a sprinter. Sometimes, as we walked along a sidewalk with no one ahead of us, she'd look at me sideways with a grin and a glint in her eye and suddenly break into a run. I had to catch her before she'd stop.

Since she hated wearing her glasses, it wasn't easy for her to locate me in a crowd. When the weather cooled, I took to wearing a red ski cap (knitted by my mother), a singular sight on the campus. The law school, like undergraduate schools of the time, had parietal rules which prohibited women from visiting men in their dorm rooms, not just at night, but during the day. Diane thought it astonishing, ridiculous and archaic that such rules existed in a graduate school whose students were adults. She ignored them, surreptitiously at first, coming into Hastings between classes through its interior entrance from the school's tunnel system. The three of us, my roommate included, would talk and read until our next classes. When needed, I'd check to see that the first-floor men's room was unoccupied and stand guard. Other friends would stop by, and word got around.

One day there was a sharp rap on the door and a dorm proctor,* peering over my shoulder into the room, said that he understood I had a woman there. Conduct of this sort wouldn't be tolerated and I was to put an end to it. He was entirely serious. I explained that the "woman" was another law student, that she came by to read and study between classes, and I had no intention of telling her she couldn't. Would he like to speak to her himself? He reddened as Diane appeared. Smiling, she said if there was a rule, it was time the rule was changed and we'd be pleased to go with him to talk to the Dean of Students. He gave us a sour look and turned on his heel. That was the last we heard of parietal rules. From then on, Diane came in the front door, from the courtyard.

We played bridge with friends during the lunch hour and early afternoon in the Austin Hall ladies' room, which was hidden behind a maze of ceiling ductwork in the basement. It was strategically located, since the only other ladies' room in the law school was in Harkness, a considerable walk from any classroom. In designing it, the administration doubtless believed it had been considerate of women's sensibilities because it was spacious, consisting of two rooms, a powder room in front and the room containing the toilets behind. The powder room had a splendid oak table and four chairs, and it was there that we and another law-school couple met to play bridge. There wasn't a lot of traffic and what there was, after an initial surprise, was amused.

---

* A second- or third-year law student whose duties were to enforce the rules and see to it that nothing immoral was happening in the dorm.

Saturdays belonged to the two of us. We had dinner in a booth in the Oxford Grille, an unostentatious, dimly lit, walnut-paneled restaurant on Church Street off Harvard Square that catered to students and students' wallets. After soup, salad, a small London-broil steak, a glass of wine and dessert, the bill came to $5.50, an amazing price, even for 1958. Meanwhile, lights burned brightly in Hastings Hall as men studied hard, long into the night.

Diane disliked the law school's artificial atmosphere and thought that its men, many of whom wore shirts, ties and jackets to class, took themselves and the school far too seriously. Real life was different, and more important. She usually dressed like a bobby-soxer, skirt, sweater, white socks and sneakers. When I left to go deer hunting, she approved. When she heard how Bart Leach had embarrassed me after my absence, she giggled, a most charming giggle. If I had a writing assignment from *Sports Illustrated,* she came along.*

She was impulsive and loved the excitement of surprises and spur-of-the-moment ideas. When I suggested on a Friday that we visit my brother in Greenwich Village, Diane was ready within the hour. We arrived at his Bleecker Street apartment in the middle of a party. It was late – very late – before the room in which we stayed – his small study – was available. Saturday and Sunday we explored Greenwich Village, rode the subway to MOMA, walked down Fifth Avenue, and visited Rockefeller Center. We poked into antique stores and art galleries. By the time we were back in Cambridge Sunday evening, it was too late to study. Diane's first taste of New York – and of my family – had been an adventure, and she was still happily in it. Tomorrow could wait.

When New England's fall foliage was at its peak, we threw a bag into the car and headed north to see the bright reds and oranges of the maple trees mixed in with the golds and browns of birches and oaks. We climbed the heights above Lake Winnepesaukee and saw the brilliant colors contrasting with the bright blues of the huge lake, its waves topped with whitecaps as the wind blew up. We looked for, and found, small and inexpensive bed-and-breakfasts in New Hampshire and Vermont, in towns off the main tourist track.

Diane brought along textbooks and notebooks and read in the car. We even discussed law along the way, but law was secondary as she absorbed the sights and sounds of a part of the country foreign to her, one where she was thinking about settling. It was early yet, but not too early, to think about that possibility.

She drew the attention of other men at Harvard, most of them fellow law students, something I did my best to discourage. One, also from Stanford but doing work in a different graduate school, was an acquaintance of a Stanford friend Diane still wrote to. He'd call her and occasionally stop by ("just a friend," Diane said). I tried to stay

---

* I had worked for *Sports Illustrated* in New York, and continued as a "stringer" for the magazine in Boston.

informed and to be there when he was. Diane described one of those occasions in a letter to her friend:

> I saw Lynn and think I must have scared him to death. He came to say hello at a time when Erik was on my bed (alone – just resting). My upstairs neighbor who looks like a whore and has approximately the life of one, was curled up on the end of the bed discussing Life with Erik, and I had just gotten out of the bath. Needless to say, Ivy League Lynn didn't quite fit – although he made an honest effort.

Ivy League Lynn was neither scared to death nor discouraged. He invited Diane to an elite party where she could meet the handsome Prince Karim, the newly-anointed Aga Khan, who was then an undergraduate at Harvard, wealthy beyond measure, a descendant of the prophet Mohammad, the leader of the Ismaili Muslim sect of Shias and already on record as intending to use his position and wealth to educate and benefit disadvantaged peoples in Africa and throughout the Muslim world.* How could I compete with Prince Karim? I wasn't happy. We discussed it. She turned down the invitation, "with regrets." I had *no* regrets, but for years afterward I would hear – as Diane smiled a mischievous smile – that I'd deprived her of a rare opportunity. She would have been disappointed, though, had I not been jealous.

She was already balancing professional ambition against traditional family plans. She wished for marriage and children, a life much like the ones her parents, and her parents' friends, and their parents, had had. She spent Thanksgiving with me in Augusta, Maine, where she met my parents and my other brother and his family.

We were both apprehensive. My family, unlike hers, was decidedly patriarchal. Right or wrong, my father expected to make the decisions and expected obedience and acquiescence from his wife and children. My mother was her own person, had had a career as a teacher before agreeing to marry, and her independence was important to her, but much of what she accomplished within our family was done indirectly. My father was skeptical about Diane and, for that matter, about any woman who wanted her own career. What if he didn't like her? What if she didn't like him? Diane understood this would be an adventure of a different kind.

My mother liked her immediately – it showed – but she, too, was uneasy about my father's reaction. None of us had cause for concern. I could see that at once from my father's eyes when he was introduced. His visage softened, and he was immediately charmed by the beautiful young woman who'd come into his house. He, too, had been nervous and uneasy, a possibility that had never occurred to us. Within minutes, he and

---

* Intentions which he later fulfilled by establishing a network of schools in Africa and by promoting economic self-reliance among developing countries and their poorest people.

Diane were seated in the living room discussing with great animation and seriousness his views on the law, its uses and its limitations.

That Diane played bridge met with his approval, but a game of bridge was serious business. He played to win. His partner on Friday night – the first of many such occasions – was Diane. When she made a mistake, he would rumble like a volcano before eruption, and my mother would kick him under the table. Then he'd smile and explain quietly – but firmly – how the hand should have been bid or played. Diane smiled graciously in return, all was well, and my mother settled back in her chair, but both she and Diane remained on the alert.

The visit wasn't easy for her. She had mixed feelings about our relationship and about where she was going with her life. The patriarchal attitude she saw in me, as well as in my family, was only part of the conflict she felt about her own freedom, ambitions and dreams. She wrote to a friend:

> I am miserable because I am emotionally involved with this Viking Lord…. I'm very much in love with Erik and I can even see it almost rationally sometimes. He wants to be married next summer and I am about two jumps from signing my soul away.
>
> I wish I were a man and could compartmentalize everything neatly into companionship, sex and so on. Instead they're all confused. I don't know what to do about Erik – I'm not being "true to myself" in letting myself need him as I do. I should have known – for a woman, sex and emotion don't come in neat separate packages. I thought that I could have my cake and eat it too. It doesn't work and I'm sure it never will. I've got to decide which part of me is to be sacrificed – does it have to be that way?
>
> Part of me – that middle-class part – yearns for some guy to feed and satisfy and scrub me in the bathtub on Saturday night. Another part wants money, fame, success, acclaim – and the rest wants to find that freedom of spirit to wander and see and experience. Which do you suppose is going to win? Are we truly what others make us? It doesn't bother me, exactly; I enjoy sex – wow, etc. – and am resigned to whatever hell there is on that account. I guess it comes back to the question whether my life belongs to me, or to other people.
>
> This is my conflict. If I were only free, I could create such an enjoyable life, I think. But there are obligations and responsibilities and those emotions pushing and pulling at me….

It was unusual that Diane would confide to someone else emotional issues she was working on resolving herself. That she did probably reflects the depths of the conflict she was dealing with. Alice Hayden, another correspondent and her Stanford roommate the previous year, was less than enthusiastic about the prospect she might decide to marry:

As for marriage vs. career, this is a difficult decision to have to make if it comes to a choice, and it shouldn't be made right away, of course, but still…. It would be a shame to tie yourself down before you're ready, as I'm convinced you could do anything you want to, even if you're not convinced. Still, no matter what you could be, it's hard to know if it would be worth the insecurity, loneliness, etc., that you would probably have to face. You will probably manage both somehow….

It was a stressful fall for other reasons, too, because her Inman Street apartment was not a peaceful place. Jimmy beat Toni regularly. Diane gave her sanctuary, her eyes blackened, smoking furiously while Jimmy pounded on the locked door demanding to be let in. Somehow, in between Toni's sad stories and Jimmy's shouting and pounding, Diane still managed to study. On more than one occasion, drunk, Jimmy demanded to be let in when Toni wasn't there. The lock was good, but the door was flimsy. Sometimes Diane called me and I'd go provide reinforcements. Sometimes I'd bring my guitar and play while Diane studied. Toni, sitting on the bed beside me, would tell me what a great talent I had. Then we'd sing a duet, Toni ever so slightly off-key. Sometimes Jimmy would appear, looking suspicious but not belligerent. Diane remained focused on her textbooks and her notes through it all.

By mid-December, events at Inman Street were getting rougher and Diane was concerned that some night Jimmy wouldn't be stopped by the locked door. She found a neatly handwritten notice on the Harkness bulletin board from Cynthia, a young woman who needed a roommate for the remainder of the school year, and called the number.* Her husband, she said, had to leave to pursue graduate studies under a fellowship granted him by a midwestern university and she couldn't accompany him until the summer. Their lease ran through June and she needed another woman to share the rent.

Cynthia, herself a graduate student working on a master's degree, lived in a respectable brick apartment building on Harvard Street, five minutes' walk from Harvard Square, with a peculiar cat named Piffles. Piffles had had a stroke and spent most of her day hanging by her front claws from the Venetian blinds, peering blankly out the window. She was no longer able, or interested, to land on her feet when she fell, an unusual characteristic for a cat, which I confirmed by dropping her onto a bed pillow from a few inches height. Piffles was friendly and purred a lot.

The two-and-a-half-room second-floor corner apartment had a small kitchen and

---

* If one believes in omens, the telephone number – TR 7-1538 – was a good one because the digits reflected Diane's birthday. It was a doubly good omen for me, because the number was easy to remember and, having memorized it, I never forgot her birthday.

was nicely laid out. There was ample room for the two women, and the building was safe. Cynthia expected to be away numerous long weekends visiting her husband in Illinois. Nice enough, she seemed surprisingly rigid at times, almost militaristic in her views and expressions, but not enough to be off-putting. Her husband, Diane later learned, was a fan of Adolf Hitler. He had photos of Hitler in an album, a collection of his writings, and recordings of the speeches he'd delivered to cheering crowds under an array of waving swastikas. Apart from those considerations, the situation was ideal, and it was an enormous relief when Diane moved out of Inman Street.

She had another shoal to navigate that winter. Since I was a skier, Diane was determined to become a skier too. When the Presidents' long weekend arrived in February, we invited two friends to ski Maine's Sugarloaf Mountain with us. One was from Mississippi, the other from Tennessee. Diane had never been on a T-bar, much less skied down a mountain. Only one of our friends had ever skied, but the other was athletic, strong and game. It promised to be another interesting adventure.

Diane returned to Sugarloaf Mountain a great many times in the next forty years, but never to ski downhill on the mountain and never to test the T-bar again. She became an avid cross-country skier on trails in Carrabassett Valley, and otherwise a fan of our wood stove while she read.

Sugarloaf was not then the resort behemoth it is today . Lift tickets were sold by the aptly named Amos Winter, who'd cut the ski trails on the mountain by hand. To the left of the rudimentary building which served as ticket office, warming hut and source of chili, hot dogs and cocoa, was a little bunny slope serviced by a short T-bar. Two other long T-bars led up from the warming hut to the mountaintop and its snowfields. There were only three trails from the top, Narrow Gauge, Sluice and Tote Road. Tote Road took a meandering course around the shoulder of the mountain and back to the warming hut. Narrow Gauge and Sluice came straight down.

Diane was dubious, but game. With some difficulty and many snowplow turns, everyone managed the bunny slope. Then we moved to the next T-bar, where Diane insisted on sitting down on the bar instead of letting it pull her. We fell off three times, but she was determined, and we made it up the fourth time. The four of us skied down together, very slowly. When we reached the warming hut, Diane said she'd like some cocoa, she'd brought a book, and the rest of us should go on skiing. We did, and she relaxed in the warm sunshine on a bench outside the hut, reading her latest mystery, warmly dressed in sweater and wool cap. She was content.

Her life during the second semester wasn't carefree, even though she was doing well with her courses, we were happy together and we had good times and fun with our friends. Coming to grips with the conflicts that confront two people who believe they want to marry, have a family and have two careers was difficult. There were no ground rules to follow, and there were no role models – none, at least, that she knew – for the life she wanted to lead. Often on an emotional roller coaster between the ambitions she had to make a difference in the world and her desire to have a husband and family and a life like that of her parents, she was torn, undecided and unsure what direction to go.

The husband she had in mind was himself trying to come to grips with the idea that the woman he hoped to marry would want a career and an independent professional life. My life would not be that of paterfamilias, but rather of partner. And what of our children? How would they deal with a family life so different from that of their friends? Neither of us knew. We had no guide, no template. Constantly wrestling with these issues, our highs were blissful, the lows depressing, confusing and troublesome.

The second semester was a grinding, grueling marathon focused on a distant point, final exams in May, the only examinations on which our class would be graded. We studied hard, conscientiously, focused and intense. Fear, as someone has said, marvelously concentrates the mind. While Diane and I still reserved weekends for ourselves, our weekdays and evenings were devoted to study and to an understanding of the issues and principles on which we'd be examined. There was precious little guitar-playing as March turned into April, and May approached. We exchanged course outlines for comparison. How would the race end?

We came out of final exams exhausted, as did our classmates. Some agonized over the outcome. Confident, Diane and I celebrated. Then we packed and returned home to California and Maine – a continent apart for the first time since September – to wait for the results. It had been an extraordinary and irreplaceable year, and it was difficult to say goodbye when I drove Diane to Logan Airport.

It had been nine months since she'd been with any of her family and she was anxious to return to familiar surroundings and the people she loved. Once there, though, she found her emotions were still in turmoil. She'd moved on, but her family had stayed the same, and her family seemed different from what she'd known when she left – and what she'd expected to find when she came home. She no longer fitted in. She wanted to talk about discrimination, women's rights and poverty, what the government should be doing to deal with these issues and the role she wanted to play in that process. These weren't subjects that interested them. She was happy and lonely at the same time, happy to be with her family, lonely because I wasn't with her, wishing that her family was interested in *her* interests, and wishing I could come visit and meet her family soon after my two-week stint with the Army Reserve in July. Seriously in love, she'd accepted each of my several marriage proposals, and was awaiting my summer visit expecting that I'd raise the subject with her parents.

Priming her parents for the event, she met mixed reviews. George sounded pleased

– he was always supportive – but Meryl was not. Unfortunately, Diane's conversations with George, who was always a rock in her life, were by telephone. Columbia Pictures had asked him to go on location for two months and he wouldn't be back until mid-July. Telephone calls were a poor substitute, especially given Meryl's disapproval. Meryl understood clearly that our marriage would deprive her of the daughter she was so proud of, and that Diane would end up living and working on the East Coast rather than close to home.

It wasn't the first time Diane had met with her mother's disapproval of her choice in men, but it was the most important. And Meryl hadn't even met me yet.

Diane wrote me about her mixed reception and mixed emotions. I wrote back that what she was feeling was the pain everyone feels on facing separation and independence from the family that had nurtured, encouraged and supported them during their entire lives. She hadn't experienced those pangs before because she'd been close to home. The thought of leaving her family had been so far off in the future it hadn't seemed real, until now. She wasn't reassured.

Her spirits had picked up by the end of June, though, and she started making plans again. Alice Hayden had been offered a lab technician's job at Boston University Hospital and had agreed to be Diane's roommate again, this time in Cambridge. They asked me to find them an apartment, and I did, on the ground floor of a Victorian house that had been converted into seven apartments, including one for the owner, midway on a quiet cross street between Cambridge Street and Kirkland Street, two of the major arteries running east toward Boston. Sumner Road was only a ten minute walk from the law school and from Harvard Square.

Her plans for my August visit had firmed up. I'd meet family and friends, and then we'd go hiking in the Sequoias with her sister Noreen and brother-in-law Carl, backpacking into the mountains. Later we'd drive up the coast of California with her parents, ending in the Redwoods above San Francisco, and then return to San Jose where Alice's family lived. Finally the three of us would drive back to Boston in Alice's brand-new Volkswagen Beetle (which she drove for twenty-five years).

Then everything changed.

First Diane received a letter from Bart Leach addressed to her and seven others (including one other woman) out of the 250 students in his two property law sections: "You have jointly and severally gladdened Old Pappy's heart by magnificent papers in Property I…. This is the first time ladies have joined my [A-plus] Club; and I am delighted, though hardly surprised, to welcome them." To his credit, Leach had put his biases aside in order to recognize merit, regardless of sex. It wasn't comfortable for him to do so, but his path may well have been eased by the recognition he'd already accorded to Diane and, perhaps, that he felt a personal bond had been forged between himself and Diane at the dinner he had hosted.

Then she received another letter, this one inviting her to join and become an editor of the *Harvard Law Review*, the most prestigious legal publication in the United States. She'd finished twentieth in our class of five hundred.

Diane had succeeded in the Harvard cauldron of trial by fire. She'd burst through to be near the head of the class, and the sense of achievement she had, the results of an intensive year of study at a discipline she felt suited her, was complete. And yet it seemed to muddy the waters of her future. Her twenty-first birthday was still ten days away. How could she fit the personal plans on which she'd been focused into this new context? How to resolve the dilemma this news presented?

DILEMMA AND DECISION

Somehow or other I goofed [Diane wrote on July 6], so prepare yourself. We did so well every other way, but someone forgot to call off my guardian angel. All this is leading up to the horrible fact that I seem to be eligible to be an editor of the *Harvard Law Review*....

I'm in a daze. I suppose this is a great and wonderful thing and I should be pleased, proud and thankful, but I'm just bewildered. I don't know what to do and *you have to help, please*. All our wonderful plans – why do nice things always have to happen to me?

A lovely little letter arrived – very pedantic – from the President of the *Law Review* asking for immediate notification – which I can't give them. I just don't know. I would have to be there by August 17. May I enumerate the thinking I've done about it?

1. <u>Problem</u>: Erik is coming to see California and my parents and me in August. <u>Answer</u>: Erik could come right away, like July 27, and we'd still have some time.

2. <u>Problem</u>: Alice and Erik and I were going to drive back. <u>Answer</u>: Not feasible. Alice couldn't leave her job early. Even if she did, Erik would have hardly any time out here and it wouldn't be worth it.

3. <u>Problem</u>: we were going to spend some wonderful, carefree weeks in Maine. <u>Answer</u>: Ha!

4. <u>Problem</u>: Hardly any free time next year to spend with either Erik or Alice. No answer.

5. <u>Problem</u>: It's a hell of a lot of work and I'm not really very brilliant. No answer.

6. <u>Problem</u>: Going back early is going to cost more money than had been planned on. No answer.

7. <u>Problem</u>: When will I see Daddy?

Balanced against all this is the feeling that this simply isn't the sort of thing one turns down in my position. This is valuable for getting a job! There is prestige involved, faculty contact, etc. It might mean perhaps I could teach somewhere, sometime.

There it is. Why couldn't I be sensible like you and take it a little easy and still do well? A nice comfortable position in the class. The only nice comfortable position about my status is that I probably will get my scholarship back. I really didn't intend anything so drastic – honest!

My feelings right now are that I'll have to accept it, I suppose. If I could just be a little more enthusiastic about it! I wish I could write them back and say, "I accept, but I can't come back early because I'm getting married." Do you suppose our life is always going to be complicated?

I'll write a sensible letter tomorrow. Right now I don't know what is what. Please write and tell me honestly what you think of the whole mess. I don't know what in the world I would ever do without you.

She reread the letter from the *Harvard Law Review*:

[Y]ou will become a participant in a tradition of legal scholarship and training which has included many of the outstanding names of the legal profession and of public life. To maintain this tradition is a task which will demand both time and effort…. The work of publishing the Review never really ends and even as I write to you, the Review's officers are preparing the materials for the early issues of next fall. To meet our rigorous press deadlines it is imperative that work begin well before classes commence….

The intensive analysis, research and writing you will do will prove to be the most valuable segment of your legal education at Harvard…. There is, too, the almost fraternal atmosphere of Gannett House itself and the opportunity for close association with your fellow editors, who represent every area of the country and every school of thought…."

The letter was flattering, supportive, seductive and elitist, and it didn't resonate with Diane. Among other things, it made explicit the obstacles presented to the future she'd envisioned for herself, should she accept. Pondering what to do, she sent me a second note on July 10:

I haven't made the final final decision on that damn *Law Review* thing, but I know I don't want it. Unless I hear something extraordinary from my father tomorrow, I will probably turn it down. I need one last talk with Mother first.

So if I were you, I'd go ahead with plans as scheduled.

My reasons are purely selfish and I hope you won't be depressed or disappointed. I rather think you won't be. I'd much rather play bridge than suffocate in the legal atmosphere of Gannett House. And I'd much rather be Mrs. Erik Lund than Miss Diane Theis, Chief Justice (or anything else). I'd much rather have an overall good standing than have *Law Review* and a deranged mind that thinks that law is God (when every sensible person knows *you* are).

To say I had mixed feelings would be a mild assessment. How could I ask her to say no? I knew what an honor it was, and the impact it would have, not only on her career as a lawyer, but on her dreams and ambitions, in the face of the sexist obstacles she knew she'd face, to become, someday, a law school professor or a judge, or perhaps both. I composed a letter I hoped she'd read as sounding balanced:

Making *Law Review* is a remarkable achievement, problems or no problems. But what about the problems? I wish I could suggest a formula into which you could put all the variables and come out with an answer, but that's impossible.... You could try to explore if you can hold on with one hand while you decide whether or not to let go. Perhaps see if you can come later than August 17 without having to decline....

We could get married right now, but I don't think that would solve the problems. I'm concerned, knowing how hard you worked last year and how run-down you became at times. Joining the *Law Review* might not only give you a much heavier workload, but also take out of our lives the times we had for fun.... *Law Review* isn't just an honorary organization. It's nearly a full-time job.... Am I being selfish? ...

This has to be your decision. In some way you have to come to grips with how important the *Law Review* really is. What does it mean now? What will it mean later for you? I can't answer those questions.... [W]hatever you decide, I'll be with you and back you. Nothing will change my feelings for you.

I was concerned that my letter would sound – accurately – as if it had been written through gritted teeth. Diane wrote again:

I really don't know what to do. I know I wrote you and said I was fairly certain, but now I'm lost again. I see both sides and can argue them equally well. Believe me, I've done it for hours. Why couldn't this have been simple? This inability to make decisions is a definite sign of emotional immaturity. Mother was just in to say good night and to tell me to stop worrying. She said obviously I didn't want it or I wouldn't be making such a problem about it. But I want to hear more from you, so I will write them about not arriving early. If they say that's all right, then what do I do? The letter you wrote said between every line, "Don't take it!"

I don't want to, but I'm afraid. I don't know what *we* want out of life. In light of the immediate consequences, I know I don't want it. But what about the significance for the future? Please, sweetheart, don't back off from this quite so far. It's not a hands-off proposition that's up to me alone. This is something *we* have to decide. It's *our* life rather than my life.

Diane didn't want to disappoint her family and friends. She'd deliberately chosen Harvard Law School because it exemplified the highest degree of education she could hope to attain, and it would have been unthinkable a year earlier to even contemplate turning down an invitation to the *Law Review*. Still, she'd never sought the honor or the recognition for herself, so the question was what impact this would have on the life she hoped to lead. She'd grown up in a family where life was balanced, and she wanted to continue to lead a balanced life. While she knew she'd make good use of her professional education, the prospect that her plans for marriage and family might be jeopardized outweighed the advantages the *Law Review* might offer her. Then, on the other side of the scale, she was concerned what impact her decision would have for women who would come behind her, and for the faculty that would evaluate them. She'd worked hard to be in exactly this position, and not just for herself.

About to join my Army Reserve unit in Boston for summer duty, I was at the typewriter again, this time describing an accidental meeting with one of our professors, Richard Baxter:

When I started asking him questions about the *Law Review* dilemma, he looked astonished – he thought I was talking about myself! He seemed relieved when I explained, and invited me for lunch today, together with two other professors and Dean Toepfer.

According to Baxter (no one at the table disagreed), this is what *Law Review* boils down to: (1) as a rule of thumb, about forty hours per week, (2) a great deal of writing, rewriting, editing, checking and research, (3) with resulting valuable faculty contacts, and (4) somewhat dubious personal satisfaction if a person is interested in doing other things besides law research and writing.

As to what effect *Law Review* has on later life and employment, he said that certainly it could be helpful, but the place you take in the world is of your own making. Concerning teaching, what you do after law school, rather than during it, is what is determinative. Teaching law is not something that can be jumped into.

In the case of a married woman planning a family, he said there will be a period of about ten years when the children are growing up and getting into school before she can contemplate returning to work. His own wife is an example.

He voiced some of the same thoughts you and I have been having. [What it all came down to was] if you want it, take it. If you don't, then decline. Someone declines nearly every year. He vividly remembered one who gave as his reason that he "had better things to do."

That clinched it. Diane wrote back on July 13:

I'll have to quote you: "…*Law Review* boils down to (1), as a rule of thumb, forty hours of work per week…." My God! And then you go on and discuss whether I should do it or not! Why would anyone in their right mind want to be extracurricular for forty hours a week? I'd *never* see you. I'd never see anybody! I'd probably lose all my hair and at least twenty pounds! …. I'll send a letter fast on the heels of the other one telling them to forget the whole thing. We'll be great lawyers the hard way!

She wrote to decline the honor. Within days she received two letters asking her to reconsider, one from the *Law Review's* president pointing out that hers could be the first class to place "two girls" on the *Law Review* the same year, and that she was alone among her classmates invited to join to decline the honor.

The other letter, from Bart Leach, began "My dear Diane." Having learned of her decision, he felt compelled, he said, to write and urge her to reconsider. Such a "rash decision" would blight the brilliant career and future prospects that otherwise were before her. It was not yet too late. While he understood the challenge presented to a young woman by the prospect of joining the *Law Review* might well be daunting, there was a solution: he would personally undertake to guide her and advise her. Any concerns she had would disappear. "Let Pappy Leach do this for you. You will never have any regrets."

The prospect of Pappy Leach assuming responsibility for her emotional and intellectual well-being was neither appealing nor persuasive. Leach would never understand that a young woman of twenty-one – or of any age, for that matter – could resist the honors and blandishments of both the institution he loved and revered, and his own. The idea that someone with unlimited legal ability would choose instead to follow a course which balanced the demands of that ability against other considerations, such as marrying, having a family and raising children, and postponing what she could accomplish until later, was incomprehensible. This was unfamiliar territory for him.

But it was Diane's territory. She'd scouted it out and he hadn't. Once again, she declined.

DISAPPOINTMENT, ANTICIPATION AND RESPITE

Perhaps it would have been different had she made a different decision, but Diane's class standing didn't translate into scholarship dollars. Her $1400 scholarship was reduced to $700, and she wondered if there was a connection. Perhaps the law school no longer felt she was worthy of its support. She was eligible for a student loan, however, and it would make up the difference. She'd manage.

Disappointment was offset by an invitation to join the Board of Student Advisors, the next highest tier of honor at the law school. Responsible for organizing, preparing and administering the Ames Moot Court program, the Board developed the factual record for each case, analyzed the applicable law and prepared legal briefing for the volunteers who sat as judges. The first-year program, in which participation was mandatory, consisted of two rounds of briefs and arguments on stipulated facts. Board members advised first-year students what was expected of them in both briefing and oral argument, and sat as "judges" to hear and to comment on the arguments and briefs. Students were organized into "clubs," each under the auspices of a professor. In the first round, each student was on his or her own; in the second, teams of two students competed against each other. If they chose, students in their second year could continue to compete in larger teams until finally, in the third year, the two surviving teams would compete in the finals, first briefing a current cutting-edge legal problem and then arguing it before three distinguished judges, often including a Justice of the United States Supreme Court.

Almost all facets of the work of the Board fitted in with life as Diane wanted to lead it. She could conceive of cutting-edge issues, and she could teach. Moreover, board members were paid $250 per semester for their work – which meant she could begin paying back her student loan – and the work required, on average, only fifteen hours per week. She accepted immediately. She could put her skills to work in a useful way, and she'd have her first experience in counseling and teaching, both career goals.

There were expectations and anticipations of a different sort when I flew to Los Angeles. In those innocent days, people meeting passengers didn't have security to contend with, and Diane was at the gate, alone, glowing and excited, when I disembarked. George and Meryl had wanted to come, she said, but she'd dissuaded them. It had been a very long time and she didn't want her parents in the vicinity when we were first together again.

She prepared me for family immersion as we drove toward North Hollywood. George and Meryl, her grandmother Beatrice, her sister Noreen, brother-in-law Carl and their two children (and other friends and relatives who might happen to drop by) were assembling to meet me. Beatrice was moving out of the little house in the backyard so I could stay there. She'd stay with her other daughter, Aldah, while I was visiting. Everything had been arranged. I should rest easy. No pressure.

There were many cars parked along Corteen Place, where they now lived, when we arrived. The gathering, although "dry," was warm and welcoming, and Diane told me my nervousness didn't show. I would come to like and admire George a great deal, and to be a little wary of Meryl, who, although curious about me, clearly felt the same way toward me.

Diane took me on rounds of friends and relatives for a few days, showing off, and I met the gang – Charlotte, Virginia, Gretchen and Donna; only Betty Jo wasn't around. One evening we had dinner with Donna and her boyfriend of the moment, and played bridge. Donna was amazing, enthusiastic and flaky, the antithesis of Diane's calm and rationality. When I tipped one of her antique chairs back to contemplate my cards, the chair collapsed, its four legs splayed out like a cat introduced to a leash, and I found myself sitting flat on the floor. I don't know whether Donna, Diane or I was the more mortified, but later, on the way home, Diane couldn't stop laughing.

Carl and Noreen rescued us a couple of days later. Carrying backpacks crammed with tents, gear and food, we hiked into Sequoia National Park and camped overnight among giant trees whose girth could only have been encircled by a half dozen people, arms outstretched. Diane and Noreen occupied one tent, Carl and I the other, while our food was stashed high in a neighboring pine, out of reach of the bears. Carl and I didn't think highly of the sleeping arrangements, nor, I know, did Diane and Noreen, but it was the 1950s, and an unmarried couple wouldn't publicly occupy the same tent, even if the public consisted of Diane's sister and brother-in-law. In the early morning, Carl and I were up and out well before sunrise, to prowl, growl and scratch around the tent in which Diane and Noreen, up to that point, had been asleep. Not far away, the real bears were foraging in the park's trash dump.

Repacking our gear and sleeping bags, we hiked another five miles up a steep trail, climbing to a spectacular pristine tarn above tree line called Heather Lake, where we were totally alone on a rock ledge by the water. On the way we'd crossed a sheer cliff on a narrow trail cleft into its granite face, and encountered a party with pack burros coming toward us. There was barely room to pass, and Carl and I flattened ourselves against the inner wall. Diane and Noreen may have done the same, but we didn't

There was no alcohol in Meryl's household, but she wasn't naïve about its use, and even occasionally tolerant. When we arrived for a visit a couple of years later, she'd saved a bottle of beer for me in the refrigerator. On an occasion when she stopped by Noreen and Carl's house unexpectedly to give them some cheese she'd bought, they hurriedly stashed their martinis in the refrigerator when they saw her car. Meryl breezed in, put the cheese in the refrigerator and breezed out again, remarking that it certainly was an "interesting way to store olives."

look. When we reached a promontory at the other end of the cleft trail, the two sisters walked out to the edge to sit and dangle their legs over the abyss, tossing their hair and laughing, as Carl and I nursed our acrophobia.

The sky over Heather Lake was cloudless, a deep bright blue that gradually and perceptibly darkened as we laid out our sleeping bags and made camp. Cooking over a campfire, we chilled out from our hike and ate while the stars began to come out. Two deer came in to browse, looking for scraps, as we quietly watched. Next day we hiked still farther, now high above tree line, to yet another motionless tarn nestled in a craggy mountaintop basin.

It was not to last. We had to return, and, a few days later, George and Meryl and Diane and I drove north along coastal Route 1. We watched the Pacific's waves crashing on the steep rock crags on the shores, stopped to sightsee in Solvang and at Hearst's transplanted San Simeon castle, and made our way to Big Sur and Monterey, then headed north into the Redwoods where we passed, car and all, right through a giant Redwood before finding a place to stay for the night. When we returned to San Francisco, it occurred to me – belatedly – that Diane was posing the problem we had to wrestle with – where would we live our life together? – and the question was not theoretical. Two families with close family ties, one family on each coast. Would there be a winner and a loser here? Did there have to be? How would we decide?

After two days roaming through San Francisco and riding its tram cars, we met Alice in San Jose and had dinner with her family. The next day, without great ceremony or emotion, George and Meryl were on their way home without us. Stuffed into Alice's Beetle, one of us unluckily sharing the rear seat with two suitcases and a dress bag, the three of us

Alice liked to drive her little car fast. We came down the east side of the Rockies like a bowling ball rolling downhill into the wide-open, endlessly straight roads of Montana. We might've set a speed record for traversing the state had it not been for the trooper who stopped Alice. He was the tallest policeman we'd ever seen. Standing beside the Beetle, his belt buckle was even with the top of the driver's side window. From above, he politely inquired where

Alice was going in such a hurry, and seemed relieved that our destination was not in his jurisdiction. Scrunched into the back seat of the Bug with the luggage, I never saw more of him than the belt buckle. Alice impatiently drummed her fingers on the steering wheel until he went back to his cruiser, while Diane pretended she wasn't there at all. He let Alice go without a ticket, but not without him. He followed us to the state line.

headed cross-country the same day. Despite the impossibility of fitting my long legs into the available space, we took turns in the rear seat, as well as at the wheel.

Our first day on the road, Diane seemed to me unusually quiet. The reason, I thought, was having to leave her family again, but I was wrong. The cause was different, and egregious. As soon as we had some time alone – and there was little of that – she came out with it, in tears. In three weeks with her family and friends, I hadn't said a word to anyone about our making plans to marry. How could I be so oblivious to her expectations – and those of her family? It was hard to fathom, and almost unforgivable. But there it was. We didn't speak about it again on the trip, but getting over it would take time.

We covered a lot of territory in the four and a half days we were on the road, stopping only for necessity and rare sightseeing, while scouting for inexpensive motels. Diane had picked up a cheap brass ring because it was important, we thought, to persuade the motel owners we were a married couple traveling with a friend who didn't mind sharing a cot in the same room. The cot would be mine. We never paid more than four dollars for a room; the low was two-fifty. Diane and Alice had brought along a hot plate, a pan and a pot. We boiled hot dogs, potatoes, and green vegetables for dinner, and fried eggs and bacon for breakfast.

Ten Sumner Road, Cambridge, Massachusetts, was (and still is) a three-story Victorian with round turrets at either end extending from the ground to the top of the roof, probably once a grand home that was later divided into apartments. One side of the house – to its right – featured a long, covered porch leading to the side door entrance to the apartments. Two rocking chairs and a small wicker table made the porch a pleasant place on a hot day. The apartment I'd signed on for them was on the first floor to the rear, and consisted of a large living room, a good-sized bedroom with two beds, a workable bathroom with sink, tub and shower – and a tiny kitchen in a space that Diane and Alice concluded immediately must once have been a clothes closet.

It was, I'd thought, ideal in every respect. I learned differently. The kitchen wasn't to their liking, so Alice and Diane decided to look

The landlady, Alice Henderson, lived in two-thirds of the ground floor, together with her gentle, senile, ninety-year old father, Peter Coyle, who'd emigrated from Ireland and owned the house. In his frequent wanderings about the neighborhood, he usually believed he was in Ireland and asked for old friends. He was well known, and someone always brought him home.

elsewhere. Diane knew I felt unappreciated, but had to take Alice's feelings into account, too, and Alice, who'd cautioned Diane against marriage in her letters, was as wary of me as Meryl was. A week of looking turned up nothing better, and they acceded, grudgingly, still making it clear to me that I hadn't attached sufficient importance to the size of the kitchen.

I wasn't there while they were looking. I'd learned that my beloved sister-in-law Sylvia had somehow contracted polio, so returned home to Maine immediately. Diane drove me to the airport the day after our arrival in Cambridge, and I was on my way north in a trusty DC-3, picking up the car I'd left at the Augusta airport.* I stayed overnight with Jon, saw Sylvia the next day and then joined my parents.

Since it was late August, they were living in a rambling summer cottage on an island on Lake Cobbosseecontee, just west of Augusta, one of the large and beautiful inland lakes in Maine. Half-mile-long Hodgdon Island could only be reached by boat. It had no electricity except for direct current generated by a gas-powered Ford Model A engine mounted on a cement block in a shed behind the camp. The generator powered a few lights and a pump that brought water up from a pipe driven into the sand twenty-five feet from the shore. A peaceful place for them, the island was for me a place of refuge and contemplation where depleted batteries could be recharged. Lunds were its only inhabitants.

Diane knew I'd spent summers there since I was five and was even then clearing land behind a sand beach in a cove some distance from my parents' cottage, where I hoped someday to build a cabin for my own family. She'd yet to see it, but just as I'd gone to spend important time with her and her family, she wanted to come spend important time with me and mine. We'd planned two weeks on the island before law school began again, but events had overtaken us, both in Maine and in Cambridge.

Alice didn't want her to leave.

Diane knew I needed her, but she asked me to come back to Cambridge for awhile, so Alice would have time to get used to Boston. I put her off for a few days, then packed a suitcase and drove south again. Two roommates and I had rented an apartment in the garret of a magnificent home on Berkeley Street, a neighborhood of grand Victorians on the other side of the law school from Sumner Road. It was owned by Avis DeVoto, widow of the Harvard historian Bernard DeVoto. Avis, an avowed feminist in a time when feminism was not in vogue, made life interesting for the three of us, and for Diane, and would later influence all our lives.

I unpacked quickly, and called, wanting to return immediately so that we could have at least a week on the island together before school interfered. Alice wasn't pleased at the prospect that Diane would be leaving so soon, and Diane was torn. I drove over

_____

* It was a traumatic time. Sylvia and Jon had four sons under six years old. Sylvia, a Wellesley graduate, had always been active and athletic, a tennis player, a horsewoman and a swimmer. There'd been no warning, no local epidemic, no explanation for why she'd been struck down. She recovered, but never regained full use of one leg. She wouldn't ride or play tennis again.

to Sumner Road, and picked them both up to have dinner at the Oxford Grille. We talked about the year ahead, the three of us and our plans, plans in which Alice was prominently included. Around 8 p.m., Diane and I said goodbye to a still-disgruntled Alice, and headed north.

Three hours later, we turned down a half-mile-long rutted gravel road leading from the paved road along Lake Cobbossee to a lot on its east shore that my family called "the landing." Family cars were parked there among towering pine trees. There was a boathouse where we stored our Town Class sailboat over the winter. Off to one side of the boathouse was a small, secluded beach shielded on the other side by an old fieldstone boundary wall. It was – for late August – unusually warm when we drove down the gravel road late on this starry, moonlit night. We were at the end of a long, stressful summer and a long day of driving. On the way north, we'd spoken about everything private we hadn't had time nor place to share with each other for nearly three months. Finally alone, we were in no great hurry to launch the boat that would take us to the island. We were happy to stay, for a time, on the beach.

That week, Diane and I swam and sailed, and lay in the sun on the sand beach in the island's cove. I showed her where I'd been clearing trees on a hillside behind the beach leading up to a granite ledge outcropping. We walked along the rocky shore on the far side of the beach to a massive boulder in the water whose flat, sloping side faced east toward the morning sun. There, I told her, I had come to sit when I needed private time. I rowed her around the island, showing off its nooks, crannies and bogs, and the spot where the edge of a granite ledge five feet above the water drops off forty feet in a straight sheer to the lake bottom. Ospreys flew overhead, screaming "kee, kee, kee." Muskrats swam low in the water, making a wake toward the clam-filled lake-bottom flats they were raiding. Great blue herons passed by overhead, majestically, looking for a spot in the

Diane in my red-and-black wool shirt a on the island in August 1959.

Diane stayed in a small guest cabin separate from the main cottage together with the ubiquitous supply of murder mysteries. She read late at night and kept the lights on in her cabin after my parents had gone to bed. My father grumbled because, whenever someone turned on a light, the noisy generator would roar to life and stay on until the lights were turned off. But he managed to limit his comments to Diane to a genial explanation of how the generator worked. She understood right away and, however reluctantly, gave up her late-night reading.

little inlets where they could fish. Loons gathered in a flock of twelve or more, organizing for the southbound flight they would soon be taking toward the sea. In the clear night air they called to each other in an eerie tremolo, sounds Diane had never heard. Owls hooted, deep in the island's woods.

Diane understood that the same question she'd put to me a couple of weeks earlier in California was now being put to her in Maine. It wasn't an easy question to answer.

Bright days full of sunshine and wind drove our sailboat as we tacked to windward and reached downwind. Diane sat on the rail holding on, leaning out and letting her auburn hair blow in the breeze as the boat heeled over precariously. August turned into September then, and the days grew cooler. Diane somehow managed to look both beautiful and seductive in the red-and-black-checked wool shirt I gave her to keep warm. We talked and we walked and we swam, and as we walked, she occasionally made the quick happy smiling bounce that always sent a thrill through me.

It was a magical time, much too short, but it was ours, an amazing time when we felt totally free and happy.

Year Two

We packed our bags, said our goodbyes, crossed the water to the landing, and drove back to face another year at Harvard Law School.

Wondering whether she could find a way to earn money to make up the difference between what she'd make at the Board and the amount of her student loan, she thought about the first-year course outlines she and I had prepared. Would first-year students think them worth buying? To be on the safe side before we went down that road, she thought we should run the plan by the administration.

The inquiry wasn't welcomed. Just the possibility of our selling our first-year outlines seemed to threaten the very fabric of the school, which evidently rested on its ability to spring its professors' confidential thoughts, ideas, doctrinal predilections and pronouncements upon an unsuspecting first-year class unsullied by the views of earlier students. Harvard intended, moreover, to take steps to protect that confidentiality. An immediate hand-delivered response from Vice Dean Toepfer stated that the school regarded "the materials, ideas and information presented in class [as] the property of the instructor. Reproduction and distribution of such materials without the instructor's consent may lead to legal consequences." While he graciously conceded that "it was thoughtful of you to bring your plans to our attention at this early point," he concluded, "I must insist that you do not go ahead with your plans." The response was intimidating, and framed a debate that would take place over the next decades concerning the faculty's prerogatives as opposed to their students' initiatives.

So much for that idea.

Even so, we had a bit of fun with the faculty that fall. One day in his Jurisprudence class, Harvard's eminent Professor Lon Fuller compared ethics in legal practice with ethics in sports. Fuller, a giant in the field, distinguished a baseball catcher's maneuvering to make a ball look like a strike as different from a football player's faking an injury toward the end of the game in order to give his team a time-out to which it wasn't entitled. The former, he said, was within ethical bounds; the latter was not. Was this subject to Toepfer's edict? Diane thought not, and I agreed. I wrote a few paragraphs and submitted them to *Sports Illustrated,* which ran the story.

The magazine's squib provoked an outraged response from a sports-loving, equally eminent law professor at the University of Michigan. I interviewed Fuller for his rebuttal. The result was a two-page spread with opposing photos of the two academicians entitled "Go to it, Professors!" Diane reported that she saw Professor Fuller leaving the Harvard Square newsstand with an armload of *Sports Illustrated*s. Apart from the fun of it, there was more, because a substantial check arrived in the mail not long afterwards.*

Diane and I now had spare money. Grasshopper-like, we threw caution to the wind and celebrated our good fortune with a more elegant dinner than our usual Oxford Grille fare, raising a toast to Lon Fuller, Michigan Law School and sports analogies. More important, I could afford to buy a modest diamond engagement ring and wedding ring. There was no turning back. I labored over a formal letter to George and Meryl describing my feelings for Diane and hers for me, and our plans, and asked for their blessing and approval. We received both (though Diane still thought my actions belated). In November, we made our way on the Red Line from Harvard Square to the Jeweler's Building on Washington Street to choose, size and order the rings. I went back there alone, before Christmas, to pick them up.

On Christmas Day, having celebrated the holiday with Alice, Diane came to Augusta to spend the rest of the week with me. The worst snowstorm of the winter had closed

---

* While the story turned out to be financially gratifying, as well as fun, my grade for the course was not gratifying. Another lesson in ethics.

down the airport, so Diane arrived in a Northeast Airlines limousine from Portland. It was late, but she wasn't tired. She knew I had the rings. I spirited her off to my father's study, dropped to one knee and asked her – for perhaps the tenth time – if she would marry me. She laughed, readily agreed and I produced the rings in their box, wrapped in Christmas wrapping and tied with a bow. She opened the package and I slipped the engagement ring onto her finger. Enormously pleased, Diane looked at it this way and that, until we could rejoin my parents and she could show her ring to someone else.

She'd bought a ski sweater for me, and I wore it faithfully. I had no other Christmas present for her. Not important. We'd passed a milestone.

The year went well.

Diane enjoyed her work with the Board so much that she barely noticed how the hours she actually spent exceeded the estimate. Throughout her professional life, what was important to her wasn't the hours or the money, it was whether she was making a difference that helped other people. Years later, I met lawyers who'd been first-year students she'd advised to think the same way, and who'd followed the counseling she'd given. Their memories of their experiences with Diane in law school were vivid and positive: she had inspired them to look at problems differently.*

We often played bridge, sometimes with Alice, a demon bridge player, and one of the upstairs tenants at Sumner Road; other times with my roommate Dick Morehead and his new friend Cindy in the garret apartment of Avis DeVoto's house.

Avis was an extraordinary figure, both in the Harvard community and in the nascent feminist community. She was constantly on the go, but on learning that Diane was a law student, she insisted that Diane stop by and have tea when she was visiting. When we did, Avis spoke passionately about what women needed to do to achieve recognition and equality. To be accomplished and passive was not enough. Women needed to be aggressive. The laws needed to be changed. Women lawyers were in a position to cause those changes and Diane could be one of those women.

Avis had an endless stream of eminent guests. She'd succeeded her husband as Mark Twain's literary executor, and when Hal Holbrook was in Boston in the early years of his one-man show as Mark Twain, he was a guest in Avis' house. She was also a literary agent. One day, she asked us to tea with a striking red-haired woman, easily six feet tall, who Avis had encouraged to put together a cookbook. Publishing a cookbook seemed a small endeavor, but Avis had great things in mind. The book would be entitled "The French Chef" and the woman was Julia Child.

On another occasion she invited us to meet her lawyer, Ethleen Diver, one of the few women lawyers working for any major law firm in Boston. A lively and bright woman in her fifties, Ethleen prepared estate plans, drafted wills and trusts and interviewed,

---

* One of those students – a decade later – persuaded her to join the faculty at Northeastern's law school, launching her on the teaching career she'd hoped for.

hired and managed the secretarial staff at Choate, Hall & Stewart, one of Boston's elite firms. Like every woman lawyer working in a Boston firm, she was a "permanent" associate, an employee who wasn't on the partnership track. Her office at 30 State Street – as I would learn – was an interior windowless cubbyhole tucked at the end of a short entrance hall that separated the men's room from the ladies' room. Whatever her private thoughts, she had nothing but good things to say about her firm, and asked what our plans were for next summer's employment. Diane, by that time, was already working at a second part-time job, assisting Professor John T. MacNaughton in revising Volume IX of the massive treatise, *Wigmore on Evidence*, a job that would occupy her full-time over the summer and part-time the next year. Hearing that I had no plans, she said I should consider working for Choate, Hall, and invited me to come to the firm's office to meet the hiring partner, Wm. Arthur Dupee. I did, and was hired.*

The second and third years of law school were very different from the first. The first year had been a trial by fire with prescribed courses covering broad legal principles – Property, Contracts, Torts, Criminal Law and Civil Procedure – most of them taught by intimidating law-school legends intent on keeping students in a state of fear. Some second-year courses continued to be prescribed (or strongly suggested), but we were largely able to choose both courses and professors who interested us. A number of those professors were new to the law school, and neither as egotistical nor as patronizing as had been our experience in the first year. Assistant professors such as Frank Sander (Tax) and Detlev Vagts (Corporations) were closer in age, life experience and temperament to their students and treated us more like intellectual equals. Atypically, they even paid attention to the women in their classes and respected their opinions. In this, they were a distinct minority on the faculty.[4]

An enormous February snowstorm buried vehicles on the streets of Cambridge up to their radio antennas. Diane had never seen so

In the snow in Cambridge.

---

* Having tea with Ethleen and Avis was our introduction to the world of Proper Bostonians, but neither of us recognized it as such. Diane would have her own experiences with Boston's Yankee elite later, but this chance encounter led to the foundation for my legal career.

much snow. Awed, she walked with me in an eerie urban quiet broken only by the sound of plows making paths through the snow, burying with still more snow what little remained visible of the parked cars. The city was paralyzed for days, but the law school's professors appeared for their classes, without fail, and expected their students to do the same.

The occasionally rocky road of our courtship had been resolved by my formal marriage proposal, ring included, and her acceptance of it, and the year proceeded uneventfully toward our June wedding date. Marriage and children were two of Diane's goals, but there was no doubt in her mind she'd also have a professional career. We were agreed that we'd find ways to make both family and career possible, though the agreement was nonspecific since we had no models to look to – but the understanding was clear and the pledge was firm. We weren't conscious of being pioneers or of blazing new paths. What we would do, we thought, would be personal to us. It was only in retrospect that we would see its significance.

Meryl began planning the wedding, and we signed a lease for a second-floor apartment at 10 Sumner Road for the following year.

A MARRIED WOMAN

It may not have been a whirlwind courtship, but we had a whirlwind wedding and honeymoon. We flew to Los Angeles on a Wednesday and went directly from the airport to a family-and-friends bridal shower at her aunt Aldah and uncle Andy Meyers's house, next day met my parents and cousin Arnold ("Tot"), who arrived after a transcontinental drive, and, later that evening, met my brother Morten, who flew in from New York carrying an enormously heavy suitcase packed with French cookware. My parents hosted a dinner Friday, followed by a late-night bachelor party organized by Carl, my future brother-in-law, a party about which I have no recollection. Saturday morning, Diane dispatched Carl, my brother Mort, my cousin and me to remove two-thirds of the folding chairs in the cavernous North Hollywood Presbyterian Church auditorium where the ceremony would be held, so that our small wedding wouldn't be dwarfed by empty chairs. Shortly after 2 p.m., with proper ceremony, we were duly married. After a reception on George and Meryl's backyard patio, we drove off for a three-day honeymoon at Big Bear Lake, then caught a flight back to Boston on Wednesday, so I could fly out to Chicago on Friday with my Army Reserve unit for two weeks of active military service.

Time slowed down during the three days at Big Bear Lake; otherwise, it was a blur.

A few things stand out in memory. Diane was happy, at ease even on our wedding day. She'd let her hair grow long and it cascaded in curls toward a traditional bare-shouldered white wedding dress. She was radiant as she came down the aisle on her father's arm, and her smile when George handed her over to me was dazzling. There was one small hitch. At the penultimate moment when George gave me her arm and we tried to walk on toward the minister, Diane couldn't move. First she tugged at her train, then said, in a whisper heard throughout the auditorium, "Daddy, you're standing on my train!"

The reception was dry, but George understood my father's Norwegian sensibilities. The two of them disappeared out the gate of the patio into the garage, where – unbeknownst to

We were married on June 20, 1960.

Meryl – George kept a bottle of banana brandy. They returned, smiling.

We were to make our getaway in George's gleaming red-and-white Ford coupe, which was parked in front of the house. When I tried to start the car it sounded as if the neighborhood had been invaded by terrorists armed with Uzis. My brother, my cousin, my new brother-in-law and my roommate Dick Morehead had disconnected the leads to the spark plugs and reassigned them randomly. After lifting the hood and rerouting the leads – amid gritted teeth and great laughter – Diane and I were on the road to Big Bear, and to the rest of our life.

We returned to Boston and Sumner Road, to the three-room second-floor apartment that would be our home for two years, first as third-year law students, then as fledgling lawyers and parents. The next day I flew to Chicago. Diane wrote me two wonderfully romantic letters over the weekend, went to work on *Wigmore* on Monday, bought curtains and became very domestic. She also got acquainted with the other inhabitants of 10 Sumner Road, some of whom became lifelong friends.

Phil and Marcia Lieberman seemed reticent when we first met them but that soon changed. Phil would eventually become a renowned professor of Cognitive Science at Brown University, an author of seminal texts in the field and an early rival of MIT's Noam Chomsky in the field of linguistics.[5] Despite her shyness, Marcia was an ardent, militant feminist and university professor who would single-handedly integrate the gymnasium and the men's locker room at the University of Connecticut (where she and Phil later taught).*

Four other Stanford graduates lived in the two apartments on the third floor, Alf and Ann Brandin, and Bill and Carol Fuller. Alf was a year behind us in law school.[6] Five years later, the Brandins became godparents to our daughter Kristin.

Then there were the exhibitionists, a couple who had a basement apartment with a street-level window in their bedroom and never drew the blinds. They made love, it seemed, at the drop of a hat, at virtually any time of the day or night, and with great enthusiasm. We didn't get to know them personally.

It was a carefree time, but we were both impatient to get through the third year of law school and out into the real world. We spent a great deal of time with the Brandins, especially on Sundays, watching Y.A. Tittle, Frank Gifford and the New York Giants on television. (The Boston Patriots, later to become the New England Patriots, were still only a gleam in Billy Sullivan's eye.) Other times we played bridge. After one game broke up late, we heard a commotion outside where, we later learned, a young woman who lived next door had come home to find a man on her porch, naked from the waist down, carrying Bermuda shorts in his hands. She screamed, he ran out to the street, jumped into a car, put on his shorts and then ran off. The unlocked car was ours. Two Cambridge detectives, looking like Joe Friday and his partner, complete with fedoras pulled down toward their eyebrows, arrived at our door the next morning, after having talked to the Brandins. Alf had been helpful: yes, Mr. Lund was wearing Bermuda shorts last night; yes, our bridge game had ended before the commotion; no, he hadn't the slightest idea what I did after the game was over….

Diane's penchant for mischief led us to get even. One warm afternoon not long afterwards, when the Brandins were gone, Diane climbed out our window, up the outside wall and in through their open window. I was the safety net. We ran wires from our hi-fi set up the outside wall. Diane let me in and I wired our system into their speaker. Before joining them for drinks in late afternoon, we put on our recording of "76 Trombones" from *The Music Man* and wired a timer into the circuit so it would start to play in fifteen minutes. When the horns began, Alf said, "There's a goddamn band out in the street!" and jumped up to look out the window. Diane was convulsed and turned beet red.

There were other, more serious things on the agenda that summer. We needed to make some money. Diane was working two jobs, one with Professor MacNaughton, and the other at the Board of Student Advisors. I'd begun work as a summer associate at Choate, Hall & Stewart, but it was slim pickings all around.

---

* The university had provided no facilities for women, and she refused to be relegated to second-class status. She'd later bring a major lawsuit against the university over its decision not to grant her tenure. She wasn't popular with the administration.

Then considered one of the larger firms in Boston, Choate had thirty-eight lawyers, all but twelve of them partners, and all male except for Ethleen Diver. Its offices were in the top three floors of the nine-story New England Merchants National Bank Building at 30 State Street in Boston's financial district. The building, now long since gone, was built in the 1890s, and had an ornate black-and-white marble-tiled lobby which led, on the left, into the main banking floor through double doors. Straight ahead were three wire-cage elevators run by uniformed elevator operators, the last of their breed in downtown Boston. The building's emergency exit was a winding wrought-iron fire escape on the exterior of the building leading from the ninth floor to ground level on Congress Street. Scollay Square was two blocks away and would soon be in shambles, razed at the outset of Boston's massive urban renewal.

There were only two law students working in the firm's gloomy seventh-floor library that summer. This room was a dark mahogany-paneled place with ceiling-high bookshelves that sometimes required the use of a handy stepladder to reach the older law books. Occasionally a partner in the firm (or perhaps an associate – we wouldn't have known the difference) would appear, bringing a memo with a research assignment.

We were paid sixty-five dollars each week, in cash.

Diane's work paid even less, but she found it challenging and interesting, which was always more important to her than money. MacNaughton, moreover, was not afflicted with sexist bias and welcomed her contributions. They became good friends and he and his wife included us in an occasional social gathering.

LOOKING FOR WORK

Law firms generally recruited from Harvard's third-year class by interviewing in October and November and sometimes, if the firms were located in distant parts of the country, by offering to fly the students they coveted to visit their offices. Harvard graduates were prized, and most of the men in the class of 1961 were offered and accepted positions at the firms they were interested in. It was different for women. They confronted overt discrimination, particularly in New York.

Two years earlier Supreme Court Justice-to-be Ruth Bader Ginsburg, who was a member of the *Law Review* at both Harvard and Columbia (where she graduated first in her class), had received no job offers from New York law firms. Her status, she later said, as "a woman, a Jew and a mother to boot" was "a bit much" for prospective employers.* She was fortunate to be offered a clerkship with a United States District Court Judge in the Southern District of New York.

Women had to devise stratagems outside of the normal Harvard hiring channels to be considered, in some instances stratagems unique to them. In the fall of 1959 Zona

---

* Guide to Government website.

Fairbanks – the Apple Pie Queen of Virginia – was hired "accidentally" by Covington & Burling in Washington, DC, one of the nation's leading law firms. Despite an outstanding academic record, she'd received no job offers through the Harvard recruiting process. Deciding on a direct approach, and believing her best chances lay in going into legal aid, public service or government agencies, she flew to Washington and began knocking on doors. The Agency for International Development was interested in hiring her but not for the positions abroad that it offered to men. Dependents of the men AID sent overseas would need legal services while their husbands were away, she was told, and that was a position they could offer her. That wasn't what she had in mind. Another agency said it had the perfect job for her: its law librarian was getting elderly and Zona could work with her for a time and ultimately take over her job. That wasn't what she had in mind either. Undiscouraged, she decided to try her luck with Washington law firms.

Without an appointment she walked into Covington's offices and said she'd like to talk to someone about a job as a lawyer. The surprised receptionist politely asked Zona to wait while she checked with someone else. Eventually a young partner came out and invited her to his office where they had a lively fifteen-minute conversation. Bemused, he escorted her to the office of a curmudgeonly senior partner who, informed of why she was there, interrogated her about her background, and asked the classic interviewer's question: why did she want to come to work for Covington?

She didn't really think she did, Zona replied, but someone had suggested she should talk to Covington. What she actually had in mind was working in legal aid or public service. Taken aback by the idea that any lawyer would want to work anywhere else ("Young lady, don't you know that *everyone* wants to work at Covington? We have our own pro bono and public service programs. You can get everything right here! If you were to come to Covington, we'd give you just the kind of work you want!"), he smiled for the first time, stood up, came around his desk, took her hand and walked with her down the hall to meet Mr. Covington himself. Two days later, back in Cambridge, a letter arrived offering her an associate's position at Covington.

Few women in law school were either as uninhibited or as fortunate as Zona. Many firms flatly refused to interview women despite excellent academic records. Others did so only for appearance's sake. Some treated the idea of hiring a woman as a joke. It was standard procedure to ask women applicants whether they were engaged, did they plan to marry, did they plan to have children? Questions not asked of men. The implication was plain.

Some women were humiliated in the job-seeking process. A classmate who wanted to work in New York, but was unsuccessful in Harvard interviews, was advised to write New York firms, enclose her resume and ask for an interview at the firms' offices. Scadden Arps, then a medium sized firm by New York standards and not the megalith it would later become, invited her to come for an interview on December 24th at 4 p.m. The date seemed an obvious mistake, so she called the firm. She was told it was no mistake, and that was when she should appear if she wanted the interview.

Dressed in a conservative business suit, she arrived to find a raucous office Christmas party in full swing. The receptionist told her, however, that Mr. Arps himself was scheduled to interview her. Arps appeared and led her to his office, where several of his male partners had collected. He offered her a drink, but she declined on the ground she didn't think it was appropriate (and thought of adding – but didn't – that it wasn't professional). She was then "interviewed," the men peppering her with questions personal and sexist. There was a great deal of laughter. With difficulty, she maintained her poise until the "interview" was over. She thanked Mr. Arps for the opportunity and left his office only too aware of the laughter behind her, and of the fact that she'd been brought in to provide entertainment for the Christmas party.

By the time Diane began interviewing, we'd narrowed our geographical choices to Boston and Portland, Maine. Portland's leading firm was prepared to offer a woman a position, but the position offered was as a secretary. Her class standing was not persuasive. The firm promised, however, that she'd be given the opportunity to do some research in addition to her secretarial duties, and, if she proved worthy, they'd consider her for a position as a lawyer at some unspecified future date. No other Portland firm was interested.

She applied for a judicial clerkship with Massachusetts Supreme Judicial Court Justice Ammi Cutter, a renowned and respected judge, probably the most learned judge on that prestigious court. A quintessential Yankee, Judge Cutter was handsome, courtly, gracious and conservative, and had a finely honed belief in the rule of law. His opinions were widely admired and cited. He invited her to come to his elegant Cambridge home for afternoon tea. Diane asked me to come along. We were dressed formally, Diane in the dress she saved for special occasions, and I in suit and tie.

We were welcomed at the front door, and Judge Cutter led us into his sitting room. The ceilings of the house were high, perhaps as much as twelve feet, the interior was oppressive and the atmosphere cool. The living room walls were dark oak or mahogany, and heavy drapes were partially drawn over windows otherwise covered in white lace curtains. His housekeeper brought in a silver tea service and some small cakes, and we carried on a polite conversation as he weighed the novel idea of having a female law clerk serving him on the Supreme Judicial Court. Judge Cutter was reserved, but the idea clearly intrigued him. Seeming shy, he spoke at length of the history and long traditions of his Court, which had never had a woman law clerk, and inquired, politely and gently, how Diane would feel if she were first, and what she saw as her career path afterwards. He promised he would give her full consideration (as a gentleman would surely do) and would be in touch at a later date.

Diane left his house feeling as if we'd been to a social occasion, not an interview, and that we'd just seen a different, parallel world, one in which we didn't belong. The experience was unsettling.

Diane's interviews with Boston's leading firms were very different from the Portland experience, professional and refreshingly focused on her academic record and future plans. That she was married was noted, but not seen as a disability. Their interest was in her law-school record, her talent and what she could bring to the firm. Whether they were more enlightened than those in New York isn't clear, but they doubtless felt they were at a competitive disadvantage in the hiring process. Each made it known to her that she was highly regarded. Diane received offers from the four major firms where she interviewed.

She was elated, but there had been other developments in the interim.

Diane understood that she was different. No woman in her family had pursued a man's career. Her career choices differed from society's expectations. Her older sister Noreen had married at age nineteen and already had two children. Her parents hadn't understood her decision to go to Harvard when she could have had a much better scholarship at Stanford. Was a career that important? She had no role model for the experiences she was going through, and she wasn't certain she wanted to be different. Her identity as a woman was important.

Marrying was an important affirmation. She'd found someone she loved and who loved her, and so she, like her sister and the girls she'd grown up with in high school, had married. But could she have children? It was a nagging concern – however irrational – that somehow, because of who she was and what she was doing, she'd be incapable of having children. We didn't decide we'd have children then, but we purposely didn't take precautions. By mid-November, she knew she was pregnant – and was delighted, not just by the fact, but because she found she enjoyed being pregnant. Both were important to her. But pregnancy complicated her life enormously.

In late November, we were invited to a cocktail party at Professor MacNaughton's house on Berkeley Street, a magnificent Victorian only a few houses down and across the street from Avis DeVoto. The company was distinguished – largely faculty and their wives – and so were the furnishings, wonderful oiled antique maple-framed chairs and tables in a living room which featured a pure white rug and a pure white Persian cat lying on the white rug, nearly invisible unless she blinked her eyes. Nervous in this social setting, Diane limited herself to one drink from the punch bowl. Unexpectedly, she became dizzy and fainted dead away, but I caught her. Except for the two of us, no one knew she was pregnant. We hadn't told anyone because the word would have spread through the faculty instantly and all would have nodded their heads sagely and wondered when she'd drop out. The pregnancy would show soon enough. Diane was determined that, by the time of the news, the faculty would clearly understand she intended to finish, get her degree and go on to practice law.

Knowing she was pregnant, however, she decided she was ethically bound to tell Judge Cutter and each of the Boston firms who'd offered her a position. Judge Cutter kindly advised her that offering her a clerkship in these circumstances was out of the question, and all but one of the firms withdrew their offers. That one, Herrick, Smith, Donald, Farley & Ketchum took a view which was extraordinarily enlightened for the times. An old-line Yankee Bostonian firm, a major part of whose practice concerned the legal aspects of investing and preserving their clients' considerable fortunes, they wanted Diane to work in their trusts and estates department. Learning of her pregnancy, they told her they were confident they could work out an acceptable part-time arrangement while her children were young, if she'd commit to work for them full-time for a year while they trained her in that field. She accepted.

In the winter, as her pregnancy began to show, the faculty nervously took note. This was the first time they'd had to deal with having a very visibly pregnant law student in their classrooms. She was well-liked among the many faculty members she'd met while working for Professor MacNaughton, and they admired the fact that she had no intention of dropping out merely because she was married and pregnant. In their experience (or so they believed), most women in that position would have done so.

Her pregnancy was the source of both titilation and concern. As her pregnancy became more and more apparent, she'd come to class, lean back in her hard chair and balance the textbook on her stomach. Ben (as he was to be called) was an active baby in utero, and when he felt the weight of the book, he'd kick at it, causing the book to bounce up and down without any effort on Diane's part, entertaining both Diane and the men around her. And unnerving her

Diane, pregnant with Ben, just before Law School graduation in June 1961

professors. What if she gave birth before taking her third-year final examinations in May? What then?

The issue was placed on the agenda in a faculty meeting in April and debated at length. A decision was made: should Diane be "disabled," she would receive in all courses her average grade for the prior two years. No one had inquired about her due date, as this was too delicate a subject to be raised, nor did she learn about the faculty vote until well after the year was out. Then she was told by a younger faculty member who thought the whole event hilarious. He added that they'd been cautioned to say nothing to her for fear that she might then decide she could avoid taking finals. They had no reason to fear. Happy and triumphant, Diane would attend our class graduation in June, with a billowing black robe serving as her maternity dress.

All these events had escaped the attention of the yearbook staff. The prior summer, having taken my last name as hers, she'd notified the registrar of her marriage and change of name. "Theis" was deleted, but a second "Lund" was not added. When the yearbook came out, she was nowhere to be found, a non-person in our class.[7]

Diane's due date was of equal interest to me because the date forecast by her obstetrician – June 28, 1961 – was the date of the Massachusetts Bar Examination. We laughed about that possibility, if a little nervously. As we were short of money, however, one thing was decided: only I would plan to take the bar exam on this go-round; Diane would take it six months later. And it would only be necessary for one of us to take – and pay for – a bar review course to prepare for the exam. She'd use my notes later.

Surely the predicted date was wrong.

But it wasn't. Late in the evening of June 27, as I was cramming for the bar exam, Diane began to have labor pains and called her obstetrician. He advised us to wait awhile to see if they continued. They did. On receiving a second call, he said he'd meet us at Boston Lying-In Hospital, where we arrived around midnight, just before he did. After an examination, he announced it was false labor and we should go home. Diane and I disagreed. After a three-way discussion, it was agreed she could remain at Boston Lying-In overnight. I was to call the next morning at 7 a.m. to determine Diane's status. When I did, the obstetrician was there and said not only had he been wrong, but Diane was now in full labor and expected to give birth in the next few hours.

I drove to the bar examination, which was being given four blocks from the hospital – an examination about which I remember nothing – and took the morning tests, then sprinted the four blocks to the hospital during the noon break. There I met our son Ben* for the first time, cradled in Diane's arms, a wonderful red-faced product of Diane's labor. She was beaming. I was elated and almost speechless. Diane laughed to see my expression.

"How's the exam going?" she wanted to know.

---

* Ben would become the first person to "graduate" from Harvard Law School twice, the second time 26 years later.

[1]   Dean Griswold and others on the law school faculty were supportive of Zona throughout her three years there, and she has only good things to say today about her treatment and about the opportunities a Harvard Law School education provided. He later wrote recommendations for her and took a particular interest in her career in Washington. They became good friends after he left Harvard to become President Nixon's Solicitor General.

[2]   Griswold's true attitude toward women's presence in the law school was never clear, even to them. Some believed, in retrospect, that in making these kinds of now-offensive remarks, he was preparing them for similar questions they would face (and did face) from professors and prospective employers. Others did not credit him with nuance.

[3]   Using the Socratic method of give and take, a professor sought to elicit from students what principles and doctrines they had gleaned from reading the casebooks, and how the principles should be applied in different, hypothetical situations. Students were expected to stand up for the principles they articulated, whether right or wrong (some professors claimed there was no right or wrong, only different points of view) as the professor bore down on them, poking holes in their statements and sometimes ridiculing them. The Socratic method (so the theory went) put a man on his mettle, forced him to stand up for himself, toughened him and prepared him for the law profession's adversary system. Many professors were loath to put women to the adversary test.

[4]   There was no sense of political correctness in that era. In his tax class, Professor Sander once posed a hypothetical question: assume a man's servant has to go to the hospital and while he is there the man makes a substantial donation to the hospital. If the servant is charged no fee on being discharged, is the man's donation deductible as a charitable gift? A voice with a deep southern accent responded, "Suh, I think that would depend on whether or not the man *owned* the servant!" Sander was speechless. The author of the response was parodying the attitudes of his native South. Actually a political liberal, he later became mayor of Columbia, SC, and a leader in promoting civil rights for African-Americans.

[5]   Chomsky's thesis about the development of human speech was that it occurred as a consequence of the development of the brain. Phil Lieberman's thesis was that it came about as a result of the physical structure that human beings have in their mouth and throat, and that what distinguishes us from other animals is not the ability to think, but the ability given us by this structure to form words and make an intelligible language.

[6]   Alf Brandin would later become the managing partner of a San Francisco firm, Lillick, McHose & Charles. Bill Fuller, who was at the business school, was the scion of the Fuller Paint Company and already well-to-do. Carol Fuller, attractive and entertaining, didn't expect to follow a career. She wasn't enthused about being in Cambridge and Boston. Carol once commented about the Boston subway (with a sidelong glance at Bill) "I've never in my life been so intimate with strange men as I am forced to be on the Boston subway."

[7]   Not long after being notified of the omission, the yearbook published a separate page with Diane's photo and law-school record on it, and furnished Diane with fifty copies, enough for friends and family and any future employer who might be curious about the omission.

CHAPTER FIVE

FLEX-TIME PIONEER

F OR EIGHT YEARS, DIANE AND I BUILT A LIFE AROUND FAMILY, work, and trust in the future. We started out in debt to Harvard and ended in debt to a bank. Diane gave birth to three children, two sons, Ben and Ted, then, miraculously, a daughter, Kristin. We moved three times, once in Cambridge, then to a small cape house in Lexington within quiet walking distance of an elementary school, and finally – at a time when both our professional lives changed profoundly – to our last home in Lexington, one largely designed by us. There we'd live as our children grew to adulthood and Diane's career progressed in ways she'd hoped for, but wouldn't have predicted.

Her focus in the early years after law school was on our children. She was content for the time being to accept the role to which law firms consigned their few women lawyers, i.e., working on estate plans, wills and trusts, but her ambitions remained intact. She never contemplated becoming simply a housewife, a mother and a handmaiden lawyer whose skills would serve only the wealthy, and not those who most needed, and could least afford, competent legal services.

It wasn't easy to strike a workable balance between family and lawyering, especially not the first year when, her son just three months old, she went to work full-time and gave over his daytime care to a stranger.

She expected to do it all. She sewed, she cooked, she cleaned, she looked after our children, and she practiced law – often in late evenings in our quiet house. But professionally she began to be left behind by her peers and shunted aside from the career she'd envisioned. To regain that lost ground, she would eventually abandon her establishment law firm and find another path, one that returned her to the ideals she'd

Some friends still use Diane's favorite recipe for serving potatoes cooked on a stove-top or grill: Peel and dice potatoes, and place them on a square of aluminum foil; dice some onions in large pieces and place on top of the potatoes; add several large pieces of butter, along with salt and pepper (and sometimes diced green peppers); firmly seal the aluminum foil packet and place on the stove-top or grill and cook until ready (which, it has been said, is approximately two gin and tonics later).

grown up with that were so important in her life before she came to law school, and before she fell in love.

Finances were a concern. My career in a white-shoe Bostonian law firm was important to us both because our assumption, given the flex-time career Diane intended to pursue, was that primary money-making responsibility would rest with me. My professional responsibilities would also be balanced against family demands, but not to the same degree. My balancing task was feasible in the Boston law firm environment of the 1960s. It wouldn't have been possible in today's quest for the last possible billable hour.[1]

It was a gentler, slower time. Copies of pleadings, letters, memos or other documents were made on carbon paper. Instantaneous changes were impossible because whenever changes were made, a new original had to be typed. The electric typewriter and the Xerox machine would soon lighten editing and copying tasks, but facsimile transmission was no more than an inventor's pipedream, and the Internet not even an Al Gore thought. From time to time we'd hear about electronic marvels to come. They'd serve (we were assured) as time-saving devices to lessen a lawyer's burden. They would enable lawyers to become more efficient in the use of their time. Lawyers would work fewer hours for the same pay and the quantity of work product expected of them would remain unchanged. How little we understood law firm economics and clients' demands.

Flex-time was interesting in theory, but the goal of having weekends and weekday evenings to herself proved illusory. Diane brought work home, worked at night and on weekends, and produced work product equal in both quality and quantity to that expected from a full-time associate. Her firm, it turned out, had made a very good deal, but that was no sure thing in that era. Employing a woman lawyer part-time was still an experiment. When it paid dividends, other firms would follow suit.

ESTABLISHMENT LAW FIRM PRACTICE – AND A GROWING FAMILY

Before joining her firm in late September 1961, Diane spent an idyllic summer in Maine with Ben, breast-feeding him during much of the period. The bottle was first introduced during early-morning feedings in midsummer so we could share the middle-of-night sleeplessness brought on by his vociferous demands to be regularly fed.

My job didn't start until early September, so we escaped north from Cambridge during the dog days of mid-July and August to live in my parents' house in Augusta. They'd moved to the island for the summer, and we often brought Ben there, motoring across from the landing several times a week. Motherhood suited Diane, and having no other responsibilities was perfect. For three months her attention could be focused almost entirely on Ben, and it was. Toward the middle of August, however, her thoughts turned to her new firm.

Her agreement with Herrick, Smith had specified no particular date in September for her to come to work full time. Nothing was in writing. To confirm the arrangements, she wrote the hiring partner, Augustus Soule, Jr., who responded immediately:

> Dear Mrs. Lund:
>
> Thank you for your letter of August 16 giving me your situation to date. I congratulate you on your son, and hope that you will be able to get things straightened out at home soon.
>
> We definitely have an office set aside for you and we will be glad to see you as soon as you can make it. There is plenty of work here for you to do and I think you will find your association a pleasant and busy one.[2]
>
> Sincerely,
>
> Augustus W. Soule, Jr.

We rearranged our three-room apartment on Sumner Road to accommodate Ben by creating an ell in the living room through the use of two stand-up bookcases, one at right angles to the wall and the other at right angles to the end of the first bookcase. Ben's crib went into the space between the second bookcase and the wall. He learned to sleep on, no matter what else was happening.

Diane arranged day-care for him with the wife of a second-year law student who had two small children of her own. Janet was an extraordinary find. But when Diane went to work for the first time in late September, leaving Ben with Janet, the separation was wrenching. Giving over her beautiful new son to someone else's care wasn't an experience for which she was prepared. Each morning at 7:30 a.m., we drove five blocks to Holden Green, a married students housing complex off Kirkland Street, and left Ben with Janet. Each evening we picked him up by 6 p.m. In the beginning, both Ben and Diane would cry when he was left off. After a time they became used to the routine, and the morning's events were less traumatic. The evening events never became less joyful.

Diane hadn't expected joining an elite Boston law firm to be a social experience, but it was. Herrick, Smith, Donald, Farley & Ketchum's important partners, generally Harvard/Harvard educated, with a sprinkling of Yale and Oxford thrown in, were Yankees through and through, with names like Taft, Guild, Cabot, Hovey, Donaldson,

Perkins and Woolsey dominating the mix. Depending on where they lived, they were members of The Country Club in Brookline or the Myopia Hunt Club on the North Shore, sometimes both if they happened to live in one place and summer in the other. The firm was a gentleman's club whose partnership agreement was simple and to the point, one sentence on a single piece of paper each one signed that said he agreed he owned no furniture, and that he would abide by the decisions of the Senior Partner.[3]

They and their families all knew one other. Many were related by marriage and old school ties. The senior partner, Phillips Ketchum, was seventy-seven years old and had been a member of the bar for fifty-three years. No other partner had access to the firm's financial statements. At the end of a calendar year, he walked through the firm's offices, stopping by each partner with a handwritten piece of paper in hand to inform him privately how much of the firm's profits he had been allocated. For most, the figure was a matter of interest, but not of great importance to their financial statements. This governance system seemed to work well until, in order for the firm to compete for clients in a more aggressive legal market, they had to hire Jews and Irish* and who-knows-what other denomination.

Neither Diane nor I thought of the Brahmin domination of Boston's major firms as an impediment to our careers.† We believed in meritocracy: everyone was on an equal footing and our merit, ability and achievements would determine the progress of our careers. We underestimated the force of elitism, both in the social world of Boston law practice, and, later, in the intellectual context of Harvard Law School. The former concerned class structure and money, and the latter, perceived intellectual superiority. While the Brahmin influence over law firms would wane over the next two decades, just as it had in Massachusetts politics,[4] elitism in all its forms would continue to impact Diane's professional life and career. The concept was foreign to her.

This was not an issue in the fall of 1961. She liked the firm's partners – they all took a particular interest in her – and she liked the firm's clients. They were intelligent, interesting, articulate people, and they all liked her. Only the idea of helping to preserve inherited wealth was troublesome for her, but that was her task. It wasn't

---

*   Boston's judiciary was dominated by the Irish, and it was customary for a large firm to hire someone Irish to handle its litigation interests in the state court system – although not in the federal courts. Herrick, Smith's Irish partner was Kevin Hern, whose Jesuit training at Boston College had been somewhat – but not wholly – redeemed by his subsequent law degree from Harvard.

†   Choate, Hall & Stewart had similar Yankee origins. The firm had been founded early in the twentieth century based on connections with the Boston & Maine Railroad, then a commercial powerhouse. Two generations of Halls and three generations of Charles Choates had been partners in the firm. Its senior partners included Harvey Bundy (father of Kennedy adviser McGeorge Bundy), DuPont and Rockefeller family members by relationship or marriage, and James A. Garfield, a grandson of the murdered president. Much of the power in the firm rested with Robert Proctor, who had married the second Charles Choate's widow, and with Claude Branch, a vigorous senior partner who commuted by train to Boston from Providence, where he reputedly maintained a mistress, and who practiced law at the firm well into his eighties.

the legal principles in tax and estate tax planning that concerned her, but rather the motivation behind legislation which served to preserve wealth for personal use, rather than encouraging the use of a fair portion of it for public benefit.

She signed on for the February bar examination* and was one of 126 people, four of them women, who passed. When the list came out, both the *Boston Herald* and Boston's tabloid, the *Record-American*, asked if they could take Diane's photo for their stories. The caption in the *Herald* read (without irony) "Cambridge woman one of four of sex to pass bar" and the photo featured her with a telephone cradled on one shoulder, her free hand holding a baby bottle and Ben, and a legal pad on her lap.† We thought it was

This photo appeared in the Boston Herald *when Diane passed the Massachusetts bar exam in April 1962.*

a hoot, but the picture was an accurate metaphor for the next few years of her life.

Ben was a healthy baby and, by that time, a big one. We calculated at his rate of growth he'd weigh 220 pounds by the time he was three and be drafted to play professional football. We had no yard, the nearest small urban park was four blocks away, and our second-floor apartment couldn't contain him much longer. We had to move. We began looking for another apartment, one we hoped would have access to a yard and not cost much more than the rent we were paying at Sumner Road.

We were in luck. A fledgling architect trying to beat the exorbitant Cambridge rents had persuaded the landlord of a sturdy brick apartment building at 19 Ware Street to let him build an apartment in the basement. It was clean, had a kitchen, living room, two bedrooms and a bath, plastic tile on the floor, no visible mold or water stains and no obvious defects. The outside stairs led up to a spacious grassy backyard which no tenants used other than the three of us. We moved in the first week of June and celebrated by buying a black-and-white television set, the only TV we'd own for thirteen years.‡

---

* Law-school graduates generally took the examination in June. Most taking the February examination had previously failed, some of them many times. Diane said it was like a reunion, with people greeting each other by name and asking how things had gone since the last exam.

† *Record-American*, April 21, 1962, p.3.

‡ We spent countless evenings watching "Wagon Train," "Perry Mason," "Rawhide," "Dr. Kildare," "Ben Casey" and other mind-numbing and satisfying shows. Our children were permitted to watch "Sesame Street" on Sunday mornings. Finally, twelve-year old Ben – anxious to see color – made a deal with a classmate to buy his family's color television set when they moved.

Diane with one-year-old Ben.

In July, we flew to Los Angeles, where we spent three weeks while Diane renewed family ties with her parents, uncles, aunts and cousins, and Ben met his grandparents, his great-grandmother, his aunt and uncle and a different group of cousins.

At the end of September, Diane began to work on a two-day-a-week schedule. By October, she was pregnant again, and we knew we had to find still another place to live – but where would we find the money?

To her astonishment, Herrick, Smith said it would share with its associates the results of an excellent year, and awarded year-end bonuses of 15% of salary. Diane paid off the balance of her Harvard loan and we began to look for a small house of our own. Our search centered on Lexington because of its excellent public school system, but everything we found was either too remote from the center of town or too expensive. Eventually we were shown 19 Ellison Road, a small cape on a 5,000-square-foot lot in a compact development adjacent to an elementary school. Although close to the noise of Route 128,* there was little automobile traffic in the neighborhood, and the two streets were filled with families with small children. We signed the purchase-and-sale agreement and moved in the first week of June 1963.

Ted was born four days later.

Three weeks after that, Diane decided we should steam off all the wallpaper in the house and paint the walls. Between managing Ted and his two-year-old brother, and renovating our new house, it was an exciting time, especially when we found that the original wallpaper, the cheapest kind, disintegrated under the force of a steamer and had to be scraped off, bit by tiny bit, with a putty knife. Ted didn't mind the activity, so long as he was fed innumerable times of day and night. Ben liked his new backyard and the sandbox I'd built for the two of them and – as it turned out – for our new cat, San Diego. We were happy to

San Diego was the first of many cats given geographical names. She would be followed by Allegheny and then twin kittens, Minneapolis and St. Paul, and there would be later cats, Tombstone (a truly misanthropic cat), and many years later (the original cats were long-lived) Annabessacook and Millinocket. St. Paul, a non-neutered male, liked to roam and was a celebrity in our neighborhood, since we called for him by name.

_____

*   Metropolitan Boston's industrial ring road.

receive used furniture from my parents, including the antique chairs my father had re-caned and refinished that became our dining-room chairs.

We had a respite on the island in midsummer, alone while my parents were in Norway. Steady on his feet now, Ben ran gleefully in and out of the water, shouting and laughing in the sun while Ted, in between feedings, snoozed under the canopy of the wheel-less baby buggy that was his crib. He was already a happy, contented child. As in the two summers before, it was an idyllic period.

By the time we returned to Lexington, Ben had become assertive ("Mommy, this is <u>not</u> your playroom!") and Diane craved conversation with people who were more than two feet tall. We'd made private day-care arrangements close by and Diane enjoyed resuming her two-day-a-week schedule and found, to her surprise, that interesting work outside of the trusts and estates field awaited her. The future looked bright.

With Ted at two months.

We were jolted out of complaisance on November 22, 1963, when President John Kennedy was assassinated in Dallas. Stunned, we were glued to the TV and witnessed – live – Jack Ruby's killing of Oswald. It was an eerie time for people brought up in the nonviolent United States of the late forties and fifties. We had to confront the reality of a presidential assassination and counter-assassination. This happened in unstable South American countries, not ours.

And what of his successor? When Kennedy debated Nixon in 1960, Diane and I were on opposite political sides. When Kennedy was elected, Diane was elated that we'd have a government that cared about the issues she cared for – education for all, regardless of origin, and the obligations a generous government in a prosperous land owed toward minorities and poor people. What could we expect now from a conservative, manipulative son of brass-knuckle Texas politics? What Lyndon Johnson actually accomplished during his term in office would astonish her, and would lay a foundation for what she would later accomplish in her public roles.

We made do as we went along. Diane created our own Christmas tree decorations: long chains made up of connected loops of ribbon that would adhere to itself (with the aid of saliva); paper cutouts; and baked plastic circles with colorful cut patterns inside them. Our Christmas wish lists were filled with practical items: pots for the kitchen, a small fry pan, a bacon griller, a pancake pan, utensils, tools for my basement workshop, fireplace tools, a new blanket for the bed. Diane managed to find something special for me, and I for her.

For a time, we celebrated Christmas twice, an early one by ourselves with our kids, and a later one in my parents' home on the real Christmas Eve and Christmas Day. There, Ben and Ted – and later Kristin – weren't so overwhelmed by presents as they would have been, had it all happened at once. In our early Christmas, usually on December 23rd, Diane and I followed the Norwegian tradition of a light Christmas Eve supper followed by presents under the tree. Ted liked the paper cutouts and the ribbons on the tree best. Ben opened presents gleefully. We opened presents to each other and told Ben about Santa (not a Norwegian tradition) arriving during the night. Almost no one was able to stay awake after the excitement had died down. After putting the two of them to bed, we stayed up, bleary-eyed, to assemble the plastic train-and-track set Santa had brought – until we heard the pitter-patter of little feet on the stairs. Ben was jumping the gun. We hustled him back to bed so he'd have the pleasure of discovery in the morning. And, finally, Diane and I went to bed.

At the end of the next morning, after the trains had been run on the tracks many, many times, we loaded our car and drove 160 miles north for the real Christmas Eve, with burning candles on the tree, Norwegian Christmas cookies and a late-evening feast of pork roast, ham and head cheese. By that time Ben and Ted were firmly asleep. They were awake the following few days to enjoy their presents.

Diane felt a strong sense of obligation to the firm that had treated her so well. When we returned to Cambridge, she decided to work three days a week to make up for lost time she hadn't worked over the holidays. The pattern continued over the winter and spring.

That summer, we flew to North Hollywood for three weeks, to show off Ted and to reconnect Ben to his West Coast relatives. George and Meryl had sold their wonderful tree-shaded lot on Corteen Place to an apartment developer for an amazing price, an offer they couldn't refuse. As part of the deal he'd moved their house, garage and backyard grandmother house to a treeless vacant lot not many streets away that had been paved with asphalt. While Diane visited everyone who wanted to meet Teddy and see Ben again, I broke up the asphalt with a sledgehammer and wedges, and George and I carted the pieces off to the dump. Soil and grass would soon replace the asphalt.

Diane was intent on completing the family of three we'd planned. Given my family history, I thought we'd probably have another boy, but she had other ideas and read all the material she could get her hands on about how we could increase our chances for a girl. A *Reader's Digest* article suggested the chances of having a girl increased if conception occurred at a particular part of her monthly cycle. Having no better advice, we gave it a try, and Diane was soon pregnant again.

Alerted to the fact that she'd have a third child in the spring, the firm didn't expect her to return, and concluded that its experiment in employing a young and fertile married female lawyer was at an end. When raises were announced at the end of the year, she received none. Given the quality of her work (which no one questioned) and the loyalty she'd shown the firm, she was bitterly disappointed and disillusioned. She'd worked hard and well, and knew she had deserved a raise.

Disillusionment takes many forms, not all of them personal. We were three years into the real world and had learned a great deal about the Brahmin social structure that permeated Boston law firms. Knowing that sexism, elitism and racism were integral to the society[5] was discouraging, but Diane was undaunted. She determined to go back to work and prove them wrong. She did exactly that, and while the firm's attitude toward her would change, so did the warm feelings she'd had toward the firm. Seeing that her sex made a difference to her employer, despite the quality of her work product, she decided her professional future would lie elsewhere, but at a time of her own choosing, not of the firm's choosing.

Diane enjoyed pregnancy and had little difficulty giving birth. She bloomed as the months rolled on, but with a special anticipation this time, an anticipation dampened when we arrived at the hospital and her obstetrician said the baby had a "good, sturdy boy's heartbeat." Kristin was born two hours later, and Diane was elated. When I came in to see them soon afterward, the joy and happiness she felt as she held her tiny daughter filled the hospital room. There was no need for words.

With Kristin in December 1965.

It was April 25, 1965, and she had no space for thoughts about her firm. The next four months would be consumed entirely by her children, with particular attention to Kristin. She wouldn't return to the firm until the second week of September.

In the meantime, we had gotten permission to build a cabin on the island, on the land I'd been clearing for more than five summers. We bought plans for an inexpensive 18 x 24 cabin made with plywood using prefabricated construction techniques. By refinancing our home, we thought, we'd have enough money to do it – and we almost did. We ran out of money at the cabin's front porch and had to tell the builder to stop.

Summer 1965, on the porch of the new cabin. L. to r.: Ben, myself, Kristin, Diane and Ted.

What we had was the cabin's plywood shell on a knoll with a spectacular view looking down on the beach and out over the bay. The weekend after the builder left, it threatened to rain. My brother Mort and I scrambled up on the cabin roof with tar and tarpaper, roofing paper and roofing tacks. We rolled out the tarpaper, slathered on the tar and nailed everything down before the rains came. Diane and I had a dry cabin. The rest would be up to us.

But not just us. My father was enthused, both about the project and about having a reasonable distance between his camp and his rambunctious grandchildren. On weekends, he and I dug postholes for the porch posts, cut cedar logs for the posts, and built, first the frame, then the porch. Using leftover plywood, he built an L-shaped counter in the part of the cabin that would be our kitchen, and then an outhouse (we had no plumbing). Since the outhouse location had a grand view of the lake, he built it with an open door facing the path leading up from the water, so that anyone using the outhouse could enjoy the view. He gave us a small gas stove and refrigerator which had once been in the big camp (which now had electricity from the mainland) and installed propane fixtures, including a small gas lamp to augment the light we had from an antique kerosene chandelier.

Diane set to our work with a will. We built bunk beds for the boys and a platform for Kristin's crib behind a 4 x 8 sheet of plywood that would serve both as a headboard for our bed and a divider between us and the rear quarter of the cabin where the children slept. She painted our side of the divider white, and transferred to its white surface a map of the entire lake drawn to scale. We built shelves, a small dining table on

Out for a paddle in the Klepper kayak.

birch legs, and two sturdy benches for the table, the children's a little higher than ours. We painted the ceiling white. We painted the floor.

My brother Jon and I cut a hole in the roof for the chimney of an Acorn fireplace – a free-standing, sheet-metal stove with an open front. Diane looked dubiously up at the hole, remarking that I certainly must have the courage of my convictions. Fortunately, the chimney installation proved impervious to rain, and the fireplace kept us warm on cool mornings and evenings for decades as we burned birch and beech and oak logs from trees we cut down, cut up and split by hand.

Jon gave us a platform bed he'd built years earlier, when he was first married, and a mattress; my brother Mort provided a Klepper foldboat he'd owned. The Klepper was a two-person kayak with rubberized skin stretched over a wood frame, its open cockpit large enough so that, for a few years, all five of us could get into it.

Having the cabin changed our lives. The island became our haven, summer after summer, where we'd have an untrammeled month with our children while they learned the value of doing hard work. Whatever else happened in the course of a year, we knew we could come here, ignore the world we'd left behind and recharge our batteries for the year ahead. As the years went on, we did exactly that.

Every day before breakfast, rain or shine, everyone had a quick dip in the lake. My father had grown up in Oslo in a family whose many males trekked down from their home on a ridge to swim in the icy Oslofjord. Lake Cobbossee was not quite the same, but the tradition continued. My mother, raised inland in Norway, was game and joined in. Early on, Diane wasn't an enthusiastic swimmer, but she ventured down the knoll each morning with our children to the sandy beach and into the lake. She became the tradition's fiercest advocate, not just for us, but for our guests and our children's guests. No breakfast unless they'd first braved the lake's cold early-morning water.

The idea of minimalist living close to nature, even for just a month each year, was important for Diane. We hauled drinking water in gallon jugs from a well we'd dug, and wash water from the lake. We used the outhouse, read by the light of kerosene lamps, cut our own wood, warmed ourselves by the wood stove, explored the lake in canoes and kayaks, and watched the fading light in the evening glow, listening to night songs and calls of loons, hermit thrushes and barred owls. We went to sleep in the quiet evenings of what seemed to us a wilderness. We woke to the early morning songs of English sparrows, flycatchers, and robins mixed in with the screech of the kingfisher and the mellifluous songs and sounds of the occasional Baltimore oriole, scarlet tanager, bluebird and cardinal. Overhead, the fish-hunting osprey called, "kee, kee, kee!" At night in the neighboring small bog, the green frogs hollered, "Unk! Unk!" We sailed, we paddled, we read, and we relaxed.

In three years we would stretch our resources again and add a bunkhouse half the size of our original cabin, with six bunks, enough for our children and the friends they'd invite. Five years after that, we'd build a deck in the rear and a "clubhouse" two-thirds the size of our cabin, with four more beds and a sheet-metal fireplace like ours, so that our children would have a private space for themselves and their friends.

Much happened in the interim, including, sadly, my father's death in 1967. He never saw the bunkhouse or the clubhouse, or the postholes for the clubhouse dug by a strong and growing Ben, or the digging of a new well that provided as much water as the entire island would need. And there were other important and difficult projects we undertook each summer that he would have approved of.

Outhouse use and the lack of electricity and running water remained unchanged for thirty years. Of all of us, Diane was the strongest on maintaining minimal reliance on modernity. We carried water from the lake to be boiled before washing dishes. We carried water from the new well a hundred or so yards to fill the small water tank we used for drinking water. She bathed in the lake (using eco-friendly soap) and

Using four-foot-diameter well tiles to replace the clogged ten-inch pipe that had served as the big camp's water source, Ben and I hand-dug a new well to a depth of fourteen feet, six feet below the water table. To replace the sump hole into which sewage and kitchen water from the big camp had drained, we bought and floated to the island a six-foot-deep fiberglass septic tank. Ben, Ted and I dug its hole and arranged its outlet pipe. We built decks by the water at the beach and by the big camp. Ben, Ted and Kristin cut down trees and cut up the trunks for firewood for the big camp, our cabin and the clubhouse. Ted would eventually install skylights in our dimly lit cabin and in the clubhouse, re-roof the cabins and rebuild the path up the knoll to divert rainwater and prevent erosion.

refused to use the shower that had been installed in the big camp. Her view was that this place, this wonderful place, should be kept pristine in its original primitive condition, and that all who came to enjoy it would have to accept and adjust.

Life in Lexington was different. Finding downtime there was difficult. We worked hard at our firms and worked to make connections in the community. Given her commitment to both work and children, however, Diane had little time to spare. After coming home from work in the first few years, collecting the children, having dinner, reading to them, and putting them to bed, we often subsided and watched television for an hour or two. Other times, once they were in bed, Diane would pull out from her briefcase work she'd brought home. Weekends revolved around our children.

One source of relaxation which had a leavening effect was a Thursday night duplicate bridge tournament* at Lexington's Old Belfry Club, a rickety two-story structure two blocks from the center of town. For many tournament pairs, these tournaments were serious business. We treated the games as fun, and enjoyed both the evening out and the luxury of having a babysitter at home.

Day care continued to be complicated. Before Ben was old enough to attend nursery school, Diane worked three full days, saving the other two to be at home. At first we drove Ben and Ted back to Holden Green in Cambridge, where we'd been introduced to another young mother, the wife of a graduate student at Harvard's Divinity School. Then, when my college friend, Jay Howard, and his free-spirited wife, Donna, came to live in half of a duplex in Watertown while Jay was doing his medical internship and residency, they offered to help out. Donna now had a daughter, Heather, who was Ben's age, so it was a good fit. With their arrival, our social life also picked up.

---

*   In duplicate bridge, a pair of partners compete against other pairs on duplicate hands. A set of four hands is dealt at each table. Once they've been played, the four hands remain the same at that table while the pairs rotate from table to table to face other opponents on four new hands.

The routine changed when Ben began going to nursery school the fall after Kristin was born, because nursery school, a half-day affair, was close by (a five-minute walk) and Diane intended both to deliver Ben in the morning and pick him up at the end of the school day. She began to work partial days rather than full days. We recruited the mother in a neighborhood family with small children of similar ages to ours to do day-care for Ted and Kristin during nursery-school hours.

Both day care and our life were simplified during our last two years at Ellison Road when our back-door neighbor, Elizabeth Rourke, said she'd be pleased to come to our house while Diane was at work. Elizabeth was a retired teacher in her sixties, and a poet. She and her husband, Gene, a science teacher at Lexington High School, had two grown sons and she thought it a good idea to practice being a grandmother, a role for which she was admirably suited. Elizabeth loved our children, but she kept a special place in her heart for Ben. *Forest Home*, a small book of poetry she published later, included a poem about him:

Each pair in a duplicate tournament is required to disclose to their opponents any "artificial bidding conventions" that is, bids which have a specific meaning that is not apparent on the face of the bid. A number of the conventions we saw were esoteric, so we created our own, the "Batz Convention." An opening bid of one diamond signified ten cards in hearts and spades combined. While this combination of cards was unlikely, we actually used it a couple of times. No one asked who Mr. Batz was; and no one made the connection to Batz in the Belfry Club.

One Cannot Tell

Intent upon his color board, Ben said
"See, I have put a cage around a star!"
Adult-wise, quick to negate, to deny
With many words such possibility,
I might have erred but for the sharp recall
Of wonder at a cross-sliced apple core.
The star deep in the sapphire's misty well,
The brief-lived snowflake caught on mittened palm,
Or, left by ebb tide, asteroids on sand
Refute all theorems to limit stars.

Ben's mind, within its sculptured cranial wall
May house a burst of stars.
One cannot tell

Our copy of the book is inscribed: "For the original Ben from whom we always expected a 'burst of stars' – Elizabeth Massie Rourke."

We commuted to work by driving twenty minutes to the train station in a neighboring town, Winchester, where the trains ran every fifteen minutes during rush hour and every half-hour during the day. This schedule gave Diane some flexibility as to when she'd return. Lexington's only commuter train left Boston at 5:30 p.m., and I'd have to scramble to make it. When I failed, she'd drive to Winchester again – this time with our children in the car – to pick me up.

Even after we acquired a second car, commuting was no less complicated. Sometimes we'd drive both cars to Winchester, leave one in the station parking lot and drive the other to Boston so Diane could return home whenever she wanted. I'd ride the train back. Sometimes I would need the car in Boston and she'd take the train back. It was important to keep track of what we were doing. I stepped off the train in Winchester one day and was unable to locate the car. It was in Boston.

There were times when it seemed the survival of our family depended entirely on Diane's being able to keep everything together, including her work life, without my help.

For several weeks while she was very pregnant with Kristin, I was virtually a stranger in the house because of a series of out-of-state depositions and local meetings. A year later, just after Ted had come down with the mumps (and I'd been shot full of vaccine), I flew to Minneapolis for two weeks of depositions and also contracted the mumps. ("Wouldn't it be something," I'd written just before leaving, "if I came down with the mumps out there?")

I had a raging temperature, but the hotel doctor said I should get on a plane and go home. I called Anne Meagher, my long-time secretary, and she told me not to move a damn inch while she made some calls. The next thing I knew, EMTs wheeled a gurney into my hotel room and rushed me to the ER at Swedish Hospital in an ambulance. For the better part of the day, I was swabbed continuously with alcohol to keep my body temperature down. Moved to the contagious ward, I was given medicine that caused several psychedelic episodes (including a vivid one in which I rode effortlessly around the room on warm bands of color). After seven days, I was allowed to fly home, where Diane met me coming off the plane at Logan Airport.

She'd been sick with concern and showed it. Unable to leave Lexington, she had received hourly reports until it was clear I was going to recover. I'd lost ten pounds and must've looked haggard coming off the plane, but the relief in Diane's eyes when we saw each other made everything well, for both of us. It would be weeks before my energy returned.

The Swedish Hospital adventure had an unplanned but enormous fringe benefit for both Diane and me. We'd been inveterate cigarette smokers, each smoking a pack or more a day. Like all smokers, we'd determined to quit and had, several times, without lasting success. Diane's latest procrastination was that she'd quit when she was thirty.

Swedish Hospital didn't permit smoking, and it had been over a week since my last cigarette. I never had one again. Feeling guilty about smoking in my presence, Diane gave it up too. (She made the point, however, that she *liked* to smoke and fully intended to take it up again when she turned ninety. I believe that, as a matter of principle, if nothing else, she would have.)

Our life returned to normal, except for one thing. With three children, nearly seven, five and three, our house was becoming small. Diane, always a doodler and a dreamer, began to construct purposeful doodles by the end of 1967. No longer depicting stylish clothes, she began to design houses. I began to notice sketches lying about on lined yellow legal pads showing house facades, room layouts, kitchens, living rooms with furniture we couldn't afford and a yard for flowers and vegetables, trees and an outside patio. The doodles were detailed and carried with them a forceful sense of inevitability.

Soon we began looking. As luck would have it, a tract just off Massachusetts Avenue, on the crest of the hill between us and the center of Lexington, was being developed, house by house, by a builder with an excellent reputation, and he was in no hurry. Nickerson Road was horseshoe-shaped and would ultimately have about twenty houses on three-quarter-acre lots. The one at the curve of the horseshoe was ideal from our perspective – if we could raise the money. The builder was willing to work from other people's plans so long as the exterior of the house looked colonial.

We met with him and, with the help of a local architect, developed plans which bore a striking resemblance to many of Diane's doodles. He agreed to begin building in the spring of 1969; by the end of that fall, we would be in our new home at 23 Nickerson Road. And Diane would begin looking toward the future in other ways.

LEAVING THE FIRM

Working part-time had limited Diane professionally. She saw her peers, none more able than she was, leaving her behind, and she began to resent the limitations that confronted her in the context of the firm. Lawyers, she believed, had public service obligations. Opportunities for public service hadn't come her way. And what of her ambitions to teach? If she were to accomplish the professional goals she'd set for herself, she needed to change course. She began to apply her talents to the public good, first in small ways in Lexington, then in larger ones. It was a start.

She joined the League of Women Voters, became involved in its committee concerning Lexington's schools and soon was the committee chair.* She was appointed

---

* Diane had attended town meetings where representatives of the LWV expressed its views on various subjects. She never forgot the response of a long-time male town meeting member after an LWV presentation: the League of Women Voters, he said, "is a wonderful organization, but it should stay out of politics."

to a town committee whose charge was to select Lexington high school seniors for scholarship aid in college or university under a nationwide program called "Dollars for Scholars." The awards were based on financial need alone – grades played no role – and this approach appealed to her. She developed application forms, distributed and collected them, collated the information and brought them to committee meetings with her recommendations. Finally, she was back on track, and after that she never left it.

She became a member of N.O.W., the National Organization for Women, then in its infancy, because of its goal to eliminate discrimination against women and its support for the Equal Rights Amendment. Up to this point she had dealt with discrimination as it affected her personally, but not as a causist. Women's demands for equal treatment were just beginning to gather steam, and N.O.W. was the organization visibly in the forefront of the movement. This was a cause with which she could identify and in which she wanted to be involved. She began for the first time to think of herself as a feminist and to consider what role she could play.

> I'd been a member of the town meeting since 1965, and was then chair of the town's Planning Board. We weren't the only husband-and-wife team in the town meeting, but were probably the only pair that didn't vote together. I recall one memorable occasion when, after I had made a presentation on an initiative my board was sponsoring, Diane rose to speak against it.

She ran for election to the Lexington town meeting in 1969, and was successful.

Her eyes were opened to new possibilities that year when I left my firm to head the business litigation section of a smaller firm, and began to bring home glowing reports of genuine collegiality among the lawyers there, a professional experience neither of us had had before. When she saw what a change the transition caused in my life, it wasn't long before she threw off the fetters in her own. The opportunity came more quickly than she thought it would.

Another lawyer and friend, Allan Rodgers, also commuted to Boston on the Winchester train, usually at 8:12 a.m., and we kept up with each other en route. Allan, like Diane, had gone from law school into private practice with an establishment Boston law firm, but his ambition, like Diane's, had always been to serve the public good. He had left his firm to become an assistant attorney general, and now – he told us – he'd recently been appointed acting director of the Massachusetts Law Reform Institute, a nonprofit public-interest law firm whose charge was to represent the interests of poor people. MLRI had become his passion, the vehicle through which he expected to realize his ambitions.[6]

It was a serendipitous time for people who believed they could remedy the country's social ills through legislation. The Civil Rights Act of 1964 had been passed, and none of the schoolhouse doors in Mississippi, Alabama or Little Rock had effectively been blocked. Preservation of the environment was on national and local political agendas.

The climate of reform embraced not only reform movements but elected officials such as Massachusetts Governor Frank Sargent, an amiable, well-intentioned moderate Republican. Sargent was pragmatic, open to reason, and didn't try to block or veto social legislation passed by the legislature, which was dominated by Democrats.* In some instances, he actually gave the bills – which dealt with such wide-ranging topics as anti-discrimination, lead paint poisoning, and eliminating from local zoning by-laws barriers to subsidized housing – his public support.

Rodgers described with enthusiasm the extraordinary legislative success MLRI and its small staff – seven or eight people – had had in its first year of existence, and Diane was intrigued.† Very little of that legislation, she knew, had concerned the rights and equality of women. These were issues that chafed at her and needed to be dealt with. Typically, working women of all economic classes who became pregnant were fired from their jobs, losing all benefits and seniority. Jobs open to women paid them, on average, an hourly wage that was half of the wage paid for similar jobs held by men. Recipients of public assistance, primarily women who were heads of households, were routinely discriminated against.‡ Young women in the public schools were excluded from vocational training and athletic opportunities available to young men. The bright ones were channeled into careers as public school teachers, laboratory assistants and dental hygienists.

When Rodgers suggested Diane come talk to him about MLRI, she jumped at the opportunity. Perhaps this could be the vehicle for her own ambitions. She gave him a very brief written resume in which she described her career at her firm ("full-time 1961-62 and part-time since then") and a practice which, on its face, wasn't particularly relevant ("general practice with specialization in the areas of estate planning and administration"). No matter. She also told him she wanted to continue to work part-time until her children were older. No problem. Rodgers offered Diane a staff attorney position, working three days per week. She accepted immediately.

On November 4, 1969, Rodgers confirmed that she could start work a month later, on December 1, adding, "[I]f in the meantime you wish to start work at home, we will compensate you at an hourly rate equivalent to the yearly rate you will receive." She was delighted. Two weeks later she had her first assignment, to review and comment on

---

* The Massachusetts legislature was led in the senate by Maurice Donahue and in the house by Speaker David Bartley. Both were receptive to reform and responsive to their constituents. Although each understood how to exercise the powers of his office, neither operated the arcane controls of the Massachusetts legislature to block socially worthwhile legislation.

† MLRI had been instrumental in the passage of more than a dozen pieces of significant legislation including changes in landlord-tenant law and the creation of legal rights for people harmed by unfair or deceptive commercial practices.

‡ Families whose heads of household were women accounted for more than 20% of all Boston-based families and more than 50% of families below the poverty line.

"proposed legislation to permit persons to register for voting on Election Day."

MLRI was a perfect fit. There she could advocate for the rights of poor people, rights which coincided over a broad spectrum with the rights of women. She saw and clearly understood the connection between discrimination against women and the consequences of women living in poverty, with their hopes for jobs and a better life cut off. And she saw the impact on their children, embedded in that poverty. Working at MLRI, she would become a moving force in the changes that occurred in Massachusetts to remedy the inequities that existed. Those changes would open doors to opportunities that had been closed to women and would have a ripple effect throughout the country.

And at MLRI she would meet another extraordinary woman whose friendship influenced and helped shape the rest of her life.

---

[1]   Law firms' determined billable hour quest wouldn't hit Boston until years later. Thirty billable hours per week was the rule of thumb in 1961, and associates were *expected* to take a month's summer vacation. Law firms in that era actually did concern themselves with the well-being of their associates.

[2]   The usual experience of a new associate is a series of research and writing projects. While Diane was to be trained in the area of trusts and estates and related tax issues, she wouldn't be exempt from the firm's other needs, given her academic record. When the firm had a particularly knotty litigation issue, the assignment often would go to her.

[3]   Given the internal squabbles that have beset law firms in the past fifty years, leading to the dissolution of many of them, a simple partnership agreement of this sort had much to recommend it, but its success hinged on a firm's social monoculture. Herrick Smith would dissolve when its monoculture was breached. As the firm's dominant Yankees aged and their authority was challenged by younger partners, their genial attitude concerning the firm would change, and that would be its undoing. In order to bow out of control in the mid-1970's they obtained concessions from the latter which included lifetime rent-free offices, secretarial help and the ability to continue representing their personal clients without accounting for the fees. It would be the first of Boston's major firms to dissolve when its younger partners decided to escape the onerous terms imposed on them.

[4]   Yankees had dominated Massachusetts life from the seventeenth century on. In the early twentieth century, Irish immigration to Boston had caused a shift in political power over the city's affairs, but not yet in the legislature. Fearful that Irish domination of Boston's tax structure would bankrupt their businesses, the Yankee legislature passed laws that prevented Boston from taxing anything other than the value of real estate. That legislation haunts Boston to this day. Had it not been for national legislators such as Ted Kennedy, and John McCormack and Tip O'Neil, both Speakers of the House who channeled massive amounts of federal assistance for public works projects, Boston as a world-class city wouldn't have happened.

5   Choate had once hired a handsome, talented and well-spoken young man named Leo Dunn, believing he would be its first Irish hire. When Dunn's name appeared among leaders of the United Jewish Appeal, his days at the firm were numbered. Its first real Irishman, Daniel Featherston, was later turned down for partnership because a Yankee member of the Supreme Judicial Court reported to one of his good friends – a partner in the firm – that he felt Featherston's advocacy was too spirited, too unrestrained, and not appropriate for a firm like Choate, Hall & Stewart.

6   MLRI had come into existence in 1968 as the result of efforts by a few activist lawyers and politicians allied with the regional head of the United States Office of Economic Opportunity, Vaughn Gearing, formerly the mayor of Pittsfield, Massachusetts. Scattered pockets of public-interest agencies existed in Massachusetts at that time to defend poor people charged with crime, usually over the opposition of the local bar which viewed those agencies as a threat to the revenue they derived from court-appointed representation, but none had the authority to represent their interests in the legislature. Gearing's vision was that OEO should be instrumental in establishing and funding statewide centers for law reform throughout the country. He could not himself originate this idea within OEO, however, and needed to receive a proposal which OEO could consider funding.

Gearing suggested to several key activists that if he were to receive an appropriate proposal from a qualified nonprofit group, he thought he could find the money to start up an organization whose mandate would be to represent the interests of the poor before the legislature. One of them was Robert Spangenburg, then the executive director of the Boston Legal Assistance Project, an umbrella organization that coordinated neighborhood legal assistance programs for the City of Boston. Spangenburg would go on to become a nationally recognized authority on legal assistance programs. Another was Joe Dee of Action for Boston Community Development (ABCD), a recipient and dispenser of anti-poverty monies.

Spangenburg discussed Gearing's idea with another attorney, Al Kramer, who was then the head of Voluntary Defenders, the Boston organization responsible for defending the indigent against criminal charges. (Voluntary Defenders' primary resources for this task were law students at the Boston law schools who, under its supervision, were allowed to defend indigent defendants in Boston-area district and municipal courts in spite of judges' impatience. I was one of those law students "wasting their time" by defending obviously guilty defendants.) A proposal was cobbled together under Voluntary Defenders' aegis and sent off to Gearing at OEO. Miraculously he found $230,000 available for this project and the proposal was approved in 1968. Voluntary Defenders changed its name to the Massachusetts Law Reform Institute shortly after receipt of the funds.

CHAPTER SIX

DOING WELL AT DOING GOOD

T HE EXTRAORDINARY WOMAN DIANE MET WAS REGINA
Healy. She'd grown up poor in the 1940s, and lived her teen years with a
maiden aunt in a cold-water flat in the grimy manufacturing city of Lowell,
Massachusetts. Coming from a devout Irish Catholic heritage, Regie had been educated
by nuns in the local parochial school, where she learned her catechisms, received frequent
raps on the knuckles with a nun's ruler and developed an abiding suspicion and distaste
for the Catholic Church. She had learned to fend for herself because her aunt worked
a full workweek pasting labels on Father John's Medicine bottles. The nuns, she

thought, were preparing her for the life of a
good subservient wife, bent on limiting her
horizons and stifling her ability. That wasn't
going to happen.*

Bootstrapping her way up the echelons of
higher education, she first won a scholarship
to a private Catholic girls school in Tyngsboro,
where she learned the hard lessons of social
class distinctions. A second scholarship
led to a bachelor's degree from Boston
University. In 1965 she became the director

Ben, Kristin and Ted, c. 1966.

---

* It wasn't just the nuns that Regie mistrusted. She remembered one piece of advice from her aunt
on being alone in the flat while she was at work: "Don't let anyone in, even if you know them – and
especially not a priest." Over five decades later, she remarked that the Church's sexual abuse scandal was
nothing new. What was new was Catholics with the courage to bring it out in the open.

of the neighborhood branch of an anti-poverty agency in East Baltimore, Maryland. The neighborhood was rough and dangerous, a mixture of races with antipathy toward each other and almost as dangerous as the urban Baltimore neighborhood in which she and her husband Robert Sloane and their infant children lived.* That neighborhood regularly hosted riots and acts of arson which threatened to burn the city down.

Regie's community center provided outreach to poor people. Its work – best case – was to help them find jobs and – worst case – to help them find food. As its director she supervised the work of both employees and VISTA volunteers, including several young lawyers. Seeing what lawyers could do because of their training and their license to practice law, she decided a law degree would be crucial to her ambitions to help remedy the unending cycle of poverty she saw and its relationship to discrimination against women. She began attending night law school at the University of Maryland, but Baltimore politics made Bob's professional life impossible, so it was time to move on.

They returned to Massachusetts in 1968 with three young children in tow, the youngest less than a year old. While Bob worked days as a planner for the Massachusetts Bay Transportation Authority, Regie was at home. When Bob came home, she'd be off, either to night law school at Suffolk University or to a job waitressing at a then-famous eatery for Boston students, Jack & Marian's.

There, late one evening, a young lawyer she'd supervised at her agency in Baltimore stopped in for a bite to eat. They were surprised to see each other, and caught up on old times. When he learned she was going to law school, he suggested she apply for a part-time job at the Massachusetts Law Reform Institute, which then consisted, he said, of five impassioned lawyers and virtually no staff. It was a fascinating place, he added, and she would like what they did. She'd never heard of it before, looked into it, and liked it. In the spring of 1969, Regie began working for Allan Rodgers and took on the writing of MLRI's newsletter.

Appointed to Mayor Kevin White's Commission on the Status of Women, she headed a task force on the root causes of poverty for women. They found a demonstrable link between poverty and the inadequate education women were receiving because of discrimination in the public schools, especially in the area of vocational training. The task force's fact-finding and conclusions became the foundation for many conversations Regie and Diane would have, and ultimately for legislation that would prohibit discrimination against young women in every aspect of public education in Massachusetts.

---

* Bob Sloane, an urban planner who then worked for the city of Baltimore, would become the right hand of Frederick Salvucci, Governor Michael Dukakis' secretary of transportation. It was Salvucci who conceived putting Boston's eyesore elevated Central Artery underground, clearing the way for the historic North End and the Seaport district to rejoin the city from which they'd been walled off for fifty years. They planned the demolition of the Central Artery and its replacement by a series of parks that transformed the city. Sponsored by Tip O'Neill and Ted Kennedy, the "Big Dig" (as it is infamously known) became the Rose Fitzgerald Kennedy Greenway.

When Diane arrived at MLRI in November, its offices were a rabbit warren of cramped spaces in a decrepit old building on Charles Street, one block from the Boston Common. She and Regie shared one of the small warrens, and not just with each other. Martha Davis, a Northeastern law student and ardent feminist, joined them during her co-op work periods[1] away from the school. Constantly in each other's pockets in the tiny office, they debated poverty and women's issues and possible solutions. Their synergy was electric and would translate into significant advances for women.

MLRI's overarching concern was the interests of poor people, not discrimination against women, but the two were intertwined. Diane's first long-term project concerned welfare benefits entitlement issues in the New England states, issues of particular importance to so-called welfare mothers. The federal government had not yet taken over welfare. Each state, seemingly arbitrarily, made its own determination of need and of the percentage of that need it was prepared to meet. The various state welfare schemes were inconsistent with each other, as were the results of hearings on these issues in the different states. Diane's objective was to work toward creating uniformity. As with all welfare issues, achieving consensus was impossible.

The following year, she drafted and helped shepherd through the legislature a bill to prohibit discrimination against recipients of public assistance *because of* their status as recipients. Massachusetts was the first state in the country to adopt such legislation. The act was important, and a significant protection for legal services clients.*

Another matter of immediate concern was a proposed cut in the Massachusetts House of Representatives, from 240 to 160 members. The rationale for this measure, on which the League of Women Voters was a moving force, was supposed economy, efficiency and responsiveness to the electorate. MLRI had a different view, expressed in a letter to the *Boston Globe*, signed by Diane and others, on February 11, 1970:

> We think that an 80-man cut in the size of the House will have a negative impact on the chances for success of further progressive legislation. Specifically we feel justified in fearing that those representatives who would lose their posts would include a number of young dynamic legislators who, instead of playing safe and offending nobody, have taken strong stands in favor of poor people.
>
> With the increased size of House districts, poor people will constitute a smaller percentage of the population of most districts and their voting power will be concomitantly diluted. The result will be the election of representatives who feel less need to respond to the poor in their districts. In short, we believe that a House cut will probably diminish the relative political power of poor people.

---

*   Allan Rodgers interview.

The League argued that if larger districts were fairly drawn, there would be a greater likelihood of minority representation in the House. Diane disagreed. Her opposition so soon after being a key League figure in Lexington is noteworthy because it reflected the traits of independence, adherence to principle, and considered judgment that characterized her life. The proposal was popular with the public, however, if not with the politicians who would be displaced, and it prevailed. Those character traits would be tested in the aftermath of events which led to the Bail Reform Act of 1970.

The bail system as it then existed smacked of cozy arrangements between district court judges and the state's bail bondsmen. The way the system worked was that in order to remain free, someone charged with a crime – regardless of prior record, either in the criminal courts or the community – would be required to pledge property (which few among the poor owned) or to post a bond underwritten by bail bondsmen for an exorbitant premium few could afford. For families unable to raise the bail bond fees, their breadwinner (then almost always a male) would be held in jail awaiting trial – and would lose his job in the interim. The impact on the individual, his family and the community as a whole was pernicious and had a disproportionate adverse effect on poor people – consequences which first came to MLRI's attention through its investigation into how judges abused the system with respect to welfare mothers.

Several district court judges in Boston had an aversion to complaints of welfare mothers seeking orders for welfare payments or for protection from physical abuse from men who may or may not have been the fathers of their children. When the judges discovered that women petitioning the court were welfare mothers, they often put them in the dock, under oath, and demanded they identify and swear out criminal complaints for nonsupport against the fathers of their children. If the mothers refused, they were charged with

> The coziness of the arrangements was known to the bar and the court clerks, but no one was anxious to offend the judges. It also presented an opportunity for graft. Following an investigation, the state's principal bail bondsmen, the Baker Brothers, were charged as bagmen to a superior court judge. The judge later resigned. The Bakers' bonding company belatedly discovered that the brothers were only reporting and remitting bail bond fees on half the bonds they wrote, and sued. Refusing to obey a court order to produce their records, which were kept in the basement of a small downtown office building, the Bakers instead tried to torch them, but the gasoline exploded, rather than burned. The company's lawyers obtained a midnight court order and seized the foul-smelling records. The case was soon settled, and the Bakers themselves had to post bond.

"intent to obstruct the due execution of the law" and immediately sentenced, without bail, to the House of Correction. The prospect of giving up the names terrified them, but given the choice of leaving their children and going to jail, most would do so. When the fathers found out what had happened, more rounds of physical abuse usually followed. Whatever one may think of the welfare system – and there were good reasons why state agencies and the courts would want the identity of the fathers in order to require them to support their children – coercing this information from low-income head-of-household mothers by threatening to jail them until they supplied the information was plain abuse. Women who had neither the means to oppose the system, nor to hire lawyers to represent them, found themselves trapped.

To build support for reform, a factual foundation had to be laid. MLRI recruited "observers" – volunteer law students – to go into Boston-area district courts to record the involuntary detention of welfare mothers. While there, the volunteers also observed – and recorded – judges' setting bail higher than defendants accused of minor crimes could afford, causing them to be jailed until their cases were tried. Many of those accused were innocent, but the consequences of being unable to post bail were visited on the guilty and the innocent alike. Once jailed, they lost jobs, were unable to support their families and sometimes lost custody of their children. For those who could raise the bail money in order to keep their jobs or their families intact, the financial burden was enormous. The volunteers interviewed the defendants' families and documented the destructive consequences.*

As a result, what began with unfairness to traditional clients of MLRI blossomed into a broader concern. Bail serves a legitimate purpose – to assure the appearance of a defendant at court hearings when there is a substantial risk of flight, or because the defendant, if released, presents a danger to others or to the community. Here it was being used for other purposes, illegitimate ones. The problem didn't lie so much with the theory as with judges who abused the system.

Michael Feldman, a firebrand and one of MLRI's founders, was its lead attorney on bail reform. An ardent advocate for poor people, his fervor carried him into community meetings in the poorest neighborhoods of Boston, Dorchester and Roxbury, areas in which he could well have been personally at risk. That risk was not of great concern to him; the cause he was advocating was. The objective was to galvanize community support for legislation drafted by MLRI that would minimize, if not eliminate, the likelihood of abuse by judges.

As Diane and Feldman talked through the issues, she developed the key structural changes which would make bail reform effective. The basic principle was simple: in the

---

* The observers' sworn affidavits proved essential and persuasive when the Bail Reform Act came to be presented to the key legislators who sponsored it, and when, after its passage, MLRI petitioned for court rules consistent with the act.

absence of a showing of danger to the community, prisoners should be released on their own recognizance. More important was a pragmatic procedural innovation which gave a defendant the right to an immediate same-day appeal to the Superior Court if the district court judge refused release on his or her own recognizance. The judge could no longer act with impunity.

Feldman and Diane met with key legislators and lobbied the Bail Reform Act through the legislature. The legislative leadership, particularly Paul Murphy, the majority leader in the House under Speaker David Bartley, was receptive to the proposed reforms. Murphy liked it, pushed it and guided it through. Promptly after the Bail Reform Act was enacted – without great fanfare – it was made law by Governor Sargent's signature.

Not long after, Rodgers received a curious call from Supreme Judicial Court Chief Justice Joseph Tauro's office asking him to attend a meeting of judges to "talk about" the Bail Reform Act. He found himself in a room full of judges and politicians, including the Governor's Chief Legal Counsel, Christopher Armstrong. Tauro said that no one had spoken to the judges about the bill before it was passed, the judiciary was opposed to it, the Court wanted the act repealed and it expected MLRI to support the repeal. Rodgers was taken aback, made a few deferential noncommittal comments, excused himself and went directly to see Murphy. Murphy told Rodgers not to worry about a repeal – there was no chance, and it wasn't going to happen. It didn't.[*]

The battle for bail reform had an unexpected consequence: a schism at MLRI and a decision by Feldman to leave the organization he'd helped found. The focus of the internal dispute was his outrage concerning certain of the district court judges, his belief they should be publicly identified and that suit should be brought against them. It came to a head in the context of MLRI's decision to petition the Supreme Judicial Court to adopt rules regarding judges' conduct in arraigning defendants in criminal cases, assigning counsel, determining bail and sentencing.

In a meeting of MLRI's board of trustees on April 18,1970, Mel Zarr, then its co-director with Allan Rodgers, advocated the majority position, which was to propose – for the future – an effective remedy to prohibit judges from engaging in the abuses outlined in the observer affidavits MLRI had assembled. The most effective way to accomplish these objectives, he argued, was without naming names, and through publicity which would educate the public on the issues. Punishment of the judges, or retribution, should not be a part of their agenda.

Feldman wanted to identify four key judges by name in the petition and in a press release. Diane was opposed. The judge whose conduct had been most egregious, and who was Feldman's key target, had powerful friends in the legislature. Diane and Zarr believed MLRI's legislative interests, here and in the future, would be better served by

---

[*]   Allan Rodgers interview.

proceeding more discreetly. How the debate was framed and resolved, and how the issues came to be dealt with before the Supreme Judicial Court, and at ground level by the district courts, reflects her role in the process. In a characteristically quiet and understated way, she argued for Zarr's position. Their view would prevail and her work served to reconcile, at least temporarily, the opposing views.

It wasn't an easy meeting. Feldman's train had been underway for some time before Zarr joined MLRI, and Zarr had a difficult time slowing it down, but he did. While he prevailed on a split vote of the board, the decision not to name names was the result of a compromise Diane suggested to the effect that the minutes of the meeting should reflect that the decision might have to be reconsidered at some time in the future.*

Diane drafted the petition, and its content satisfied everyone for the time being. When submitted to the Supreme Judicial Court on May 22, 1970, the petition charged that court rules and the constitutional and statutory rights of defendants, especially the poor and members of minority groups, were frequently ignored or denied by some district court judges. It asked the Court to adopt rules providing minimum standards of fair procedure and to provide stenographers in the district courts to ensure compliance. It did not name names and was signed by Rodgers, Zarr, Feldman and Diane. MLRI's press release featured Michael Feldman:

> The petition is the result of a six-month investigation…. More than 110 pages of affidavits from lawyers, law students and qualified observers were collected …. The petition, the first of its kind to be submitted to the SJC for relief, states that this mistreatment of poor people is not unique to the Boston area … and alleges that at present there is no effective way of stopping these practices.
>
> "The situation is obviously critical," said attorney Feldman. "I am convinced that many poor people are unjustly imprisoned every day because they lack money to pay for excessive bail or because they are denied the due process and equal protection of the law…."
>
> The petition is only MLRI's first initiative in insuring that district court judges give equal protection to all people…. A proposal will be submitted to the Governor asking him to use new procedures in selecting persons to fill judicial vacancies. These procedures will include consultation with and recommendations from representatives of the communities to be served.†

The petition listed rights of a criminal defendant, rights which MLRI sought to ingrain in the process:

---

*   April 18, 1970 MLRI board meeting minutes.
†   This proposal concerning the method of selection of judges would be embraced by Governor Michael Dukakis when he created the Judicial Nominating Commission in his first executive order after taking office in January 1975. And Diane would be one of his first appointees.

To be adequately informed of his right to counsel if he cannot afford one.

To assure a defendant who does not have a lawyer fully understands the charges, the kinds of defenses available and the consequences of pleading guilty.

To assure that a defendant who is being tried without being represented by a lawyer is adequately informed of safeguards protecting his right to a fair proceeding, e.g., 5th Amendment, to produce witnesses and require them to attend and to cross-examine.

To have appointed counsel given adequate time to prepare and present the case in full.

To ensure that a verdict is rendered on the evidence before the judge can consider a probation officer's information concerning any prior record.

To ensure that a defendant who has been found guilty is adequately informed of his right to appeal for a jury trial in the Superior Court and that he not be improperly induced to relinquish that right.

To release a defendant on personal recognizance without having to pay for a bail bond unless the Court determines there is a need for bail in the case of the particular defendant.

It alleged that defendants were being deprived of rights and protections guaranteed by the Declaration of Rights and by the 5th, 6th, 8th and 14th Amendments to the United States Constitution, and requested the Supreme Judicial Court to issue rules of practice and procedure governing these matters.

The neutral and nonconfrontational approach that Diane had advocated raised no judicial hackles and resulted in an effective process. The Court referred the petition to the Chief Justice of the Massachusetts District Courts, Franklin Flaschner, a revered figure in Massachusetts judicial circles. Judge Flashner consulted with various court committees – and at length with Rodgers.

The reception Rodgers received from Judge Flaschner was very different from his encounter with Chief Justice Tauro. Flaschner didn't quarrel with the new law. What he wanted was to implement it constructively, and provide guidelines for his judges. Rodgers brought drafts for discussion to their meetings. The result for the judiciary was a set of guidelines which Judge Flaschner approved and issued for the use of all judges on his court. The result for poor people – criminal defendants and welfare mothers alike – was the elimination of preventive detention and, in the case of the latter, detention for no criminal reason whatever.[*]

Judge Flaschner reported in July 1971 to Chief Justice Tauro that he would be submitting a draft of "Initial Rules of Criminal Procedure for the District Courts" as

---

[*]   Allan Rodgers interview.

the "first stage in the development of a comprehensive set of rules … framed to protect certain fundamental rights of the defendant." His letter was careful not to be critical of any particular judges and to say that the rules were in essence a formalization of existing practices. He acknowledged the contributions of MLRI and the Lawyers Committee for Civil Rights Under Law.* The rules proposed by Judge Flashner addressed all the concerns expressed in the petition and provided the relief requested, including MLRI's enumeration of defendants' rights.

Diane counted among the signal achievements in which she was involved, the Bail Reform Act and the rules of court that followed it.[2]

Michael Feldman came to believe that the petition and the rules hadn't gone far enough and that charges should be lodged against a particular judge before the state's judicial ethics commission. He couldn't overcome, however, the opposing view that taking a proactive stance against the judge would be harmful to MLRI's basic mission. Alienating members of the judiciary and legislature whose support was needed, not only for *this* legislation but for legislation MLRI would propose in the future, wouldn't be in its interests, or consistent with its mission.

Diane viewed the fact she was a moving force in events like these as nothing short of miraculous. She'd spent eight years in a context in which she could only use her legal training and talents in service to people who could well afford to pay for them. Little more than a year earlier, she'd felt resigned to a limited career important largely for the income it generated and the stability it gave to her family. Now, more surely with each passing month, she found herself serving the public good and working with people like herself, selfless in spirit, hope and ambition, people she could rely on to be her compatriots and who she knew were

Feldman left MLRI and moved on to the Boston Legal Assistance Project (BLAP), which was willing to take an aggressive, naming-names stance and did so.

The evidence showed that so-called "right to counsel" slips supposedly signed by the judge contemporaneously, had been blank at the time and filled in later. While this evidence was dramatic and damning, evidence regarding the judge's other activities was even more damning – and he was both removed from the bench and disbarred from the practice of law.*

* *In the Matter of Troy*, 364 Mass 15, 73 (1973). This case is one of two seminal cases in Massachusetts which have confirmed and defined the inherent power of the Supreme Judicial Court to adjudicate petitions concerning unethical conduct and personal conduct of judges.

---

* Judge Flaschner's report referred to the "cooperation with MLRI" in the work of his task force. "While the separate functions [of court reformers and the courts themselves] preclude a partnership, I do believe we have developed a healthy working relationship which will continue to mature and contribute to the sound improvement of the administration of criminal justice." (July 11, 1970 Report of District Court Chief Justice Franklin Flaschner.)

relying on her for those same reasons.

The first year at MLRI was a testing period, a time to explore, to find out what was within the realm of the possible for her. She'd found a kindred soul in Regina Healy, and the two of them soon spread their wings together and took flight in ways that served women everywhere.

Eliminating Discrimination Against Women in Massachusetts

Mayor White's Commission had linked poverty for female heads of households directly to their exclusion from vocational training in the public schools. The Boston Trade School for Boys trained its students for jobs that paid $4.50 to $6 per hour, while the Boston Trade School for Girls trained its students for vocations which were, in some cases, hopelessly outdated. And those vocations that still existed paid only $1.85 to $3.16 per hour. While 80% of the girls graduating became employed, only 6% were employed in work for which the school had trained them.[*] Most important, young women were excluded from skilled trades such as carpentry, plumbing and electrical work. Homemaking and home economics were the order of the day. Little had changed for decades.

Regie was working on a law review article addressing these issues and focusing on the need to recognize that protective laws for women were anachronistic and that the times now required opportunities for women equal to those of men, both in education and in the workplace.[†] The assumptions underlying these paternalistic laws were that women should be trained for marriage and, once married, would be taken care of by their breadwinner husbands. The laws limited the hours women could be required to work and the physical loads that could be imposed on them. They excluded women from education and training for employment deemed better suited for men, in which it was feared women would be exploited. And they disqualified women on moral grounds from certain kinds of jobs (e.g., bartender). Regie wrote about the unintended consequences of such laws:

> Discriminatory practices against women have come to be regarded … as the norm, and the correlative increment of poverty in female-headed families has been accepted and summarily dismissed by many social historians…. Women without men to support them are a growing minority. The numbers of wives and mothers who, although married, continue to work and make essential contributions to the family income are growing at an even faster pace. It is unrealistic to fall back on the assumption that all women and children are financially supported by men. This is simply not true.

---

[*]   Ellen Goodman article, *Boston Globe*, August 26, 1973.
[†]   Regina Healy, "Protection, Poverty and the Woman Worker," *Suffolk University Law Review*, Vol.V, No.1, Fall 1970. Very little had been written on this subject matter at the time, and this article would be much cited over the coming decade.

In the spring of 1970, Diane, Regie and Martha began analyzing those issues and developing solutions for them. Martha's focus concerned discrimination against women in the workplace who became pregnant; Regie's agenda concerned young women's opportunities in the public schools. The two of them were still law students and looked to Diane for advice, criticism, evaluation and guidance because of her experience and reputation both within and outside of the office. Ultimately they looked to her for direction. She made them think differently about the problems and their solutions and lent an air of gravitas to what they were doing.

Working with Regie and Martha, Diane began developing the inclusive teaching techniques that would characterize her teaching career. Regie and Martha thought of themselves and Diane as three activist lawyers engaged in a common cause. "Diane never talked down to us although we asked her about everything. We were equals and our opinions and ideas mattered. We explored those ideas together. She included herself in our thoughts and us in hers. She never dictated what we should do. We worked it out together."*

The results justified their trust in each other and the confidence they developed in working together. By December 1970 (Martha's second co-op quarter) they knew what they wanted to do and how to do it and were given a green light by MLRI. The results were the Maternity Leave Act, which guaranteed maternity leave to women and the right to return to their jobs without loss of benefits or seniority, and Chapter 622 of the Acts of 1971, which ended sex discrimination in all aspects of public education in Massachusetts. Both had an extraordinary impact on women's rights, status and opportunities in the workplace.

The former proved easier to implement than the latter.

Before the Maternity Leave Act was passed,† if an employed woman decided to leave her job because she was about to give birth, the common practice was to treat her as having voluntarily quit. Employers routinely fired women who left work for childbirth and wouldn't hire them back. A key consequence was to keep women employed at low-paying jobs because, having left to give birth, they lost seniority rights and other benefits to which they would have been entitled.

The act put an end to this practice. Diane conceived of its structure and guided the other two in its preparation and drafting.[3] The proposed legislation required that after three months of full-time employment, a woman who was absent from work for a period not exceeding eight weeks on "maternity leave ... *shall be restored* to her previous, or a similar, position with the same status, pay, length of service credit and seniority" as she had on the date she took the leave. "Said maternity leave shall be with

---

* Regina Healy interview.
† Chapter.790, sec. 1 of the Acts of 1972.

or without pay, at the discretion of her employer." In short, the taking of maternity leave couldn't affect a woman's rights to the employee benefits she'd earned as of the date of the leave. And for the first time, employers were *required* to grant maternity leave to female employees.

The right to maternity leave was enforced through an amendment to Massachusetts's anti-discrimination law* which made it an "unlawful practice … for an employer to refuse to restore certain female employees to employment following their absence by reason of a maternity leave … or to impose any other penalty as a result of a maternity leave of absence."

This was a major step for women in the workplace – a forerunner to and model for similar legislation elsewhere. Conceived, researched, drafted, proposed and lobbied through the legislature by Diane, Regie and Martha, its enactment would have made for a heady time even if that were their sole accomplishment – but it was not. They were responsible for even more important legislation, Chapter 622 of the Acts of 1971, which eliminated sex discrimination in the public schools.

There, the solution Diane hit upon was deceptively simple, and was built on the efforts of a renowned Boston attorney a century earlier. In 1848, Charles Sumner[4] had unsuccessfully represented Benjamin Roberts, a black man who tried to enroll his five-year-old daughter in a primary school for whites that was closer to his home than Boston's segregated black schools. Outraged by a decision that compelled his client's daughter to attend a segregated black school, Sumner took his case to the legislature and caused to pass – and the governor to sign – legislation outlawing segregation in public schools.†

Sumner's law provided simply that "No child shall be excluded from or discriminated against in admission to a public school of any town on account of race, color, religion or national origin." MLRI's proposed amendment added the word "sex" to the list – but it also added more complex language which proved critical to its success. That language was "… or in obtaining the advantages, privileges and courses of study of such public schools…." The amending bill was presented without great publicity and was passed without fanfare, but not without intensive lobbying efforts by Regie, Martha and Diane.

They started with House Speaker Bartley's executive assistant, Connie Kaufman, a woman whose judgment Bartley trusted. Kaufman was taken by the background and overwhelmed by the statistics – and by the stories. One of the required parts of the courses women could take was "millinery," the making of hats. No one wore hats anymore, and the course didn't prepare women for anything useful. When women had

---

*   Massachusetts General Laws, c. 151B, sec. 4.
†   The Roberts decision by Massachusetts's Supreme Judicial Court originated the "separate but equal" principle which was overturned by the United States Supreme Court in *Brown vs. Board of Education* in 1954.

to find work as single heads of households, no useful skills had been taught to them. They had been excluded from training in well-paying vocational jobs – plumbing, auto repair, electrical skills, bricklaying – skills which translated into work that would support a family. Bartley, whose background was in education, may have become interested for other reasons, but it was Kaufman who persuaded him to endorse the bill.*

Boston home rule presented another obstacle. They had to obtain City Council approval. Mayor White was all right with the bill and Council President Gerry O'Leary decided to support it. At a City Council hearing, there was a verbal duel between competing representatives of the American Civil Liberties Union. A woman stood up and said she represented the ACLU, which supported the legislation. A man stood up in the balcony and said, "She doesn't represent the ACLU. *I* represent the ACLU and the ACLU is against it!" Exactly who represented the ACLU was not resolved. Nevertheless, O'Leary managed Chapter 622 through the City Council.

MLRI joined forces with N.O.W. Between them, they lobbied every member of the Legislature. Poverty statistics drove the effort. Regie did a great deal of the lobbying, Diane less, including meeting with Bartley. They both met with Representative Michael J. Daly, the co-chair of the Education Committee, at his home. Daly's wife – independently a political force – became a supporter and lobbied for Chapter 622 with other legislators. Daly committed to it. Representative Ann Gannett, his co-chair, endorsed the bill. Another key legislator, Senator Jack Backman, called Diane because he had a concern that the bill could have an adverse effect on the racial imbalance law. They talked it through and Diane tweaked the bill a little. Backman was satisfied. It sailed through the legislature and was signed into law by Governor Sargent.

As a result of the language "… or in obtaining the advantages, privileges and courses of study of such public schools …" Chapter 622 served to outlaw discrimination on account of sex in every aspect of the public school system. ("We weren't sure how the language would be interpreted, but it sounded good and seemed to encompass everything," Regie said.) For the first time, young women had equal access to vocational training of every kind. They also were to be treated equally in extracurricular sports programs.†

It was the first legislation of its kind in the United States, and preceded by a year Congressional passage of Title IX of the Education Amendments of 1972, which had the same effect nationwide in all federally assisted education programs. Passage of the one served as an example and model for the other – and young women's lives and

---

*   Regina Healy interview.
†   Ultimately this requirement was interpreted to mean that women's sports were to receive equal funding, but it also meant that young women who wanted to try out for previously all-male teams could not be excluded from them.

expectations were altered dramatically.

Little attention had been paid to the funding needed to implement the bill, and the legislature appropriated none, leaving that to local school boards, city councils and town meetings. Nor had attention been given to what structural changes in the public school systems would be required. Establishing the principle was the first order of business.

Nor had there been any talk at the outset about the effect the legislation would have on Boston's elite sex-segregated Latin Schools (Boston Latin and Girls' Latin). In truth, no one had thought about it. Those issues arose after Chapter 622 became law.* Edith Fine, then counsel to Mayor White, when asked for her opinion whether it applied to the Latin Schools, stated that it did. That brought West Roxbury's representative Charles Doyle out swinging. Doyle introduced a bill to make its adoption a *local option* for all cities and towns – not just Boston and the Latin Schools – a bill which, had it passed, would have emasculated Chapter 622. When Doyle's bill came before the legislature's Education Committee, eleven elected Boston officials, including a majority of the Boston School Committee, then headed by Chairman James Hennigan, supported it. Wilfred O'Leary, the headmaster of Boston Latin, and Margaret Carroll, the headmistress of Girls' Latin, spoke in favor of local option, arguing that the schools should not be forced to become coeducational.†

It was a brass-knuckle battle.‡ Doyle argued for Boston Latin's special place in Boston's educational firmament in an interesting way:

> Boston Latin is one of the outstanding schools in the country. What would happen if we did not exempt it from this law? Within a short time, Boston Latin would be 50 percent women – an injustice to the boys.
>
> Last year we excluded taverns from the law [barring sex discrimination in public places]. Don't you think the parents of our children should be given the same consideration as the tavern owners of Massachusetts?

O'Leary said the separation was necessary "to give the boys a fair chance":

> At that age, the girls are three years ahead of the boys. If anything happens to these schools, there will be an exodus out of Boston the likes of which you have never seen.

Daly accused O'Leary of trying to harass him into supporting the Doyle bill by

---

*   Regina Healy interview.
†   Boston *Herald-Traveler*, February 17, 1972.
‡   As described in the *Herald-Traveler* article, ibid.

having students call him at home. Daly showed a bulletin written by O'Leary giving Daly's home phone number and address. "Several students," he said, "called my home and my office and used obscene language."

Doyle's bill was opposed by the Governor's Commission on the Status of Women, the Boston Commission to Improve the Status of Women and by MLRI, represented at the hearing by Diane and Regie. Speaking for MLRI, Regie noted that because the student capacity of Girls' Latin was only slightly more than half of Boston Latin, girls had to score 15 points higher than boys on a competitive examination in order to be admitted. As to O'Leary's argument that requiring coeducation at Boston Latin would be unfair to the boys, she responded that "One of the assumptions made by opponents of integration is that boys are sleepers … that they will ultimately exceed girls in intellectual ability. There is little evidence to back this up."

Mrs. Helen Sherwood of the Boston League of Women Voters said that public schools are "tax-supported without regard to the sex of the taxpayer. Life in the real world is heterosexual."

Students and former students from the two schools spoke on both sides of the question. Andrea Mulhern, Student Council President at Girls' Latin, said she'd intended to support continued segregation but had changed her mind during the course of the hearing because she was "appalled at the sexist attitude of people" who had spoken in support of the bill.

While there was drama, the political reality was that there was no chance of repeal or amendment over the opposition of representatives Daly and Gannett, and Speaker Bartley. Their support never wavered. The Doyle bill was referred to a study committee and never reached the floor of the House.

The more difficult and long-term tasks were to persuade the Department of Education to adopt regulations implementing Chapter 622, which took the better part of four years, and educating local school committees, which, lacking state guidance, created a patchwork of rules, principles, *ad hoc* decisions and regulations of their own across the state. Despite the clear mandate of the law, its implementation was enormously difficult.

Diane and Regie had their first meeting at the Department of Education on December 20, 1971.* Diane had drafted a proposed set of guidelines, and much of the meeting consisted of other participants, particularly the Department's representatives, chipping away at them. The meeting was attended by Fred Lewis of the Department and Joe Robinson, its general counsel, and representatives of the governor's office, the

---

* By this date, neither Diane nor Regie was still employed by the Massachusetts Law Reform Institute, but they continued to serve as its representatives on all matters pertaining to Chapter 622. Diane had begun teaching at Northeastern Law School; and in the fall would begin teaching at Harvard Law. Regie, having graduated from Suffolk Law School, had accepted a position at Harvard's Community Legal Assistance Organization as a Reginald Heber Smith Fellow.

Governor's Commission on Women, the Bureau of Equal Educational Opportunity, and the Equal Employment Commission. The process wouldn't be concluded until 1975.

Both the Department and the local communities were resistant to the concept of genuine implementation in the vocational area and in the area of athletics. Lewis and Robinson in particular were not reconciled to Chapter 622 and had no interest in implementing it. Their bureaucratic foot-dragging lasted until Robinson was replaced as general counsel to the Department.

In the interim, Diane and Regie continued the battle on local fronts, working to bring pressure to bear on the Department from both above and below. They stood firm on equality of vocational training, as that was key to the legislation. On athletics, where there were genuine grounds for separation of the sexes, they insisted on equal per capita *expenditures,* something which would prove critical to the development of women's sports at both secondary school and collegiate levels.

In early 1972, Diane was appointed to the Massachusetts Advisory Council on Vocational-Technical Education. Its tasks in implementing Chapter 622 included bringing young women into courses from which they'd previously been excluded, e.g., carpentry, plumbing, electrical work, machinist training, ironworking and construction. Locally, she served the same function on an advisory committee to the Minuteman Regional Vocational-Technical High School located on the Lexington-Concord line. In May, representing the Council, she spoke at a statewide conference of guidance counselors in Hyannis who brought the message back to their communities.

Progress was made on all fronts except the Department of Education. Publicity and community involvement were critical. In March 1973, Regie and Diane appeared at a Cambridge Forum presentation in the First Parish Church at the edge of the Harvard Law School campus:

Lawyers Cite Sex Discrimination in Schools*

Two women's rights advocates told a Cambridge Forum audience last night that the crucial area of concern over women's rights in education lies in children's education. Diane Lund, assistant professor in the Law School, and Regina Healy, instructor at the Radcliffe Institute, who in 1971 drafted Chapter 622 of the General Laws of Massachusetts, explained that the Massachusetts Board of Education is still considering how to enforce Chapter 622, which prohibits discrimination in the public schools on the basis of sex.

"It took a long time for the state to realize that it had a responsibility to implement change. We're looking for some self-executing way of implementing

---

* *Harvard Crimson*, March 1973.

this law. One would like to see the schools themselves change," Lund said. The part of the law which has the most significance, she said, deals with sex discrimination in areas such as shop, homemaking, textbooks and teaching materials.

Healy added that chemistry textbooks are still being used which show girls bleaching their hair and "concocting chemicals to make themselves look prettier."

"At every level of American life, it seems clear that sex discrimination is carried through, either overtly or covertly," Lund said. Discrimination is even present in those with the "highest level of consciousness." She explained that one of the final exam questions she gave in her course at the Law School, "Women and the Law," dealt with an unidentified public school principal, who all 55 students identified as a male.

"We don't know yet how to assess the success of the women's movement in education," Healy said. "But if we would have to evaluate it now, we would be using a male standard of measurement. What we're talking about is a variety of lifestyle choices. People should be able to determine for themselves what options they choose."

Diane and Regie fought to end sex discrimination in Massachusetts public schools.

A few months later *Boston Globe* columnist Ellen Goodman wrote an article which proved instrumental:

Dick and Jane and Chapter 622*

It seems there's a law in Massachusetts barring discrimination against any child in obtaining the privileges and courses of study in the public school on account of, among other things, the sex of that child. Jane doesn't have to sew while Dick saws. But so far that's true in only a very few communities. When are the rest going to implement it?

* * *

It is two years now since Massachusetts became the first state to outlaw sex discrimination in the public schools. Yet, when most classes begin a week from Wednesday there still will be secondary schools that refuse admission to either

---

* *Boston Globe*, August 26, 1973.

boys or girls. There will be thousands of textbooks that only portray men at work and women in aprons. There will still be dozens of school systems that require boys to saw and girls to sew. And in other school systems there will be ample funds for football uniforms but none for cheerleaders. Chapter 622, the law that is envied by women's groups all over the country, has been more a statement of intent than a law.

The crucial paragraph said simply: No child shall be excluded from or discriminated against in admission to a public school of any town, or in obtaining the advantages, privileges, courses of study of such public school on account of race, color, sex, religion or national origin. It passed simply, too, without guidelines, without funding, without a separate implementation clause or staff. Enforcement was to depend on individual action, on the parent or guardian of a child bringing suit against an individual school.

But what constitutes sex discrimination? What constitutes an "advantage" or a "privilege" or even a "course of study" in the public schools? These things were never defined. As Connie Kaufman, a staffer in House Speaker David Bartley's office who did much of the original work for the bill says, "It gets depressing when everyone calls to inquire two years later – and not much has been done."

But now at last 622 is beginning to be used effectively on more than a token basis. A catalogue of sex-discriminatory activities has been drawn, a checklist of what may be considered sexism in the schools:

- Schools that refuse admission on the basis of sex.
- Courses of study that similarly refuse admission on the basis of sex.
- An athletic program that allots more time, space or money to male sports than female sports.
- Extracurricular activities, including clubs, etc., that are open to only one sex.
- Guidance departments that routinely track girls into "female" vocations and futures, and boys into "male" ones.
- Textbooks and other educational materials that discriminate by insult, neglect or stereotyping of either sex.

These things and more can be interpreted as illegal under 622. But the question remains, as with the racial imbalance law, how do you implement a revolution, how do you enforce social change?

To begin with, how do you end sex discrimination in education in a statewide school system that itself is open to charges of discrimination in employment. In Massachusetts 80 percent of the teachers are female but 70 percent of the principals and all but one of the superintendents are male. Even the State Board of Education has only three women among its twelve members.

* * *

With all these built-in problems, how do you implement Chapter 622? Slowly, steadily, says [the head of the Equal Education Department of the State Board]. "The real trick is to move forward steadily, one step at a time, never going backwards. You have to do it like Grant won the Civil War. Not by lightning raids but by steady pushing. Every position that you take has to be kept."

The General Grants of Chapter 622 have been Regina Healy, a lawyer for the Cambridge-Somerville Legal Assistance Project, and Diane Lund, an assistant professor at Harvard Law School. Over the past two years an enormous amount of their "free" time has been spent writing letters and opinions and dispensing information about the law. Ms. Healy became involved in the issue of action in the schools while she was still a law student. "I was working with MLRI on poverty issues. One of the things we discovered was the relationship between sex and poverty. [The trade schools] all operated on the theory that the man on the white horse would cart the girl away so all she needed were housewifely vocations," said Ms. Healy.

As Ms. Healy adds, "It's more than vocational training. It's attitudes. Education teaches women to be passive and dependent. Don't move the chairs in the auditorium. Don't play dodge ball. Don't run the projector. They grow up to be mothers just as they're supposed to and then when they are on welfare we call them all kinds of parasitic names. Well that started way back when the schools prepared them for the treadmill."

* * *

In Lexington, a group of "Grant-style" women began by integrating the industrial arts-home economics course in the junior high school. They were once mandatory and separate. They are now mandatory and integrated in the eighth grade. In Brookline, industrial arts and home economics will be completely co-ed next year through grade five and within two years the whole program will be co-ed.

* * *

The area in which the greatest economic discrimination against females in the schools occurs is in athletics. * * * In Brookline, for example which has 19 varsity sports for boys and eight for girls, the budget spends $10 for boys' sports for every $1 for girls'. And that budget is more equal than most. Athletic directors argue that boys' sports simply cost more than girls', noting for example Brookline spends $160 for every football player. Prof. Lund says – only half-facetiously – that she can think of several expensive sports for girls, "like horseback riding or skiing, that would make up the gap. It's a question of attitude. The attitude is that sports are for boys." She also notes the number of times the boys get their uniforms paid for by the town while the girls make or buy their own.

* * *

Prof. Lund says that the [segregated] playground scene is still the same. In Lexington, where her son is a student, she noted the difference and wrote a letter to the principal. His response was to integrate the playground the next day without any planning or preparation. "There was no activity that week except for boys chasing girls. It was obviously his way of showing resentment. My son lived in terror that someone would find out his mother did it."

* * *

Teacher attitudes are the most difficult to get at legally or to change. The school systems in the state number 395. There are 1191 elementary and secondary schools. There is no possibility of monitoring what happens in every school room, even if this were desirable. In Prof. Lund's opinion, "any time there is a distinction shown on the basis of sex alone, you probably have discrimination. To change the school system is an enormous undertaking. To change it without funds, with a law which has counted on parents for enforcement can seem impossible." The last two years have been spent putting wedges in doors and having scatter-shot success. They have been spent preparing for action. "The general level of sensitivity is higher than two years ago, but we haven't changed that much," admits Prof. Lund.

* * *

Finally after two years a group has been formed to write up guidelines for the law. The Ad Hoc Committee expects to finish these guidelines by some time in October and set up six regional hearings in the winter. The guidelines will become rules and regulations only after this process is completed. Then there will be a legal reference as to what constitutes sex discrimination.

* * *

As Ms. Healy says, "Theoretically one of the aims of education has been to prepare students for a self-sufficient adulthood. In practice, self-sufficiency has been promoted only for boys. It's not that we want the schools to preach a political philosophy, but to stop preaching one. An accident of birth is not the school's business. What is the school's business are the attributes a kid brings to it. This is what the school has to deal with. The school must not be able to decide that a child's athletic skill is not to be developed because that child is a girl or that language skills are not to be developed because that child is a boy."

Another year came and went with no action by the Department of Education. In late 1974, a statewide coalition had been formed. It circulated a letter, signed by Diane and Regie, among others, to Chapter 622's supporters:

Dear friend of Chapter 622:

A [discouraging] status report on Chapter 622 was recently sent to us by the Department of Education.

[T]his law, which was enacted by the state legislature in 1971 can potentially be used as a wedge to expand educational opportunities for all students in Massachusetts. It complements both the Racial Imbalance and Bilingual laws by offering students not only access to schools but also access to courses of study and to all the advantages and privileges offered by a public school, and of course it provides full protection against discrimination.

The potential of the law can only be realized if the Board of Education approves strong regulations, and if the state approves funds for implementation. To date the legislature has never appropriated any funds for Chapter 622.

We, the undersigned, ask you to join us in our efforts to support the implementation of Chapter 622 by forming a coalition. The purpose of our group will be to urge the Board of Education to adopt regulations at least as strong as the existing recommendations.

If you believe, as we do, that Chapter 622 requires a commitment from the state of adequate funding and strong regulations for enforcement, we ask you to sign the enclosed petition and send it....

Fortuitously, political events in late 1974 resulted in a power shift within the Department, a shift which led, finally, to its 1975 adoption of regulations to implement and enforce the intent of Chapter 622 throughout the state.

The events arose out of another battle against discrimination, the high-profile issue of segregation of blacks and whites in the public school systems of Boston and Springfield, segregation perpetuated by decisions of their school committees. In 1965, a study and report commissioned by the Department of Education had concluded that racial imbalance was educationally harmful and should be eliminated. As a result, the Massachusetts Legislature passed the Racial Imbalance Act, which obligated the school committees to correct the imbalance. The Department attempted to force the local committees into compliance, but without success. Litigation followed.[5]

In 1973, the Supreme Judicial Court upheld an order of the Department to the Boston and Springfield school committees to implement a racial balance plan by September 1974. In the interim, in 1972, a coalition of Boston parents had brought the momentous Boston School Desegregation case in the United States District Court before Judge Arthur A. Garrity, and had named as defendants, among others, the Department and the Commissioner of Education, Gregory Anrig, Jr. A parallel action was brought in Springfield, again naming the Department and the Commissioner as defendants.[6]

When the Boston and Springfield cases were brought, the interests of the Department and Anrig were aligned with the plaintiffs even though the Department and Anrig were defendants in the cases. The Department requested Attorney General Robert H. Quinn to appoint counsel to represent the Department's interests, and Quinn delegated the task to Howard Mayo, an assistant attorney general. In the early fall of 1973 Mayo assigned a new and relatively inexperienced assistant attorney general to represent the Department, working under his supervision. Sandra L. Lynch, a graduate of Boston University Law School and an editor of its law review, came to the attorney general's office after a two-year clerkship with U.S. District Court Judge Raymond Pettine in Rhode Island, the first woman to have served as a clerk for Judge Pettine. She and Mayo and Anrig would form a team to pursue the objectives of school desegregation in Massachusetts.*

In the summer and fall of 1974, however, Quinn was seeking the gubernatorial nomination in the Democratic primary against Michael Dukakis and made political promises to politicians in Springfield that he would not push desegregation there. He, Mayo and Lynch were at odds. Anrig, understanding the situation, offered Lynch the job of General Counsel within the Department, which she promptly accepted. There were two lawyers in the Department when Lynch arrived, one being Joe Robinson, the long-time general counsel who she was displacing, and the other being his assistant. Robinson was a trouper and a good lawyer, and he stayed on, in charge of school building construction matters.

Lynch came in at a tough time for the Department: South Boston High was in receivership, and there were daily marches and protests in opposition to Judge Garrity's orders requiring busing to remedy the racial imbalances in the Boston schools. The Boston School Committee had defied Garrity's orders, and its chairman, John Kerrigan, had been held in contempt of court.

It had been three years since Chapter 622 had been enacted, and the Department had as yet done nothing with it, as its attention had been taken up entirely with the Boston and Springfield desegregation cases. Lynch, however, also wanted to deal with the intractable problems that Chapter 622 had presented for the Department, and hired Sandi Moody, a contemporary and another feminist, into the Department.

Moody had to wrestle with both political and substantive issues before regulations could be promulgated. Politically the Department could not simply impose the regulations from above – it had to go out and get local and regional input. The points of most bitter convergence and dispute were in manual arts/home economics and in athletics. The Department's position became – and was ultimately embodied in the

---

*   In 1995 Lynch was appointed by President Clinton the first woman judge in the United States Court of Appeals for the First Circuit. (In the federal system, the Circuit Courts are one level below the United States Supreme Court.) In 2008, she became the Circuit's Chief Judge.

regulations – that if young women wished to try out for a formerly all-male team, they had the right to do so; if they wanted to learn woodworking, then they had that right, just as any male had the right to learn cooking skills.

There were downsides. Some high schools dropped manual arts and home economics as required courses. Vocational high schools, however, opened their doors and courses to young women. In this area and in athletics, Chapter 622 had a major impact on young women's opportunities. They were brought on a par with the boys, and the result was a vast increase in the number of self-confident and competent young women graduating from the school system.

It had been a long haul for Diane and Regie. In the intervening years, much had happened in women's fight for equality that had an enormous impact on Diane's life. In retrospect it is difficult to fathom how she could also have remained involved in the initiatives for which she and Regie had worked at the Massachusetts Law Reform Institute.

The first of those events had occurred in the fall of 1971, when Diane was approached by Professor Steve Subrin* of the Northeastern University School of Law faculty asking if she'd be interested in applying to become the first woman on its regular faculty.

Northeastern's approach to the study of law included reexamining the effect of laws on groups and individuals who had been disenfranchised in the United States, a markedly nontraditional approach which Diane found fresh and exciting. The opportunity represented, moreover, not just a milestone for women, but a continuation of the career path on which she'd set out when she had joined MLRI two years earlier. Northeastern's approach in combination with its emphasis on small classes, the close relationships it encouraged between faculty and students, and the practical opportunities its students had to work in the real world during their co-op quarters, appealed to her.

So did the challenge. No woman was a regular member of the faculty in any major law school in the Northeast. For this very reason, however, there was internal opposition at Northeastern concerning its solicitation of and consideration of Diane's candidacy. The internal stir dissipated, largely because she won the opponents over in the course of her interviews with the faculty. She began teaching in December 1971.

Within weeks, her classes began to be monitored by members of the appointments committee of Harvard Law School, where failure to hire women had become a cause celebre, not only among its students but with the federal government, which was looking into Harvard's lack of diversity in all its departments. She was soon invited to join the Harvard Law School faculty as the first woman it had ever hired on a tenure track.

She was torn. Northeastern suited her perfectly, both philosophically and because

---

* When Subrin had been at Harvard, a year behind Diane, she'd been his advisor on the Board of Student Advisors, an experience he recalls vividly.

of its approach to the law and the teaching of it. She had no personal ambition to go on to Harvard because Harvard represented the establishment antithesis of everything for which she'd been working for the past two years. Weighing heavily on the other side of the equation was the opportunity to blaze a new trail for women in a prestigious institution whose doors had been closed to them. It was an opportunity she felt she couldn't turn down, but she never said in any private conversation with me (or with Regie) that she really wanted to do it.

In the end, she accepted Harvard's offer and began teaching at Harvard in September 1972.

---

[1]   Northeastern operates on a four-quarter basis, alternating between academic quarters and co-op quarters in which its students receive practical legal experience working for law firms, nonprofits and government agencies.

[2]   The Bail Reform Act has endured and served its intended purpose. Over the years, the statute has been chipped away at, but it remains in substantially the same form today. Except for offenses punishable by death or where there are specific findings based on evidence of a danger to the community or to individuals (as by a person who has violated a restraining order in the abuse context), burglary, arson, or an offense calling for a mandatory three-year sentence, the judge "shall admit such person to bail on personal recognizance, without surety," although the judge has the discretion to determine whether release will "reasonably assure the appearance" of the individual at a later date. The statute continues to provide a same-day appeal to the Superior Court. In the 1990s, Republican Governor William Weld succeeded in amending the Bail Reform Act to allow district court judges to take additional factors into account in making their decisions – but apart from that effort the act has survived largely intact.

[3]   Although the Maternity Leave Act wasn't formally passed and enacted until 1972, when all three were elsewhere , they knew before they moved on – because of promises made by the legislative leadership during their consideration of the act in 1971 – that the legislation would be passed and signed. All three volunteered their time to make sure that the promises were kept.

[4]   An abolitionist who later became a U.S. senator, Sumner was the victim of an infamous caning in the United States Senate which nearly killed him. The caning came at the hands of Preston S. Brooks, the nephew of a southern senator, Andrew Butler, who had been singled out by Sumner in a fiery anti-slavery speech in the Senate. It was more than three years before Sumner was able to resume his seat in the Senate in 1859. He'd been reelected by Massachusetts in the interim.

[5]   Lynch, Sandra L., "The Boston School Desegregation Case," *Massachusetts Law Quarterly*, Fall 1977, p. 137.

[6]   Anrig, a highly respected career educator, was and had been sympathetic to the cause of desegregation and had had the support, through 1969, of Massachusetts Attorney General Elliot Richardson in attempting to enforce the Department's order to the local committees. After Richard Nixon was elected and Richardson was named Attorney General, Richardson was followed by Robert H. Quinn, who had been Speaker of the Massachusetts House. Quinn was not an enthusiastic supporter of racial balance in the schools, but the state's position, and that of the Department, was well-established by the time he assumed office.

CHAPTER SEVEN

CHANGE COMES SLOWLY TO HARVARD

WHEN DIANE GRADUATED FROM HARVARD AS ONE OF SIX women in the law school class, women weren't protected under anti-discrimination laws, and their second-class status was a given. The masters of the universe, the university and the law school were men, and their decision to admit women at all was an act of noblesse oblige.

Eleven years later, women's status had changed in the eyes of the law, but not in the hearts and minds of the law school's male faculty. Its attitude at the prospect of having a woman colleague was negative and skeptical at best. For some, the thought gave rise to a palpable and visceral animus. The idea was unthinkable. For others who claimed to be open to the idea in principle, the reality was that they believed it should happen somewhere other than at Harvard.*

Professor Arthur E. Sutherland's aptly-titled 1967 history, *The Law at Harvard, a History of Ideas and Men,* contained, in its 369 pages, one reference to women (on page 320):

> The profound conservatism of academics had fostered many worries about the effect of such a radical innovation [as admitting women students]; when it happened there was no difficulty at all. Thirty to forty women now register each year in a class of 550 or so first-year students. Many of them live in Wyeth Hall, on Massachusetts Avenue at Everett Street, a university dormitory for women graduate students. Some are appointed senior residents of the smaller

---

*   Frank Michelman interview, March 22, 2005.

Radcliffe houses. About the same percentage of women as men make the *Law Review.* Now and then a woman student marries a classmate and outranks him in grades; from this disparity no domestic disaster has thus far ensued. Women find appropriate employment after graduation. One now wonders what caused all the worry between 1871 and 1950.

It is telling that Sutherland defined women's achievements by reference to domestic family tranquility and to their finding "appropriate employment," whatever that might have meant. Answering his own question, he mirrored the attitudes of the times.*

As to the faculty, the mantra that disguised the discrimination that was actually practiced, and justified it, was plainly stated by Professor Milton Katz:

> Of course we want women, but our great duty is to never reduce our standard of excellence. It is our conscientious duty never to flinch or falter in pursuing excellence.†

The subliminal message remains strong, even now. It doesn't admit of the idea that an appropriate "standard of excellence" in scholarship and teaching might differ from standards formulated exclusively by aggressive white males for other white males.

Professor Duncan Kennedy, a rebel at the law school, expressed it well in discussing gender-based norms: women, he said, had to confront the male stereotypes of "one who is verbally aggressive, analytical and possesses a 'surface insensitivity to social and emotional subtleties.'"‡ The idea that cooperative and nonconfrontational conduct and methods of teaching might be equally effective, even preferable to the 2000-year-old Socratic method, wasn't something that academics at Harvard – raised, trained and disciplined in the adversary system – could accept. Diane, like many women, didn't espouse or endorse that system. There were other choices.

Change was brewing at Harvard despite faculty opposition. Empowered by the Kennedy and Johnson administrations, Harvard women began attacking the status quo, first in small ways, later in significant ones. An unaccredited organization – the Women's Law Group – was formed in 1969. Its early focus was to seek coed housing for women, as they had none of the housing privileges of men. There were no law school dormitories for women, and only a handful of accessible women's bathrooms on the entire campus.

By 1970, now accredited as the Women's Law Association,§ it undertook to recruit

---

* Harrington: *Women Lawyers – Rewriting the Rules,* pp. 46-47.
† As quoted in Basile, *Integrating Women into the Law School Faculty,* 28 Harvard Journal of Law and Gender, p. 155, quoting from Seligman: *The High Citadel, The Influence of Harvard Law School.*
‡ Ibid., p. 164.
§ While the law school had recognized the WLA as a legitimate campus organization and given it office space, the space had previously been a closet under the stairs at Austin Hall.

at women's colleges and sponsored a series of conferences and forums. The *Harvard Law Record* (HLR) described their purpose, condescendingly, as "to find out what women are really thinking about," * perhaps a paraphrase of Freud's notorious question: "What do women really want?"†

A third-year law student, Dorothy Glancy, carried out a survey (Harvard funded its $700 cost) designed to explode the myth that women law graduates simply married and didn't use their legal education. Her work, published in the fall of 1970, showed that women lawyers stayed longer in their first jobs than men did, and that they continued to practice law after they had families and throughout their lives. Perhaps, said Ms. Glancy, "we can present this information ... in the hope that it will affect hiring policies and do away with discrimination against women in hiring." It was a vain hope. Writing of "our girls" at the law school, the *Record* quoted a law firm interviewer as saying that his firm *never hired women* because the firm expected them to leave.‡

There were no women on the regular faculty, nor even among the fifteen lecturers and teaching fellows listed in the 1970-71 catalogue. A course in family law was taught by a male, the estimable Frank Sander. No course was offered in employment discrimination. The professional responsibility course encompassed only criminal law, and not a lawyer's responsibility to assist the broader community in matters of public interest such as the reforms Diane and her colleagues at MLRI had addressed.

However, the 1970-71 catalogue did feature women. The "student activities" section had a photo of the "The Law School Show Chorines," four shapely women dancing in tights and miniskirts. They were not law students, but they weren't identified as anyone else.

Under the *Record's* headline "Basta to Women's Lib," Rodolfo de Nova, a visiting professor from Italy, was quoted as saying, "What is important is the influence that women have in the community.... The legal decisions which the man makes as to place of domicile, money, etc., aren't important compared to the woman's role in raising children. I fear that children may be neglected if women try to be too much like men. It is distressing that women are stirring up discontent at a time when America is facing so much discontent in other areas...."§

Harvard's Paul Freund, then a leading candidate for the U.S. Supreme Court, opposed the passage of the Equal Rights Amendment, saying that it was "the pursuit of

---

* *Harvard Law Record*, March 26, 1970. The *Record* had only one woman on its staff at this time, Michelle Scott, one of the two news editors. Over the next two years she became Managing Editor, then Editor. The *Record's* approach toward and tone in describing women's concerns would then change dramatically, illustrating what has become all too familiar in recent times, the importance of control of the media, even at the university level.

† Harrington, *Women in Academe*, p.5.

‡ HLR, April 19, 1970 and October 29, 1970.

§ HLR, October 15, 1970.

a mirage rather than of a productive reality … [with] possible foolish, unpredictable or chaotic results." The matter, he said, should be left to the courts and the legislatures on the ground that it was "more economical and would allow the retention of necessary differences in the legal status of men and women." Special provisions for women should reflect "realistic policies that recognize the average woman's limited savings and earnings power."*

Linda Matthews, a second-year student who'd previously been a lobbyist, called Freund's views "hopeless."†

The Women's Law Association proposed a non-credit course entitled "Women and the Law" to cover topics such as abortion and birth control, day care, housing and welfare, legal relations between men and women, and employment discrimination. They invited women from Yale (which already had such a course) to come to Cambridge and help with the project, and they did.

Boudin would later become a key figure in the Weathermen and would serve more than twenty-five years in prison for her part in an infamous robbery/murder.

The WLA petitioned the faculty concerning the need for this course, asking each one to respond. Only two professors, Vern Countryman and Frank Sander, bothered to reply. Undeterred, the WLA decided to seek out a qualified woman to come teach the course, and settled on Kathy Boudin, a firebrand feminist. When he received wind of what the WLA intended, Dean Bok rejected the proposal. ‡ He assured them, however, that the school would soon address the issue of recruiting a woman for the faculty.§

In February 1971, the WLA sponsored a conference at Radcliffe on "Law as a Career for Women." A *Harvard Crimson* staff writer reported on the conference:

> [O]ne member of the Law School appointments committee said yesterday that the faculty "has issued an invitation to a distinguished woman teacher" from another university to teach a special course on "Women and the Law" to second- and third-year students. He said that the faculty has "become interested in finding women members for the faculty," adding that "there isn't a large pool of excellent women law students who are interested in a scholarly life." Part of the reason for this, he asserted, was that women have "no models of women faculty members at Harvard."
>
> Only recently has the "lack of women faculty members been perceived

---

*   HLR, October 1, 1970.
†   Ibid.
‡   HLR, January 21, 1971.
§   Alice Ballard interview, April 7, 2005.

as a problem," he commented, adding that the increase in women law students would probably soon be reflected in the number of women on the law school faculty.*

Gloria Steinem criticized the law school's "inattention to women's studies" and its "insensitivity to women students' concerns and career goals":

> "The humanization of Harvard Law School is inevitable," [she] told a group of Law School students, faculty and alumni Saturday at a closed banquet of the *Law Review.* "Part of living the Revolution is that the scales fall off our eyes a little bit every day." Speaking at the Sheraton Plaza Hotel – "probably so I wouldn't have to come in the back door of the Harvard Club" – Steinem sharply criticized the Law School for its insensitivity to anti-female biases. "I am here to talk about the half of the human race that is women," she said. "The first problem for both men and women is not to learn, but to unlearn." †

Steinem's suggestions to the WLA included "recruitment of women students, with a goal of 50 percent in mind; that qualified women be sought out immediately for positions on the faculty; that a course on women and the law be added for credit; that firms suspected of discrimination against women in hiring and promotion be investigated, and denied use of the Law School's placement facilities if discrimination is found; and that the Law School become a place for human beings, not a work-obsessed skill bank for big firms." She criticized the Law School curriculum for ignoring legal problems relevant to women: "In Constitutional Law there is no mention of the Equal Rights Amendment, in Family Law there is no mention of how women lose their civil rights when married, and Labor Law doesn't mention the protective legislation that applies to women.

"Just last night," she added, "an eminent professor of law admitted he didn't know what the Equal Employment Opportunity Commission was. The same man replied to the demand that a female full professor be hired by saying that this would cause too many problems on the faculty 'because of sexual vibrations.'"‡

When the Visiting Committee invited students to an open meeting in 1971, the lecture hall was packed, and the committee was unprepared for the sentiment it

---

* *Harvard Crimson*, February 18, 1971. The writer, Patti B. Saris, then an undergraduate, is now U.S. District Court Judge Patti B. Saris of the District of Massachusetts.

† HLR, March 17, 1971. Steinem may have been being facetious, but the reality was not a joke. At that time, the all-male Union Club on Park Street in Boston didn't permit wives of their members to enter by the front door, even if they were arriving to have dinner with their husbands. A side door at a lower level existed for that purpose.

‡ *Crimson*, March 15, 1971.

encountered. Asked if any student had views to express, a woman raised her hand, strode to the front, turned, and asked those students who supported the Women's Law Association to stand up. The entire audience – men and women alike – rose. They remained standing as she made a fiery speech about the school's attitude toward women, its discrimination against them and its failure to rectify the discrimination practiced by prospective employers. She received an ovation.

John Quarles, a member of the Visiting Committee that had been challenged by the Women's Law Association – and a law school classmate of Diane's – recalled the era. "We were products of a half-generation earlier – the silent generation – and change hadn't been part of our agenda. Now it was part of the national agenda and we were swept up into it." When protection of the environment became a cutting-edge issue, John joined the Department of the Interior, whose umbrella in 1969 encompassed environmental protection. Two years later, Congress passed – and Nixon signed – legislation creating the Environmental Protection Agency, and John moved over into a lifelong career, both within government and, later, in private practice.

Young people were fighting to change the system. "The times, they are a-changin'," sang Bob Dylan. Change was happening nationally. The Chicago riots were still fresh in mind. The conclusion of an unjust war in Vietnam was at hand, an end hastened by the militant opposition of young people in colleges and universities. Their success and their tactics spilled over into other areas of change, not least the women's movement and its efforts to have the Equal Rights Amendment passed and adopted. Passed by Congress in 1972, what remained was its ratification by the states. What the Visiting Committee witnessed was a facet not just of the women's movement, but of a broader movement demanding change.

An important shift occurred at the law school when Derek Bok left the deanship in 1971 to become Harvard's president, and was succeeded by Professor Albert Sacks. While Bok himself was married to an extraordinary woman, Sissela Bok,* he was attuned to his faculty's views regarding women colleagues. He hadn't quite turned a deaf ear to bringing women on, and had in fact given assurances that the issue would be addressed, but doing anything concrete was left to his successor.

The discrimination Sacks inherited at the law school was university-wide. Informal complaints concerning Harvard's bias against hiring women faculty in any of its graduate schools (and in the undergraduate

---

*   Sissela Bok would commence an important twenty-year academic career in 1972, focusing on moral and ethical choices in living one's life.

school, which had not yet been merged with Radcliffe) had been lodged with HEW in Washington. Harvard needed to respond affirmatively. A plan to rectify inequalities in employment patterns based on sex, race, national origins, etc., submitted in 1970, had been rejected by HEW as inadequate. Revised and resubmitted in February 1971, the plan's new focus was on the conspicuous absence of women among tenured faculty ("very much a concern of the University"). This time it was accepted.*

Once – briefly – the law school had had a woman on its faculty. Soia Mentschikoff, a 1937 Columbia graduate and an outstanding practitioner and legal scholar who'd become the first woman partner in a major New York law firm, had been a visiting professor in 1948-49 (before women were admitted at all) teaching Commercial Law to the men. She wasn't offered a tenured position.†

Other than Mentschikoff, the only female presence on the faculty had been, and continued to be, Elisabeth Owens. Owens, who received her law degree from Yale, had come to Harvard in 1955 to do research for Professor Stanley Surrey in his then-new International Tax Program. Over time she'd developed and begun teaching courses in her specialty, and on water management and gas laws, and succeeded Surrey as director of the International Tax Program. Not a feminist, not involved in the women's movement, not an advocate for change and not on the tenure track, she didn't regard herself as part of the regular faculty. She wasn't the role model the WLA envisioned.

Sacks proactively approached recruiting women for his faculty, not because the faculty had had a change of heart, but because he had a longer-term – and more prescient – view of the future than his faculty did. Sacks understood not only that the issues women were raising needed to be addressed, but that they needed to be addressed responsibly and substantively. He intended to give more than lip service to the plan approved by HEW. Hoping he would gain his faculty's acceptance, however, his own plan was only incremental, a one-at-a-time approach.

He began with Ruth Bader Ginsburg, who already had an outstanding reputation and had built a significant academic career. Ginsburg had been a law professor at Rutgers for eight years, the second woman on its faculty. She was skeptical about Sacks' proposal that she come lecture at Harvard for a year, with tenure in the offing, and it wasn't an easy sell, in part because of her earlier experiences there as a student. She'd married and had a child before entering Harvard, but became a member of the *Law Review* in her second year, the third woman to be so honored. She transferred to Columbia for her final year to join her husband, who'd begun practice in a law firm there. She became a

---

* HLR, November 12, 1971.
† Later tenured at the University of Chicago, Mentschikoff became the first woman president of the American Association of Law Schools and dean of the University of Miami School of Law.

member of Columbia's Law Review as well, and finished first in her class – but Harvard refused to award her a degree.* She had not, after all, finished *there*.

Ginsburg was wary for other reasons. On graduating from Columbia, she had received no job offers from New York law firms, nor was she able to obtain a clerkship interview with a Supreme Court justice. "[H]er status [she recalled] as 'a woman, a Jew and a mother to boot' was 'a bit much' for prospective employers."† She finally obtained a clerkship with a U.S. District Court Judge. "The second-class treatment I had experienced," she concluded, "was a symptom of a larger problem – social conditions that denied women choices and opportunities open to men." While teaching at Rutgers she began litigating sex-discrimination cases for the American Civil Liberties Union.

In each of the two years prior to the Harvard offer, she'd sponsored "consciousness-raising sessions on the subject of women" at Rutgers. The first year, "not one of my male colleagues showed up." In the second year, "we rescheduled it and sent subpoenas to all the male faculty. This time most of them came."‡

Although she accepted Sacks' offer, she had no intention of leaving behind what she'd achieved and throwing her lot in with Harvard. She and her husband had a solid professional and social base in the New York area. Although her husband agreed he would move to Boston if she were offered a tenured position, in the interim, she would keep a foot in both places. She would maintain her status and a full course load at Rutgers, and commute between Boston and New Jersey.

That she agreed to come at all reflected the importance she attached to a woman's joining the Harvard faculty. She described the seminar she would teach, "Legal Aspects of Sex-based Discrimination" in an interview with the *Harvard Law Record* in April 1971:

> The major comparison we will be making on the status of women will be with Sweden. When I was in Sweden in 1962-63 that country was in just about the same position as the United States is now vis-à-vis feminism. The debate was just beginning. Now it's finished [in Sweden]. Not only is there no discrimination, but there is a genuine sharing of roles.

It's noteworthy that while male professors from other schools were termed "Visiting Professors of Law," Harvard's catalogue listed Ginsburg as a "Lecturer on Law," a title usually reserved for local Boston practitioners such as President Nixon's attorney, James D. St. Clair, Esq., who lectured on trial practice, not a mainstream subject at Harvard.

---

*   HLR, April 23, 1971.
†   Guide to Government website.
‡   Ibid.

And while none of the male professors or lecturers were listed as "Mr.," Ginsburg was accorded the designation befitting her marital status: "Mrs."

Teaching at two law schools and working on the ACLU's Women's Rights Project, she was stretching herself precariously thin, and although she was creating a national reputation, it would not serve her well at Harvard. Judging from the *Harvard Law Record*, however, women's hopes were high in November 1971, two months after Ginsburg's arrival:

> Harvard Law School may soon be able to boast the first woman professor in the history of the school. An intensive search is currently in progress to discover female candidates for a faculty appointment leading ultimately to the granting of full professorship and tenure. "We are conducting a very thorough search," explained Dean Sacks. "We are reviewing all possible females who might be qualified for a professorship and we will do what we can to attract them." Sacks stated however that no quota or firm commitment had been established with respect to hiring one or more women by next fall … According to Sacks, the present quest for a woman to fill the role of a professor reflects a definite change of emphasis gradually fostered in the last year or so under both Sacks and Dean Bok.*

An editorial titled, "A Woman Professor?" appeared in the same issue of the HLR:

> There are some who fear that the quest for a woman professor at the Law School may be only a brand of tokenism. While that remains to be seen, it is at least true that there must be one woman professor before there are two. As a practical matter, Harvard Law School is unlikely to break traditional ice more than one crack at a time.
>
> But will the School have even one woman professor – be she only a visiting professor to start out with – by next fall? No firm commitment to that goal has been made…. Moreover, it would be imprudent for the administration to concentrate its recruiting efforts prematurely on only one or two individuals, leaving other candidates aside. No insurmountable obstacles loom to block the path of real intent.

Ginsburg's path to tenure, however, was blocked by Philip Areeda, a distinguished member of the faculty who, having attended one of Ginsburg's classes, reported that in his opinion her performance did not meet Harvard's standard of excellence. In

---

* HLR, November 12, 1971.

December 1971, to Sacks' dismay, the faculty rejected the idea that she should be offered a tenured position.

Urging her to stay on for the full year, he explained to her that he thought, given another semester's experience, the faculty would change its mind. She was not of the same view. Columbia had offered her a tenured position. She decided to accept it and advised Sacks accordingly. In a letter to the Women's Law Association concerning these events, she was circumspect:

> During the holidays I accepted a tenured professorship at Columbia Law School and next year will spend half-time there and half-time at the ACLU heading up its women's rights project. With these new assignments and much deck-clearing to do this spring, the Harvard commute seemed a heavy burden and I asked Dean Sacks to relieve me of it. His understanding and Betty Owens' agreement to take over the first-year spring seminar on sex-based discrimination made life much easier for me.

Ballard, a feminist activist and a physics major as an undergraduate (Radcliffe/Harvard '70), something both remarkable and unusual for a woman of the time, says that she and other women found themselves out of place when they arrived at Harvard. They were a 15% minority and felt they were regarded as entertainment for the men.

A month later, Ginsburg said she was "mildly critical of the Law School's hiring practices toward women." She noted that Harvard's history had made it difficult. "There is a feeling on the part of some faculty members that women don't really belong…."* The Women's Law Association was outraged by Harvard's rejection of Ginsburg. Its spokeswomen Alice Ballard and Janet Benishook said that the Association "had felt that confidence had been building up between the administration and the WLA but this [Ginsburg's leaving] has completely destroyed it." As for Areeda's criticisms, they noted that no effort had been made to contact Ginsburg's students – particularly women – for their views about the quality of the course.

Ballard said she was "pessimistic about the possibility of there being a woman professor on the faculty next year and she would be astounded if one were hired."†

In a bind, Sacks turned to a woman who'd had a superb academic record at the law school, who was highly thought of by a number of faculty members based on personal experience and who'd just begun her teaching career at another law school. She didn't have Ginsburg's academic background and reputation. What she had

---

*   HLR, January 28, 1972. See also end note 1.
†   HLR, January 28, 1972.

was teaching ability, charisma and students who admired and related to her and her teaching methods.

When Sacks called, the idea of teaching at Harvard wasn't even a glimmer in Diane's mind. She had just concluded the two most exciting and rewarding years of her professional life, her children were ten, eight and six years old, all in the most interesting periods of their young lives, and she'd secured a plum position at Northeastern, an institution whose philosophy and faculty she liked very much.

PROFESSOR OF LAW DIANE THEIS LUND

Northeastern's law school had opened its doors in 1968 and was unique in several respects. Its emphasis was on social change in light of the inequities of existing law – much in line with Diane's views – so its faculty and student population had a liberal bent. Like the undergraduate university, it operated on a four-quarter co-op plan under which second- and third-year students spent alternative quarters at work as interns where they could gain practical experience for their new-found legal skills. Its physical environment was very different from that at Harvard:

> There are no wood-framed portraits of distinguished-looking alumni hanging from the narrow, low-ceilinged corridors of the Northeastern University School of Law. [T]he law school is engaged more in establishing its reputation throughout the country than it is in providing the traditional trappings of a legal education. And even if, in the future, the school does get around to decking its modest halls with the images of graduates-made-good, it is unlikely that the paintings will display bushy-eyebrowed judges in their robes, nor silver-haired, pipe-smoking scholars of the law. Instead, they will probably depict a long-haired man working in a tenants' organizing office, or a tee-shirted woman advising welfare mothers of their rights.*

These weren't areas of the law in which Harvard was interested. They were "soft" subjects not worthy of attention because they were merely matters of community interest rather than the serious work of lawyers. Elizabeth Bartholet, who would come to teach at Harvard in 1977 after a remarkable twelve-year career as an activist lawyer in the public sector, was astonished to find, even then, what little respect the faculty had for what she'd been doing so well for so long. What she encountered was total disinterest. What one might have learned or accomplished in the real world was suspect and raised a question whether one was, or could become, a serious academic.†
Harvard's male students, taking their cues from the faculty, put down what women

---

* *Crimson*, May 29, 1974.
† Elizabeth Bartholet Oral History and June 2005 interview.

were teaching, what women students were interested in and the uses to which women saw the law being put. These issues weren't important.

Northeastern, by contrast, had as goals that women should constitute 50% of its student body and that social justice and activism – suspect areas of the law which had been of great interest to women in the previous twenty-five years – should be a focus of its legal training.

The 1950s and '60s were transitional decades for women. They had been brought up and socialized into caring kinds of work, whether at a paid job or at home. The paid jobs available to them before law and medicine opened up were people-oriented, caring kinds of work, e.g., social work, teaching, nursing, dental hygienist, etc. Women were less focused on themselves than they were on what they could do for others. When law opened up, their natural instinct was to gravitate toward those areas of the law, social justice and social change, that had a similar theme. Not only were these fields intellectually challenging but they provided a path for ambitious women to become power players. It was not until some years had passed that they began thinking of legal practice in terms of public office, private practice, money and other kinds of personal ambition.

Even at Northeastern the appointment of the first woman to become a full-fledged member of the regular faculty hadn't been an easy process. During Diane's appointment process, there had been uproars within the faculty which had to be quelled. At issue was not only the idea of hiring a woman, but of hiring her under a flex-time schedule no other member of the faculty enjoyed. The objections had been overcome and the position had been offered on a two-thirds-time basis – a unique opportunity in regular law-school faculty circles. This schedule allowed her to divide her time between professional obligations and family. She wouldn't have accepted otherwise.[2]

She began teaching in December 1971 for the winter quarter and found that Northeastern suited her. She enjoyed the teaching, not least because of the interplay Northeastern encouraged between faculty and students. Its faculty was small and the law school already had a high proportion of women students – 40% – most of them drawn to the school by its dedication to social justice and activism – and all of them enthused by the opportunity to engage intellectually with a charismatic teacher from their own sex.

It was, Diane said, a "propitious time" for her to appear at Northeastern.* She had three courses to teach. For two of them, Constitutional Law and Gratuitous Transfers, she used standard texts. For her course on Women's Law she developed her own – something unheard-of for a novice teacher. She enjoyed the freedom given her, and the fact that Northeastern provided a very different education than Harvard, one that did not glorify competition and the adversary system, but rather explored "ways of

---

* HLR, April 13, 1973.

changing things rather than preserving the status quo."

Cooperative approaches to the law and its uses were attractive to many women. Northeastern's students responded to Diane and to her approach toward the study and uses of law. (There was rigor to her teaching, but infused with the rigor was a strong sense of "fairness." Diane taught that they should strive for the "right" result. She had a "gentle persuasiveness" in guiding students toward the right result that resonated immediately with them.*)

Consequently, Harvard's overtures in January 1972 didn't present an easy decision. Far from it. We had managed a reasonable balance between the competing demands of family and profession. She'd always concerned herself with the twists and turns of my career, was enormously supportive of me, especially during this important period, and tried to accommodate its demands on my time. Northeastern's low-key approach – both professionally and socially – made it seem likely we could keep that balance. Harvard's demands would be something else entirely. She knew it, and she agonized.

We talked at length about the effect accepting Harvard's offer would have on us and our family. Diane was our linchpin, the one who organized our family's life. The rest of us helped with setting the table and cleaning-up, but Diane prepared dinner. I could boil potatoes, steam vegetables, boil and fry and scramble eggs and run a vacuum cleaner. With some guidance, perhaps, I could make more complicated meals. Ben was almost eleven and we wanted our kids to learn to cook. This would be a good time to start. I would learn to cook, then so would Ben, and then Ted and Kristin, in their turn.

We were fortunate to have living close by a family with five daughters, the oldest a senior in high school, all pleased by an opportunity to earn money sitting our kids on afternoons when neither Diane nor I could be home. During the next four years, we made our way down the ranks of the three eldest daughters. And Ben on occasion – not to his siblings' delight – would assume a supervisory role.

Our month on the island in August would continue to be sacrosanct. That was Diane's sanctuary as well as mine, our time with each other and with our children, when we could reflect and recharge our batteries. She needed that time and she'd have it, but not without the press of work.

She had two lengthy meetings in Cambridge with Sacks and members of the faculty appointments committee, meetings in which she expressed her misgivings and – typically – questioned her own qualifications to teach at Harvard. Sacks assured her that Harvard had no misgivings or reservations. It had sent observers to her classes and they'd come back with positive reports.

She raised issues concerning her family responsibilities and her public interest activities, and bargained for a less-than-full-time appointment: she would only be

---

*   Margot Botsford interview, March 2008.

willing to consider teaching at Harvard if she were working on a part-time basis. No one – certainly not someone interviewing for an assistant professor's tenure track position – had ever made such a request of Harvard. Sacks and his committee were taken aback. They would have to get back to her. That evening she said – hopefully, I thought – that Harvard would likely conclude it wasn't willing to consider such an arrangement. Then she'd have no decision to make. That would be a relief.

She was wrong. In their next meeting, Sacks said Harvard would extend its offer on a two-thirds-time basis, the same arrangement she had at Northeastern. He impressed on her not just the magnitude of the honor Harvard proposed to bestow but the importance of her decision to Harvard, to its women and to women law students and teachers to come. She was offered a four-year contract. The opportunity she would have to influence matters affecting women at Harvard and beyond was extraordinary. Her decision, she concluded, involved much more than its effect on her alone or on our family. The question wasn't simply could she manage it. The answer to that question was "of course."

In the end, Diane concluded she couldn't turn Harvard down. Her friends and colleagues treated the opportunity as a matter of great moment for women and for the feminist movement. What she might accomplish could influence the future for many women besides herself, could change both the way in which law was taught and its subject matter, and, not least, could garner support for the Equal Rights Amendment.

It was hard for us, in the middle of it, to get that kind of global perspective. Given her druthers, Diane would have preferred that nothing be made of the significance of her decision, but that wasn't what was happening. Perhaps she would have accepted Harvard even without its implications for women and for reform of the law-school educational system, but the latter was the basis for her decision. Soon afterwards, she called Sacks, who said he was delighted.

Official confirmation came from the President and Fellows of Harvard College on March 13, 1972, in a curious letter advising her of a one-year appointment. This wasn't the agreement. Sacks assured her a mistake had been made and the mistake would be rectified. On May 8, 1972, the President and Fellows sent a second letter:

> I beg to inform you that at a meeting of the President and Fellows held May 1, 1972, you were appointed Assistant Professor of Law, to serve for four years from July 1, 1972, subject to the Statutes of the University and the rules concerning retirement, and that consent to the appointment was duly given by the Board of Overseers at their meeting of May 8, 1972.

In the interim, Harvard had done what it could to mend fences with the Women's Law Association. Its first step was to announce in late January 1972 that Elisabeth

Owens would become its first tenured woman professor.* Two months later, it announced the following:

> Mrs. Diane V. T. Lund '61, assistant professor of law at Northeastern University has been appointed assistant professor of law at HLS…. Elisabeth A. Owens will become professor of law…. Ms. Owens is the first woman to hold a tenured position at the Law School; Mrs. Lund is the second woman to hold a regular faculty appointment. Mrs. Lund, a 1958 graduate of Stanford, will teach Trusts and a course on the legal status of women.†

The WLA, meanwhile, had presented Sacks with a petition signed by 80% of the women enrolled in the law school calling for increased enrollment of women. Sacks met with the WLA and agreed "in principle" to hire a woman administrator who would participate in the admissions process and to the "future placement" of a woman faculty member on the Admissions Committee. Diane, still four months away from beginning her employment at Harvard, would be asked to take on the latter role.

On March 30, 1972, her unusual two-thirds-time status was noted in the *Record*, as Harvard congratulated itself on its flexibility in meeting women's needs:

Second Woman Prof Will Work Part-Time

> Harvard Law School's second woman professor will become the first person to be accorded professorial rank for less than full-time work. Diane V.T. Lund '61, recently named assistant professor, will work on a two-thirds-time basis in order to allow time for family responsibilities, according to Dean Albert M. Sacks. He said the appointment was arranged in this manner at Lund's request.

The appointment was formally announced in the Harvard Law School Bulletin in April:

> Diane Lund will become Assistant Professor of Law in July 1972. She will be the second woman to receive a tenured faculty appointment at HLS. Ms. Lund presently is an Associate Professor at Northeastern University where she is teaching courses on women's law and Constitutional issues concerned with

---

* HLR, January 28, 1972. In her oral history, however, Owens acknowledged that her tenured appointment was a reward for her years of faithful service at a time when the law school's administration – if not its faculty – was actively seeking women for its faculty and had failed with Ruth Ginsburg. She never attended faculty meetings.
† HLR, March 17, 1972.

the First Amendment. At Harvard she will teach Trusts and in the spring a new course, The Legal Status of Women. While at HLS, she was invited to join the *Law Review* but declined the honor. She received the LL.B. degree *magna cum laude* in 1961 and was 13th in her class.

On April 25, at Sacks' request, she attended a faculty-overseers dinner where Sacks made the rounds before dinner to introduce her. One member of the faculty asked her, archly, how it felt to be stepping into Austin Scott's shoes and teaching his Trusts course. (Scott, a law-school icon, still maintained an office at the school.) The remark was not intended kindly. Smiling, Diane deflected the question and said she had seen nothing about foot size in her appointment letter – had she missed something? He had no choice but to smile himself, and they went on to other topics.

How Scott's course would be taught had already been the subject of conversation between Sacks and Diane. He'd asked her what text she intended to use, and held his breath until she said she'd be teaching from Scott's book (though a year later it would be a different story).

On meeting her before dinner, another member of the faculty, Professor Mansfield, assumed Diane was a law student and was stupefied to learn that she was about to become his colleague. Sacks was embarrassed and Diane was bemused as she looked at Mansfield over the top of her horn-rimmed glasses and gently corrected him. Mansfield, with nothing more to say, wandered away.

There were other conversations, some friendly, some awkward, but most of the men made little or no effort to come by, or even to acknowledge her presence. She could, perhaps, have remained at Sacks' side, but that would have been demeaning. She intruded, sometimes successfully, sometimes not, into the male clusters of the cocktail hour. Apart from the waitresses, she was the only woman in the room, and she had never felt more alone.

When she was introduced at the dinner itself, there was polite applause, but the applause covered palpable tension, if not hostility. Animosity – or even taking offense – was never a part of Diane's personality, but she wouldn't forget – and would often re-tell – how she'd been received at the first Harvard event she attended.

Northeastern had accepted her decision with good grace, not least because of the impact she had made in her short time there. She'd been so well accepted by both faculty and students that barriers to women had been broken down permanently. Northeastern hired two women to start teaching the next fall, and the arguments raised against Diane's appointment were not raised against the newcomers.

Her life during the spring quarter at Northeastern had a normalcy to it that she would not see again for four years. She was able to be both a teacher and a mom, and to delight in her children. "[C]ircumstances," she wrote to Meryl, "have made it imperative that Kristin in her first year of organized activity should be both a Bluebird and a Brownie. I've become a specialist in uniform management and an expert in sorting out wishes, promises and similar ritualistic forms. My ultimate challenge lies ahead. In this somewhat remote outpost of the heartland of America we faithfully celebrate Patriot's Day with an early-morning parade of all the children's groups in town, each child marching proudly with his or her own group … Brownies in a cluster … Bluebirds in a cluster …" and so on.

And in another letter: "Kristin's after school hours are filled with dancing, piano and engaging in an all-girl neighborhood game called World War One. I haven't inquired into the mechanics of this one at all; I sense that my feminist bent and my pacifist leanings may come into conflict.… Ben's cousin Scott has interested him in chess, so much so that he spent his lawn-mowing earnings on his own chess set.… He's beaten Erik twice in their regular matches (so far).…"

We spent as much of the summer as we could – weekends and the month of August – on the island doing those things we'd always done. "Ben has became an advanced swimmer," Diane wrote. "Teddy's had a magnificent fishing season, catching both a two-pound pickerel and a two-and-a-half-pound bass. He even complied with our rule that those of us who catch fish eat fish, but this policy may dampen his fishing spirit.… I bought a license and have had some luck too – but I'm not sure I'm going to master the art of hitting them over the head."

"Some luck" was an understatement. Diane had caught the largest bass that summer that any Lund had caught in all our summers. It was 6:20 a.m., and she was casting a surface lure from her seat in the bow of our canoe when the water erupted as a 4 ½-pound large-mouth took the plug and leaped in the air. She set the hook (I hesitate to say) manfully as the rod doubled over and the bass dove. Diane resisted, putting tension on the line, and urged the fish up to the surface little by little. When the bass tired, Diane brought it over to my net, I lifted it on board and hit it over the head.* She came ashore wearing a pleased

Showing off the big bass.

smile. It wasn't so much that she'd bested the Lund men as it was that she'd caught this magnificent fish on her own. The event could have been a metaphor for what was to come.

It would be a long time before we'd have that kind of summer again, but it was still a different kind of summer than we'd had before. Diane spent much of her time developing

---

* This was well before the days of catch-and-release and we weren't concerned about the later-discovered mercury contamination of freshwater fish in Maine.

her teaching plans and materials, not only for Trusts, but for her spring course, "Women and the Law: the Legal Status of Women," a course for which there was no prescribed text but the material she herself developed. There was no extant legal treatise on the subject (or none that she considered adequate) and the course would be taught at Harvard for the first time. She didn't intend to leave its preparation to the end of the fall.

While she had no illusions that life and a career at Harvard would resemble in any way her experience at Northeastern, she was naïve concerning the extent of Harvard's demands on her. She predicted there would be nights when she couldn't get home for dinner and late nights working at home, even when she did. But she didn't envision how Harvard's non-teaching demands would eat up the time she had expected to spend with family, and that her flex-time arrangement would fail to permit her to live a balanced life. The juggling act would become difficult, and ultimately impossible.

Pioneering women of the time were intent on demonstrating they could do anything a man could do, but the pool of experienced and accomplished professional women was small, and corporations and institutions under pressure to demonstrate fairness toward women asked them to do too much in a representative capacity. Those in the pool felt an obligation to other women to respond to the demands made of them in order to set examples of accomplishment. Individually they took on burdens which today would be viewed as unthinkable for any one person.

Diane's experience at Harvard became a case in point. The theory of a two-thirds schedule proved ironic* and, like Ruth Ginsburg, she stretched herself thin by continuing on with what she viewed as her public responsibilities. As a member of the Lawyers Committee on Civil Rights, she worked to see to it that the Bail Reform Act became effective. Together with Regie she crisscrossed the state to meet with local school committees in support of Chapter 622, and proposed to the Department of Education regulations to implement it. And she served on the Massachusetts Advisory Council on Vocational-Technical Education, a key governmental body for its implementation in the trades. Already elected to the Lexington Town Meeting, she continued serving through several reelections. As coordinator, she headed and oversaw the work of the Citizen's Committee for the Lexington Public Schools. She was a board member of the League of Women Voters and the co-chair of the League's Education Workshop.

And she still insisted on taking responsibility for home and family, just as her mother had done. She wouldn't consider (even if she could have afforded it) hiring someone to

---

* A male partner in one of Boston's major law firms put flex-time succinctly and correctly in context when one of Diane's students, who'd followed a similar flex-time career, decided to leave the firm to accept a judicial appointment. "What a good deal flex-time was for the firm," he said, reminiscing about her career there. "We had a superb full-time lawyer at two-thirds pay!" That was the reality. (Fernande Duffly interview, March 23, 2005.)

do household work. That smacked too much of having a servant, a concept with which she was not comfortable.

Taking Office at Harvard

Diane's office was in the ground-floor stacks of the law school library in Langdell Hall (where many of the less-frequently used volumes were stored). It was a tiny room compared to some adjoining faculty offices (one of which belonged to Austin Scott), but there were other tiny offices. Her shelves soon filled with materials from which she would develop her courses, leaving a few vacant spots for the occasional green plant that required watering. She was on her own. No one on the faculty felt that the first woman hired as an assistant professor, someone who had just entered the teaching profession, could use

In her office at Harvard Law.

any guidance, assistance or advice in preparing to teach Austin Scott's course to the first-year law-school class. None was offered, nor did she ask for any. Sacks, however, regularly took time from his busy schedule to come by.

Although Diane had agreed to use Scott's book to teach Trusts in the fall, she viewed the traditional teaching of the course – focused on legal principles, estate planning, trustees' investment and fiduciary obligations and drafting legal documents – to be too narrow, particularly given the views she'd developed concerning lawyers' obligations to serve the public good. She thought, to put it bluntly, that the course as previously taught was obsolete, an artifact of an earlier era. Her description in the 1972-73 catalogue reflected her intention to concentrate on broader duties lawyers and fiduciaries owe in other contexts: "An examination of the principles which govern the responsibilities of a fiduciary and the rights of a beneficiary in the context of a trust arrangement *will be followed* by an inquiry into the extent to which these principles are transferable to relationships which are similar in nature but dissimilar in origin, with emphasis on those which arise in the public sector." Fair warning.

Diane approached her first Harvard class with trepidation, and was buoyed at the end of the week by the reception from her students. They were engaged, they liked her, and they responded to her teaching techniques. She herself responded to the intellectual challenge of an elite law-school class. This could work out.

On September 15, 1972, she attended her first faculty meeting. There the reception was more restrained. Her presence was not deemed important. The following week she invaded the previously all-male Faculty Club for lunch. She wasn't warmly welcomed there, either. After that, more often than not (generally unless a point of it needed to be made), her lunch would be a sandwich brought to work in a brown bag. Given the various tasks Sacks would ask her to undertake, it was probably just as well. She would have little time for the leisurely and companionable lunch enjoyed by the men, even if that prospect had presented itself.

Soon after she had taught her first Trusts class, Sacks stopped in to ask her to serve on the Admissions Committee. In that capacity, he told her privately, causing change in admissions policy would fall to her. (It was something he wouldn't acknowledge publicly.) She accepted immediately, confident of the impact she would have. The appointment was announced at the end of September:

Admissions Group Adds Woman Prof *

> Assistant Professor Diane Lund has been appointed to the Admissions Committee as the result of a request made last spring by the Women's Law Association…. Asked to comment on Lund's appointment, Sacks said that "each member of the committee brings individual judgment" and that he did not foresee any significant change in admissions policy as a result of the appointment.

Sacks' public comments notwithstanding, she took her appointment as a directive to advocate the admission of qualified women, and she did exactly that. To gain their admittance she had to demonstrate that women applicants were not only equal, but superior to the male candidates with whom they were competing. This task required a detailed examination of competing applications and skilled advocacy without bias. She reviewed applications at Harvard during the day and at home, night after night, making detailed notes of the qualifications and records of the applicants. Her advocacy occurred in afternoon and evening committee meetings. Her preparation for the meetings, she said, was akin to preparing to argue her clients' cases in court.

Apart from advocating for individual applicants, there were broader admissions issues that needed to be addressed. The law school had long had relationships and tacit understandings with favored men's colleges, such as Bowdoin, Williams, Wesleyan and Amherst, to the effect that a certain number of slots in each year's class would be held for their graduates. No such relationships or understandings existed with women's colleges such as Smith, Wellesley, Vassar or Mount Holyoke. Diane found it

---

*   HLR, October 6, 1972.

a Sisyphean task to persuade her male colleagues on the committee it was time to abandon this anachronistic approach.

But persuade she did. Not only were these understandings unfair to women, she said, they were unfair to men and contrary to Harvard's being a national law school. Each applicant should be considered on his or her merits, without regard to their college or university. Ultimately the principle was adopted, even if its practice was somewhat uneven.

Her two-thirds-time position quickly became not only full-time, but more than that. Her work on the committee took up all her spare time that fall after preparing for and teaching class. When she arrived home to meet her children after school, she had a briefcase bulging with applications. The same scenario would be repeated in each of the next three years.

Diane took on other responsibilities as well. Professor Clark Byse,* for many years chair of the Appointments Committee, had her appointed immediately to his committee, one of whose objectives was to identify and seek out women to be offered faculty positions. That portion of the committee's charge, while not as time-consuming as admissions– largely because there was only a small pool to draw from – was a daunting one because persuading the faculty to approve the appointment of a woman was even more

There were thirty-eight women in the graduating class of 1973. The class of 1976, the first on which Diane had any influence, had ninety-four women. The class of 1977 included 116 women, three times the number in the class of 1973. There were 118 women in the class of 1978 (twenty more had been admitted and had declined). Of the 211 women offered admission to the class of 1979, 138 accepted. The dam had been breached. *

---

* Assistant Dean and Director of Admissions Patricia Lydon, who had joined Harvard's administration in September 1975, denied there was any "conscious effort" on the part of the Admissions Committee to increase the number of women at Harvard. Rather, she attributed the increase to the substantially higher number of women applying. "Statistics," she said, "reveal a small but steady increase...." (HLR, December 3, 1976.)

difficult than the obstacles confronting women in the admissions process. Byse once recommended the appointment of a woman who had clerked on the U.S. Supreme Court for Justice Thurgood Marshall. Professor Charles Fried inquired whether she was "a super-hot prospect," to which Byse responded that he regarded her as very able. Fried then asked "if we wouldn't do better, later." That was the end of her candidacy.†

It was unprecedented for a first-year assistant professor to be appointed to either the Admissions Committee or the Appointments Committee, much less both.

---

* The intimidating professor depicted in "The Paper Chase."
† Clark Byse interview, July 12, 2004.

Each assignment, by itself, was formidable. Having to do both presented an almost intolerable burden for anyone.*   That was the nub of the dilemma confronted by the woman who was the guinea pig – she was expected to represent women's perspectives in all of the institutional contexts in which those perspectives were important. Not to accept meant woman's voice wouldn't be heard at all, and that result, for Diane, was unthinkable.

She wasn't free from other demands either. One came from N.O.W. There then existed in Massachusetts a voluntary statutory exemption from jury duty for women who chose not to serve if they had children under the age of sixteen. Lexington treated the voluntary exemption as mandatory, so that only one percent of the Lexington jury lists were women. N.O.W. enlisted Diane in the fall of 1972 to challenge this practice. She interviewed women who agreed to be representative plaintiffs, drafted a complaint and brought suit in the U.S. District Court in Boston. Faced with an injunction, the State conceded and stipulated that the practice would be abandoned wherever it existed. Lexington itself agreed to use a randomized computer jury selection process.

There were demands from me, as well. I'd taken up the cause of low- and moderate-income subsidized housing as chairman of the Lexington Planning Board, and then as head of the Lexington Interfaith Corporation. Delighted that I was working pro bono on the side of poor people, Diane was not only supportive but worked on strategy with me and helped research and frame the legal issues.

She was on the go, often out several nights a week, either at Harvard or at meetings in Lexington or other communities, and occasionally at out-of-town conferences. Her most difficult task was to prepare materials and a lesson plan for her spring course on the legal status of women. She was writing her own textbook while she prepared to teach the course.

Then there were Harvard's social obligations, a ritual for any new assistant professor (or visiting professor), a seemingly unending round of faculty cocktail parties and dinners. Every two weeks, we went to another. Fortunately Diane hadn't lost her social butterfly skills, but it was hard work to have to carry on intellectual conversations with male colleagues whose primary focus was on life and in-fighting at Harvard.

"Erik and I are both fatigued by the effort of keeping up," Diane wrote. "He as the faculty spouse may have the harder job since he doesn't appear inclined to give the internal affairs of Harvard (the primary topic of male conversation) their appropriate amount of importance and he's shy about his own good works (which, if revealed, would make him a winner among the females). [3] As for me, I'm learning that token women must be highly visible, i.e., they must serve on committees. But teaching is fun and students are very nice people."

---

*   Frank Michelman interview, March 22, 2005; Elizabeth Bartholet interview, June 29, 2005.

A male spouse of a faculty member was a novelty, if not an oddity. Chief Judge Andrew Caffrey of the U.S. District Court in Massachusetts, in whose court I'd often appeared, was an invited guest at one event. We knew each other well. He asked – since I had no obvious connection – how it was I was attending a Harvard function. I said I was there as a spouse. Caffrey, a plain-spoken man and an excellent judge, but an unreconstructed Neanderthal, was stunned at the thought.

Neither Diane's hiring nor her appointment to the Admissions Committee mollified the WLA, which wanted concrete evidence of changes in admissions policy and hiring practices, changes which were not yet evident. Late that fall the WLA filed a formal complaint with HEW:

> Dear Mr. Pottinger [HEW's Director]:
>
> We are writing to file with you a formal complaint individually and on behalf of all women students currently enrolled at Harvard Law School and on behalf of all present and future applicants and admittees to the Law School.
>
> We charge Harvard Law School with the following discriminatory practices, unlawful under Title IX of the Civil Rights Act of 1964:
>
> I. Admissions Policy: Harvard Law School weights the grades of the applicant according to the past performances at the Law School of graduates of the applicant's undergraduate college. In light of the fact that Harvard Law School did not admit women as students until 1951, and thereafter admitted only a tiny number to each class, the present admissions process carries forward the discrimination of the past. In particular, it perpetuates bias against colleges which women attend in large numbers.
>
> II. Recruitment: Harvard Law School does not, indeed has not recruited male and female applicants in comparable manner over time. Harvard continues to accrue benefits from past recruiting relationships with predominantly and all-male undergraduate institutions that have fed their male graduates into the Law School for the past century. It has failed to establish similar relationships with women at all-female colleges or with women at the predominantly male colleges. Among the discriminatory practices to which we refer are the use of male Harvard Law graduates as advisors to pre-law societies at the predominantly male colleges and recruitment efforts by Harvard Clubs, some of which still exclude female graduates from their membership.
>
> III. Discriminatory Faculty Hiring: Faculty hiring at Harvard Law School is done on the basis of the "old boy network." Reviewing the results, it is apparent

that Harvard hires its own graduates. Thus given the exclusion of women as students until 1951, and the extremely small numbers of women admitted thereafter, the perpetuation of this hiring practice has led to the near exclusion of women from the Harvard Law School faculty. We should note, in addition, that the admissions committee has been and is comprised of faculty members hired pursuant to this policy.

IV. Discriminatory Administrative Hiring: In violation of Executive Order 11246 as well as of Title IX, Harvard Law School has virtually excluded women from positions of responsibility in its administration.

We request that you act according to your mandate to enforce the Civil Rights Act of 1964 and investigate the charges which we have outlined above. We request as well any further action necessary to eliminate these discriminatory practices.

Sincerely,
Rosalind Avnet Lazarus
Alice Walker Ballard
of the Women's Law Association

While Sacks responded that the charge of male bias was "groundless,"* the complaints were well-founded, as were complaints of sexist attitudes in other contexts.† Harvard was slow to address them, but Diane would do so in her spring course, "Women and the Law."

Her description of the course illustrates and reflects in practical terms the concerns and issues with which women were dealing, and did so for the first time in a Harvard academic setting:

An examination of laws which reflect the premise that women as a class occupy an inferior or dependent position in our society, laws which classify persons according to sex rather than by reference to functions or physical capabilities and practices which proceed from the assumptions underlying these laws. The extent to which changes in those laws and practices should be made and the extent to which they can be made, either through judicial or legislative action, will be explored. Close scrutiny will be given to the operation of those remedial statutes which already exist, with particular attention paid to those which pertain to

---

* HLR, January 26, 1973.

† Such as juvenile sexist graffiti on the walls of the elevator in Langdell Hall and the length of time it stayed there before being removed. The elevator had painted metal walls, something that could easily be incised with a ball point pen. Typical graffiti read that "the best pussy in Harvard Law School is [followed by names of women students]." No one bothered to paint it over. It was embarrassing and frustrating. (Alice Ballard interview, April 7, 2005.)

employment and educational opportunities. Questions relating to the methods of implementing changes in laws and the effect of such changes upon the sources of sex-linked distinctions will be fully considered.

The practical side of these issues would also be addressed:

> Participation in a course-related project will be required. It may be a research paper, a proposal for specific legislative or executive action or materials prepared for litigation.

The description embodied what the WLA had been fighting for and what women wanted and needed to have taught in a formal course setting in a prestigious law school. This course, like the big bass she'd caught, was reeled in on her own despite faculty antipathy and tacit opposition. It was original, innovative and successful. On her last day of class, she received a standing ovation – and a potted plant. While it was customary to applaud a professor at the end of the year, she was the first to receive a potted plant. She was touched, placed it in her office and watered it faithfully.

Dean Sacks followed her progress and her other contributions closely. He wrote her "to express my appreciation for all you have done to help the School function this year. I am most grateful."

He and Harvard still had a long road to travel so far as its women were concerned. Three months after he had appointed Jeanne Kettleson Assistant Dean and Director of Administration for the Clinical Program in the winter of 1973, the following editorial appeared in the *Harvard Law Record*:

Women and HLS*

> The quiet that has settled over the Law School since the filing of a sex discrimination complaint with HEW by two members of the WLA in December should not be interpreted as signaling the end of the Law School's crisis over the increased admission and representation of women. In truth that crisis is growing and will continue to grow until important changes occur. And the Harvard Law School administration has not yet begun even to perceive what those changes will mean to legal education at Harvard.
>
> The status of women at the Law School today is still little more than that of unwanted stepchildren. The sense of alienation they continually feel in the predominantly male atmosphere throughout the Law School is pervasive – and more oppressive for the fact that most men here are not even aware of it.

---

* HLR, April 13, 1973.

Members of the Women's Law Association.

Diane brought to the table something important: women identified with her, she confirmed the legitimacy of their views concerning women's abilities and their societal objectives, and she personified who it was they themselves hoped to become. When she was appointed to the faculty it felt like a miracle to them.

"She changed the feel of the place."* She was from the real world and had been in the trenches, someone who'd had the gritty experience of fighting meaningful feminist battles. "We saw we could *be* like her," said Ballard in describing Diane's impact on the Women's Law Association. "She was an inspiration. *We* could do what *she* had done! She'd had real clients. She was an activist. She was accessible. She showed us the kind of life we wanted to lead was possible. She had different priorities than those the law school put in front of us. She made us legitimate." And she was a genuine friend to activists at the law school. "Having a friend there was important," Ballard concluded.

In April, Ted, then ten years old, appeared as Richard Henry Lee in his elementary school's production of the musical *1776*. He rode off for the afternoon performance on his bicycle, in Continental costume and white-powdered wig. Both of us were home in time to see him off and go to the performance. For Diane, this was one of the signal events of the year, at least as important as anything else that had happened. Ted's tenor voice, a little hesitant at first, but then resolute, soared through the auditorium on his solo. She couldn't have been more happy than to be in that time and place at that moment and to share it with him, and with me.

Ballard and Lazarus, meanwhile, did not let up on the administration: they carried the WLA's discontent forward into the law school's yearbook:

> To write this article we have drawn upon personal observations made during three years of study at the Law School and work outside. We still feel like strangers at the school....
>
> We do not charge Harvard Law School for any direct responsibility for the ways other institutions such as Harvard College and the Rhodes Scholarship Foundation preclude or limit opportunities for women. But in its refusal to make a more substantive value decision in favor of more women at the Law School,

---

* Alice Ballard interview, April 7, 2005.

Harvard builds these past and present discriminations into its own admission process. Its passivity in failing to remedy the damage which others have done is exactly the substantive choice inherent in any formalistic system. It is a decision in favor of the status quo, however ugly that may be....

Our three years here are spent marking time until we can become part of the progress of the legal profession. Harvard barely participates in that movement and does so, if at all, because of student pressure. To refuse to act is not to remain neutral. It is to make a choice, to act in favor of maintaining the present situation. The sluggishness of this institution's responses has taught us what the classroom ignored – that where liberalism prevails, the status quo has the strongest defense of all.

The HLS faculty in 1973. Diane is just to the right of center, wearing a turtleneck sweater.

On the yearbook's inside front cover and back cover were photos of the faculty en masse. Diane looks out of place, a female face in a sea of male faces, but amused by the situation. Elisabeth Owens seems uncomfortable to be in the photo at all. In her personal bio under the yearbook's photo of "Diane Theis Lund, Assistant Professor," Diane poked sly fun at the formulaic bios used by her male colleagues. "Married 1960," she wrote, "to the former Erik Lund."*

That summer, Ben and Ted left us for a month in July to go to Birch Rock Camp in Maine, the first time they'd both been away (Ben was there the prior summer). Kristin went to day camp at MIT where – to Diane's discomfiture (but not dismay) – she became a sharpshooter in the .22 caliber rifle competition.

---

* Diane's photo appeared again later that year, in *Esquire Magazine's* June 26, 1973, issue, in a section entitled "300 Women Who Look Cute When They're Mad." She laughed when she saw it, and sent copies to friends.

We were all on the island in Maine in August, regrouping in different ways and in our different lives. It had been a draining first year at Harvard, and Diane was preparing for a year that would extend still further the boundaries of anything she'd ever done before. Others of us were coping with the fact that her life had become so completely absorbed by Harvard's demands.

TEACHER, ROLE MODEL AND INSPIRATION

The institutional attitude at Harvard, that the way to make it was to look like a man and act like a man, was not a good fit for women, both for obvious reasons and because, as a group, their approach toward problem-solving was less confrontational and more relational. How were they to know how to react and what to do in the context of such male-formulated institutional and professional expectations? Not only did the male professors provide no role models for women, they failed to recognize that women might approach issues differently.

A woman in the Trial Advocacy course challenged Professor (later U.S. District Court Judge) Robert Keeton on the fact that no women were involved in teaching the course. All the teachers were excellent lawyers, he replied, and had been brought to Harvard from all over the country. Why did it matter what sex they were? Her response was that he simply didn't understand the fact that a huge difference exists between the way in which men and women approach a problem and deal with it: watching a man in a three-piece suit demonstrate his bravado courtroom technique and style wasn't going to help her to develop techniques and style that would work for *her*.*

In the fall of 1973, there was one role model to help women deal with the law school's "in-your face-test-your-mettle" approach. Diane showed that women needn't be men and needn't feel they were "others." Her presence and teaching methods made it clear for the first time that fitting the mold was an option, not a necessity.

Here was a real human being who nonetheless was a member of the faculty, someone not aggressive but firm in her principles and views, and, besides, warm, compassionate and nurturing. She reached out to men and women alike, teaching them that they could succeed through collaboration, through addressing problems of society together rather than through confrontation.† In the Harvard context, her approach – that people should think, reason and work together to solve community issues – was revolutionary. While many of the issues she addressed were women's issues, the principles she taught had general application, and their appeal wasn't limited to women students. Men in her class were also influenced by her teaching.

Unlike many male faculty who were intentionally ambiguous about their own values,

---

*   Larry Field interview, June 23, 2005.
†   Within the WLA, she was occasionally referred to as "St. Diane."

Diane was clear about hers. They were community values with social implications that she made her students think about, focusing on the mundane problems faced by ordinary people. She taught that lawyers *should* think about those problems and that they had an obligation to *do* something about them, regardless of the career paths they would follow. While she was passionate on issues affecting women, she approached those issues objectively and analytically. The law, she posited, was an important tool that could be used to help ordinary people deal with unfairness and discrimination in their lives, issues which confronted not only working women, but many others.

In some respects, her first year at Harvard had been tentative, not knowing exactly what was expected of her, feeling her way. Now she was on firm footing, confident of the worth of her teaching, and now, in all the courses she taught and would teach – Women and the Law (The Changing Status of Women), Fiduciary Responsibilities, Employment Discrimination, Lawyers' Professional Responsibilities, and Family Law – she made her students understand that they were on the cutting edge and dealing with evolving areas of the law. She used real material, current material, not the dry contents of traditional law school textbooks. She brought to her classes xeroxed or mimeographed material on matters that were in process toward resolution in the real world. She used the Bail Reform Act and Chapter 622 as examples, debated with her students the rationale for the Equal Rights Amendment, and made them think about the underlying lack of fairness in statutes supposedly enacted to protect women, but used to discriminate against them, such as the jury selection process in the Lexington case she'd prosecuted, and in anachronistic common law concepts of real estate ownership.

Importantly, she introduced a clinical element into her courses, another rarity in the Harvard curriculum. While the first semester of her Women and the Law course was largely traditional and classroom-oriented, the second semester provided experiential opportunities through collaboration with the Massachusetts Commission Against Discrimination (one of whose commissioners was Regina Healy). The MCAD was over-worked and understaffed, overwhelmed by its caseload. Under Diane's supervision, and with Regie's help, student volunteers helped alleviate the burden by assuming actual caseloads, performing investigations and drafting fact-finding reports and recommendations. Sometimes a complaint would issue based on their work. Sometimes decisions would incorporate their

One former student recalls with glee that two of the more confident women in the class undertook personally to integrate a men's bar. Since bars were licensed, they couldn't discriminate in admitting their customers. The effort succeeded with the bar's owners, but didn't change the attitudes of their long-term male customers toward the women who'd invaded their domain. (Susan Lennox interview, May 25, 2005.)

recommendations. Their stints exposed them to civil rights issues in real life and enabled them to apply their legal training to those issues in ways which had real-life consequences. The opportunities were inspirational.

These experiences proved important for a number of reasons, including the fact that they exploded the myth underlying the law school's aggressive male adversarial approach.* Also, students who'd had no previous interest in family law as a career discovered the field was entirely different from what they had thought. Traditional legal concepts pertaining to the family were changing. The course put human relations into the context of societal change, and was not only interesting but contained so much information of current significance that they understood they were dealing with how a critical aspect of the law was being developed. One student was inspired to go on to a distinguished career as a family law practitioner and then as a judge, first in the Probate and Family Law Court and then in the Massachusetts Appeals Court. She wouldn't have gone into the field at all, had it not been for Diane. †

Another, who had worked in human resources for two years before coming to Harvard and came in wanting to be a civil rights lawyer, became fascinated by employment discrimination issues. Diane opened this woman's eyes to the evolution of these issues and the direction the law was headed, and made the field interesting and rewarding to pursue from many perspectives. Instead of a civil rights lawyer, she became a defense lawyer in the employment discrimination field. There, working on problem-solving with corporate executives, many of the community values and objectives important to her were achieved through counseling her own clients.‡ Diane supervised third-year papers on subjects ranging from sexual inequality in public school curriculums to real estate ownership by husband and wife as "tenants by the entirety," a ancient common law doctrine that discriminated against women.§ She introduced her student to a legislator prepared to sponsor remedial legislation, and worked with her to draft a bill which changed the common law and eliminated the possibility of seizure or sale by a creditor of one spouse so long as the property was the principal residence of the other.¶ She was an advocate for poor and disadvantaged people and didn't focus

---

* Later studies in professional adult education and training have shown there is very little factual support for the effectiveness of the approach. The way adults learn is experiential in a supportive environment. (Susan Lennox interview, May 25, 2005.)

† Fernande Duffly interview, March 23, 2005.

‡ While Diane made it clear to her students that they could – and should – make a significant societal contribution in their careers, exactly what they should do and how they should do it was up to the individual. (Susan Lennox interview, May 25, 2005.)

§ Under a tenancy by the entirety, spouses did not have equal rights in property held by them. The husband had the exclusive right to income, possession, and control of the property during his lifetime; the wife's rights were solely those of survivorship.

¶ Fernande Duffly interview, March 23, 2005.

exclusively on women's interests. Her teaching style was different, neither intimidating nor designed to showcase her own intellectual superiority. She encouraged her students to cooperate, both with her and with each other, in solving problems. One of her male students recalls her in the classroom "sitting on a battered desk, a slim and attractive woman with large horn-rimmed glasses, long hair in a ponytail, asking questions of us in a quiet and earnest way, but always with a twist of irony and bemusement."* Her style was a sea change from what students had experienced with their male professors. Some described her classes as the most intellectually stimulating and enjoyable they'd experienced at the law school, while others thought her style was not sufficiently challenging, not enough like the thrown-gauntlet approach of her male colleagues.†

Perched on her desk in the classroom, 1976.

One student described Diane as a "great teacher" who helped him survive Harvard. He found her Women and the Law course exciting, in part because of the ardent and talented feminists in the class, but more because she challenged existing assumptions in the law. Pointing out how oppressive the law was and could be, she led her students to challenge those assumptions themselves. An approach which refused to accept existing limitations in the law appealed to the imagination and opened her students' minds to new concepts and ways of thinking. She was, moreover, extraordinarily accessible to her students, and this didn't end with law-school graduation.‡

Another student had the unique experience, through mischance, of taking the Professional Responsibility course twice, once with a male professor and again with Diane. The former taught the course in traditional abstract and pedantic academic style, using the professional code and a casebook, and posing hypotheticals for class discussion. Diane used mimeographed materials and engaged in dialogues with the

---

* Larry Field interview, June 23, 2005.

† Student evaluations.

‡ Although one student's third-year paper – on the topic of sexism and the stereotyping of women in school textbooks – was written for another professor, he relied heavily on Diane's critiques to guide him through the project. Then, when he became a lawyer, she counseled him on both ethical and tactical issues. Years later, when he was sworn in as a judge, Diane, in the middle of her final illness, wrote a note apologizing for the fact that she couldn't attend but that she was enormously pleased and proud. (James Wexler interview, January 23, 2006.)

class using real-life contexts, with an emphasis on legal services problems one was likely to encounter in the field. The ethical issues came alive in her course in ways that weren't possible in the other class. She interested the class in the subject matter and worked her way through the ethical issues by building on what the students had to say.*

She quickly developed a loyal, devoted following. Early on, she had to head off a demonstration her students had planned on her behalf at the dean's office. Their impression was that her part-time appointment was the law school's doing, not her own, and that it was discriminatory. As they prepared to storm the dean's office and demand she be given a full-time appointment, Diane got wind of their plans in time to head off the demonstration, explaining that it was her doing, not the school's.

Diane kept and treasured a letter from a student to whom she'd written praising his work. He wrote:

> Your kind letter arrived today and I want you to know how honored I am to have received it. You have supervised my entire education in employment discrimination law, beginning with your course in my first year at this law school and finishing with my third-year paper.... [M]y single most rewarding intellectual endeavor since I came [to Harvard] was writing that paper under your guidance.
>
> As I suppose was obvious from my frequent appearances at your door, I especially enjoyed conversing with you on legal topics, even totally unrelated to the paper. You have a singular gift for instructing without a hint of demeaning, of letting a student discover rather than be intimidated. If I "sought opportunities to learn from others," as you kindly put it, that was simply because those "others" were exceptionally open persons who understood the art of teaching.

Teachers at every level need to establish authority to control their classes, and women in particular need to be strong and show confidence in their knowledge of the subject matter. Diane was treated with deference and respect. She was experienced, she knew her subject matter, she was not cowed by the aggression of male students. (She was, if anything, amused by it, which showed in the friendly ease with which she dealt with it.) She confidently developed her own style out of her own personality, and demonstrated that the ability to teach and to inspire was not sex-related, either in the teaching process or in the learning process. Importantly, she emanated good will, and her students understood that she was in utter good faith. Students were attracted to her because of who she was, her knowledge and experience, and how she taught. She knew how to engage her students and make them a part of the process of teaching.

Declining to emulate her male colleagues' teaching style (in the words of one of her

---

* Larry Field interview, June 23, 2005.

woman contemporaries, "Diane and I were not going to do that!"*) she never put down her students, male or female, but she made it clear who was in charge in her classroom. At least two-thirds of her students were male, and she was well-received by them. None questioned her credentials or her ability and all felt warmly toward her. Had she shown weakness or lack of confidence, Harvard's males might well have attacked her like piranhas. She was (to again quote her contemporary) "rock solid!"

Diane's importance as a role model and mentor for other women took many forms.

She was approachable and supportive and had an aura of competence and understanding about her. She opened intellectual doors for women. She made women feel welcome and she brought a very different perspective to the table than the other members of the faculty, in her persona, in her approach to teaching, in keeping her courses alive and current. And she was highly regarded in the broader feminist community.

A 1974 letter from Joan Dolan, Special Counsel to the Massachusetts Teachers Association, reflects her stature there:

> I've always felt that a person's success is best gauged by the girth of her files. In keeping with this basic philosophy of life, I'm sending you yet another piece of information which I hope will be used in the apparently endless battle against sex discrimination. Dammit, I'm going to flush me some good plaintiffs out or expend a hell of a lot of words and ink trying! Last batch I thought I had just faded away. Most discouraging.
>
> Seriously, though, as those awful stand-up comics say, I thought you might have some interest in this pamphlet. It's being mailed early next week to the 52,000 members of the MTA and I have high hopes that somebody will read it and be motivated to bring a sex discrimination case. Should you have the time and inclination to (1) read it and (2) comment on it, I would be very happy to have your thoughts. Caveat: the presses have stopped rolling and if there are any potentially fatal errors of law or fact in it, ain't a thing I can do about it.
>
> P.S. Last night, Margot [Botsford], Betty [Gittes], Barbara Burke, the Cathys – White and Farrell – and I had a most enjoyable dinner. One of the topics of conversation was the possibility of forming a women lawyers' group which would be a source of companionship, intellectual stimulation and ideas for constructive work on women's problems. In a few moments we came up with about 20 names of potential members.
>
> What think you? Margot's going to give you a call.
>
> As I write this, I'm realizing something which never occurred to me before. Among the trails you've blazed must be counted that of role model for a generation

---

*   Mary Ann Glendon interview, June 23, 2005.

of law students. We're all sitting last night talking about the idea of a group and we decide that the first step is to call Diane. She'll know if there is such a group, whether it's been tried, whether we should try to become attached to one of the bar associations, etc. Betty brought up the point that individually we seem to turn to you for advice rather frequently. We agreed that this was true and wondered if it became burdensome for you. You seem to handle so many different things so well, but everyone has a limit. The point is that we really don't mean to lay things on you in a way which leads to an unfair increase in your workload or a decrease in time available to meet your constituents. Your brief time at Northeastern has reaped you a harvest of eager neophytes who admire your personal, legal and political talents.

In short, we all appreciate the varied forms of assistance which you've given us. We hope you feel perfectly free to say no when you want to.

She never said no and she never acknowledged that her workload might have a limit. This was probably a personal failing, but it was also a reflection of the demands of the times on the few women who were in prominent positions and how they responded to other women looking for advice.

Joan Dolan was less than two years out of Northeastern law school when she wrote the letter and she, like many other young women lawyers, looked to Diane for reinforcement and confidence-building in what they were doing. Those were "very rocky times for young women wanting to be lawyers," says Dolan. "The sexism was almost overwhelming." Earlier, she had been told by the Association's general counsel that he would have hired a man, but for the demands of the Association's membership, 90% of which was female. ("I've had better welcomes to jobs," she says.)

She'd written the pamphlet on sex discrimination ("endemic in hiring, promotions and virtually every aspect of a teacher's working life") in response to the women teachers' urgent requests for guidance. Retaliation against anyone who complained was widespread and vicious, and the stories so hair-raising that persuading women to become plaintiffs and be identified was an almost impossible task.

Diane managed to deal with these issues, both personally and in advising others, with "magnanimity, calm and humor," qualities young women lawyers who knew her wanted to emulate. They had no hesitation in seeking her advice because of her "unfailing kindness, interest in others, generosity with her time and the way in which she treated everyone and their opinions with respect and interest," regardless of their difference in age and experience. They admired her for who she was and what she'd accomplished, but most important, perhaps, they felt comfortable with her.[*]

For women married while in law school or about to be married, she demonstrated by example and the way in which she went about her work that it was possible for a

---

[*] Joan Dolan interview, March 2008.

woman to achieve a balance between working at her profession and her family life. Her friends at home didn't think of her as a lawyer or a law professor. She was just a mom. That she could achieve both personal and professional objectives in the way she appeared to do was reinforcing to all the women law students and lawyers who knew her.

The reality for Diane, however, was different from the appearance. It was a lonely existence, and the stress of trying to perform all the roles she assumed took its toll on her. But she saw no need to share this with her students and friends.

Harvard faculty meetings were a special source of stress. The order of the day was elitism, and elitism translated in practical terms to sexism and racism. Diane, the only woman to attend faculty meetings, sat with Derek Bell, the only member of the faculty who was black. None of the white males in the room were interested in what either of them might have to say or what opinions they might offer. She and Bell usually spent much of the time in discussion with each other, but Diane didn't hesitate to speak up on issues where she had something to contribute – despite the infuriating reaction of no one looking in her direction and the meeting's moving along as if nothing had been said. She kept her fury to herself and participated as if she weren't being ignored.

Regardless of reality, Diane didn't accept sexist limitations on her role, or limitations on her own capacity to fulfill all that was asked of her, because what she was doing was important to women. However, actual limitations did exist. They were both physical and psychological, and came into play as the 1973-74 academic year proceeded. Her failure to accept them and to impose limitations on the activities she undertook would have consequences.

The 1973-74 catalogue wasn't an accurate gauge of what her teaching workload would be because it only listed two courses, one in the fall and one in the spring. The fall course, "Women and the Law: The Changing Status of Women," made no mention of its (optional) accompanying clinical course in the spring. It was not a repeat of the prior year. Rather it was "intended to introduce students to the methodology of legal problem-solving in the area of social change and to do so in the specific context of changes affecting women." The course dealt with the premises underlying sex discrimination (which had once justified protective legislation), e.g., that women are weaker and have reproductive potential, and how the "structure of our society, with the nuclear family as the basic unit, affects the status of women, what changes are occurring, whether others are necessary, and optional modes of initiating them."

In the spring Trusts course, she abandoned Scott's textbook and moved on to contemporary issues. It was no longer a course in "Trusts" but rather a course in "Fiduciary Responsibilities" – "a study of the accountability of persons and institutions which administer property for the benefit of others or act on behalf of others in contexts in which there is an interest on the part of the state in the performance of the fiduciary." This was the forerunner of the professional responsibilities course she would originate and teach at the law school during the following decade, a course that became a requirement of all law-school curriculums.

Her shift in emphasis was no doubt observed, and no doubt accepted. It represented a major shift in Harvard's teaching concerning lawyers' responsibilities.

Hers was a full teaching load, not one diminished for a part-timer. Nevertheless, Dean Sacks asked her to fill in for an absent professor and teach still another class in the spring, a section of Family Law. She'd have to teach three classes that spring, even though Harvard had no budget money to compensate her for the extra workload. Sacks said he would add 50% of her salary into the following year's budget as a "research stipend," but her two-thirds-time contract for her second year had become a fiction. She carried a full teaching load in the 1973-74 school year, in addition to her work on the Admissions and Appointments Committees, and her public commitments.

None of the three courses had standard texts. She prepared and circulated the written materials to be used in all three. In effect she was inventing three new courses at the law school simultaneously. No one on the faculty before or since had undertaken such a challenging task.

The winter and spring of 1974 was the most difficult period she had ever encountered personally, and the hardest on our family and our own relationship. She was carrying an enormous teaching load and had little time or energy left over for anything else. *
On the positive side, our children took a tremendously helpful attitude, and between us, we did what had to be done at home. Ben, at twelve, was particularly diligent and responsible. Diane needed every bit of support she could get.

Further complicating matters, Governor Sargent, running for reelection, asked if I would serve as counsel to his campaign finance committee. With Diane's approval, I said I would. It wasn't a good decision.

At this point, our summer respite seemed a long way away.

Things looked cheerier on a Saturday in late April when Diane returned from an early morning shopping expedition transporting delicate green sprouting plants in flats in the back of our station wagon. Spring was here, the sun was shining and we spent a good part of the day clearing last year's weeds from our raised garden beds, preparing the soil and planting the sprouts of flowers and vegetables, the radishes, tomatoes, cucumbers, lettuce and basil we'd harvest throughout the summer.

In mid-May she taught her last class. She was exhausted, totally spent – but she would rise to the occasion when her parents arrived for a long visit in June:

---

* I was concerned "because of the tremendous number of personal problems, pressures and decisions which Diane and I have to confront on almost a daily basis....Our attempts to cope and still to lead a balanced life vis-a-vis our kids and ourselves have led us to an inward-oriented life. Our outside contacts are business, political and professional. Our social life is ourselves."

> You may not have noticed the wonderful effect your visit had on Diane [I
> wrote at the beginning of July] because you didn't see what a difficult time she
> had this past winter. Her spirit lifted when you came. She was able to free her
> mind from the sheer burden of work and worry about the future and devote
> time to the things she really liked and wanted to do with you. That feeling has
> carried over – her battery's been recharged.

Their visit was a wonderful tonic, and the tonic seemed to carry over for the summer. We tried to do new things, exciting and interesting things that would give her an early respite from the demands of the coming fall.

We went bicycling on Nantucket in July, just for fun. The history of Nantucket appealed to Diane. It had started out a religious refuge for persecuted people and was for over a hundred years dominated by Quakers before it turned to profitable pursuits such as sheep-raising and whaling. The sheep ate up the sparse vegetation, so the island had to get rid of the sheep and concentrate on whaling, an industry in which it took the national lead. Then a large section of Nantucket burned down, a sandbar closed the harbor to large ships, and whale oil became obsolete when oil was discovered seeping out of the ground in Pennsylvania. Yet the island survived until, eventually, off-island summer people became its principal stock in trade.

Its history was a metaphor for survival and renewal, not unlike what Diane was facing.

We had another adventure in August. In the spring freshet, the earthen dam in Augusta had been breached and the Kennebec River – on which Benedict Arnold

One of our excursions on Nantucket threatened the survival part of the metaphor. Following an outdated map we'd bicycled to S'conset at the far end of the island and taken a different route back – the "shore road." The road became a path, then a track which grew steadily deeper in sand until we had to dismount, wheeling our bikes until we were blocked by a ten-foot-tall fence topped with five strands of barbed wire. The airport's runway had been extended across the old road to accommodate small jets. It was already late afternoon. We scaled the fence, lifted our bikes up and over, avoided the barbed wire, and wheeled our bikes over a wide grassy area separating the fence from the runway. Looking left, then right, we scurried across the runway nanoseconds before a private jet came in for its landing. Shaken, we weren't surprised to see an official vehicle with a flashing light headed our way. We imagined the headline, but happily there was none.

had transported his rag-tag army on the way to attempt to take Quebec – was at its original level for the first time in a hundred and thirty years. After the river had become industrialized and polluted, the surrounding communities had turned their backs on it, and its steep banks were virtually pristine, just as they'd been two hundred years earlier. At my brother's suggestion, we and our families and a couple of friends launched a flotilla of canoes and kayaks from a riverside gravel pit ten miles upriver.

We were alone on the broad, fast-flowing river as a world Diane and I had never seen opened up. We herded flocks of ducks, gannets and great blue herons before us. Deep in the river valley, we rode the current and the occasional small rapids past a series of enormous log towers filled with boulders erected to hold log booms during a hundred years of log drives to the paper mills. The limitless recreational potential of the river with the dam removed was evident.* The feeling of exhilaration was palpable as we reached Augusta and sped on a narrow raceway sharply down through the breach in the dam. Renewal was in the air for the river, as we hoped it was for us.

The first three weeks of August that year were glorious, one bright, sunny day after another. While Diane was pleased to be able to spend time with our children, something important was missing – her initiative, vitality and energy. For the first time, she seemed subdued and passive, and not looking forward to the fall, a time projected to be set aside to research and to write. She already knew the prospect was illusory. The last week before Labor Day was grim, mostly gray, cool and rainy.

The weather matched Diane's mood, except for one bright spot on her horizon. For two years she'd been the only visible woman on the faculty. That was about to change, and she would be joined by a contemporary who was making a name for herself on the other side of the Charles River. Mary Ann Glendon, for six years a professor on the Boston College Law School faculty, had agreed to come to Harvard for the 1974-75 year as a Visiting Lecturer to teach Property – a required first-year course – and then, in the spring, The Legal Process. Her presence created a stir. Two weeks into the semester, the *Law Record* noted her arrival:

> Visiting Professor Mary Ann Glendon finds that it is "really a little early" to contrast her two weeks at Harvard Law School to her six years at Boston College Law School. Yet numerous HLS students have had time to find that with her, Harvard has acquired for a year both an expert in European comparative law and a professor of Legal Process quite a bit more attractive than Dean Albert M. Sacks.

---

* The dam, alas, was rebuilt. It would be twenty-five years before the efforts of sportsmen and conservationists, spearheaded by my brother, would cause its permanent removal after the federal government declined to renew its license for electricity production. With the dam gone, the river has renewed itself and filled up with the salmon, striped bass and shad that have returned to their historical spawning grounds.

Having been instrumental in Harvard's inviting Glendon, Diane was optimistic that the faculty would finally ask another woman to join it – and that she'd accept. It was a "look/see visitorship." The task, she thought, would be to persuade Glendon to overlook the sexist attitudes she would encounter and to accept the offer she would inevitably receive. We spent a couple of pleasant social evenings with Mary Ann and her husband, Ed Lev, who'd been a partner at Mayer Platt in Chicago where they both had practiced, and who'd moved to Boston to become a partner in Sullivan & Worcester when his wife began teaching at Boston College. Like us, they had three children. Mary Ann, like Diane, juggled the competing demands of her professional life and her family life.

Glendon wasn't the only one coming. Women were beginning to trickle in, it seemed, even if the atmosphere was unwelcoming. Raya Dreben, a Boston practitioner, would lecture on copyright law from 1974 to 1977. * There was no sense of collegiality between the women and the male faculty, however. On a few occasions, Diane and Raya went together to eat lunch in the faculty dining room, but stopped because they found it unpleasant and hostile. Conversation would cease when they entered the room and was tense when it resumed, as if the men didn't want to have conversations which could be overheard or in which women could participate. "It was impossible," Glendon told me, "to have an intellectual conversation with male faculty members. The conversation usually degenerated into 'So, who takes care of your kids?' The attitude was, 'If you have children, why are you teaching at Harvard?' Women had no support system except for what the few of us – Diane, Raya and Elisabeth Owens – could generate ourselves."

Harvard was not yet ready for Mary Ann Glendon. At the end of the year Sacks reported that the faculty felt they had not really gotten to know her, because she hadn't often had lunch in the faculty dining room. This comment, which was in a sense true ("I had three kids under ten. I came over in the morning and I ate my box of yogurt at my desk so I could get home to them in the evening."), was particularly ironic in view of the reception Diane, Raya and Mary Ann had experienced in those hallowed precincts. Glendon returned to Boston College at the end of the academic year.

Except for the presence of Glendon and Dreben, the fall of 1974 marked the nadir in Diane's life at Harvard. When she'd agreed the previous spring to teach two courses in addition to her scheduled catalogue course, she knew she wouldn't be teaching in the fall. That semester was to be a sabbatical period during which, theoretically, she would have the time to research and write the learned article that would earn her tenure. In the chilly, short day's light of the previous fall and winter, the dean's request to tack on to her teaching load an additional course in the spring seemed reasonable and she

---

* Raya Dreben was eight years Diane's senior, but it was important for her, as it was for other women, to have Diane as a colleague and friend at the law school. It would have been "very lonely," otherwise. (Dreben interview, March 23, 2005.)

viewed the fall's freedom as "comp time" for what she'd been asked to do. Perhaps she should have foreseen the toll the teaching load would take on her, but she didn't.

She'd had little or no time to reflect on the task of writing for publication, or even to begin to prepare for it. The fall was little better, despite having no classes to teach. She continued to spend untold hours on the admissions process and the appointments process. She continued to work on recruiting other women to teach. She continued to respond to the ongoing demands of the Massachusetts community. And I was little help, as I was caught up in the Governor's reelection campaign and a complex jury trial that lasted for several weeks.

Diane used what little free time she had to research and write, but she wasn't inspired. For the first time since I'd known her, she was unable to compartmentalize and exclude distractions. Concentration took enormous effort, and writing was a chore. Coming off the stress of the prior year, she found the process she now faced exhausting, and the article became her *bete noire*, a stumbling block, something menacing that she couldn't seem to overcome. We discussed her topic, its objective, its organization and the approaches she could take. Nothing seemed to work. The stress became physical. She developed such excruciating back pains that she had to lie flat on the floor to try to alleviate them. Ben was distressed to come home from school and find his mother lying in pain on the floor.

She knew she was radically different from the vast majority of her colleagues. She wasn't driven by ego or personal ambition, but by a desire to serve, to make her life worthwhile. She also understood that she probably had been first invited to join the faculty at a difficult time for the school and because those on the faculty who knew her viewed her as safe. They felt comfortable with her. She was feminine but not strident, competent but not pushy, intellectually capable but not threatening to the males on the faculty. Diane feared that her written work might be accepted because of who she was rather than because of what she'd done. That fact, in and of itself, was unacceptable to her, not just for herself but for the women who would follow her. She was unwilling to expose to her colleagues work that they might find wanting.

She concluded that she was in a no-win situation. She could never be sure that her work – even if she herself thought it was acceptable – would be judged on its merits. She could, perhaps, have confided in a colleague and looked for guidance, but she was never one to take her problems to others. She was the one from whom others sought advice and guidance. Internalizing these issues took a singular toll. Even her mother became concerned, although she thought the cause to be more prosaic:

> Why don't you try to figure out why your energy level keeps declining!! It would be my guess that you just have too much on your mind – you feel pressured and your subconscious feels that you're trying for the impossible, that you'll never get done all the things you have to do....

You have the idea that you must do all these things yourself instead of getting help in many many ways, that is, by hiring people to do some of these things – which would give you peace from the nagging feeling that they must be done sometime soon. Just keeping up with the washing and folding of clothes takes hours each week. And that easily could be done by someone else, giving you those hours to put on your book work. If you only would! Having someone clean your house once a week would give you another eight hours of freed time – and peace of mind that it is done. But I'm wasting words as I know you do not think this way – your feeling that you must not be dependent on help in any of these fields is really foolish. Isn't your health and well-being more important?*

We sent out no Christmas cards that year, and for the first and only time in her adult life, Diane sent no Christmas newsletter to friends and relatives. She apologized a year later: "Life overwhelmed us last year. The Christmas cards never got sent, but we did manage to hang the stockings, fill them, grade the exams and win the cases. This year we're trying to gain perspective. I can't really remember how our hectic 1974 life went."

She wasn't prone to exaggeration. Diane had been burned out. She needed to find a way back.

The Return Trip

The process began with the holidays and continued during the first two weeks of 1975 as Diane's sabbatical wound down. We talked through the issues at length from the perspectives of what was important and what should take priority in her life, in my life and in our life together. It was a complex equation because as time and achievement pressures had built up for her, similar career pressures had built up for me.† Very likely, although I don't recall it that way, we were at a crisis point in our marriage. Not surprisingly, we agreed that our family came first and our focus on the issues should begin from that premise and its two components, time with each other and time with our children. Surprisingly, perhaps, gaining tenure at Harvard wasn't a priority for Diane in our conversations. It wasn't her ambition; it was an ambition others had had for her.

Continuing to teach was important, as was her Harvard committee work, because change was occurring. She could see it in increasing numbers of women admitted, and in genuine efforts to bring women onto the faculty – but the change was painfully slow.

---

*   Letter dated November 28, 1974.
†   My workload (I wrote) was "huge, overpowering, almost incapable of being coped with." I was "surviving by working with extraordinary intensity and concentration."

The satisfaction Diane had from teaching, and from teaching by a different philosophy than Harvard espoused, was personal, and different from the satisfaction she had from her work on the Admissions and Appointments committees. There were other matters of personal satisfaction that were important: she wanted opportunities to continue to serve the broader public good, something she'd had at MLRI and wanted to regain. The personal and professional relationships and friendships she'd developed in the course of her public work were something on which she wanted to build.

She decided to abandon any thought of tenure at Harvard and to concentrate on other matters of importance. One of those matters, something of great importance to Diane and, she believed, to the profession as a whole, was the professional responsibility course she had introduced to Harvard. It had not yet been accepted into the regular curriculum and she was intent that it should be. Those about to become lawyers needed to understand what their public and private responsibilities entailed. Harvard could lead the country's law schools by establishing her course as a part of the regular curriculum. She lobbied the faculty and the administration and in March 1975, Harvard accepted the course. *

When we turned to personal matters, her decision made the road map easy. We would make time for each other and for our family. Exactly how and what we'd do remained to be worked out, but the principle was plain enough, as was the need: Ben would be fourteen in June, Ted twelve and Kristin ten in April. They needed us no less than they had before, and probably more.

For the first time in a long time, we did some long-range planning as a family. Ben had become interested in archeology and in the Aztecs. We promised him (and Ted and Kristin) that we'd take them to Mexico that summer to see the ruined remains of Tenochtitlan, the Aztec pyramids of Teotihaucan, Mexico City's wonderful anthropological museum and the castle fortress built by the Spanish viceroys on a towering rock above the city. After Mexico, we'd go on a long visit to Diane's parents and other relatives in California. We promised to take them to Norway a year later to meet the relatives they'd only heard about, to explore the country from which their Norwegian grandparents had emigrated, and to go on from there to London and then west to the Cotswolds, an introduction to the country that had spawned New England.

The day we sat down with our three children to talk about our plans was a wonderful day. The prospects excited each of us in different ways. Ben wasn't the only one who had wanted to go to Mexico. It had been in my mind and Diane's for a long time. Diane hadn't been on an extended visit to her parents and her sister's family for a much longer time. Norway promised to be an extraordinary adventure. England would be

---

*   Professor Keeton, among others, applauded the decision, saying that failure to instruct students in the misunderstood and often overlooked issues of professional responsibility posed a "far more serious problem" than failure to instruct in the required law-school courses. (HLR March 21, 1975.)

icing on the cake. Our lives were reopening to a bright future we couldn't have begun to think possible, had it not been for the decision Diane had made.

Her decision was a personal watershed. An unwanted burden had been lifted and she became herself again. There would be challenges ahead during the coming eighteen months that would impinge on her priorities – but not on her resolve as to her future at Harvard. Removing the onus of ambition freed both of us to look at decisions differently. It would take time, and there would yet be frustrations and conflicts, but little by little our life would change.

The first order of business was her mid-January return to the classroom. She had a sense of foreboding, as if the world would know what she'd privately concluded and it would be held against her. The world didn't know. No one but I knew about her decision, least of all her students. When she began teaching again, she found strength, excitement and vitality from the interaction with her students. She settled happily back into her teaching routine. It was, I wrote, "an upward cycle. We'll make it through another semester okay."

A challenge to her new view of life wasn't long in coming. The public sector needed her in a new role. Michael Dukakis, who Diane knew well and who'd been at law school with us, had been elected governor. One of the planks of the clean government platform on which he'd run was to make the selection of judges nonpolitical, public and on the merits.[4] On taking office, his Executive Order No. 1 created a new – and unpaid – volunteer entity called the Judicial Nominating Commission, which was to consist of both lawyers and non-lawyers, with the latter being the majority. The JNC's task was to solicit applications for appointment to vacancies at every level of the courts in the Commonwealth, from the judges who ran the courts to the clerks who served them. The JNC was to submit to the governor a slate of three qualified applicants for each position and the governor would make his choice from that slate.

When Dukakis took office, there were thirty-eight vacancies to be filled.

One of the goals of the Massachusetts Law Reform Institute five years earlier was going to be achieved, and Diane was elated. When Dukakis asked her if she would serve on the JNC, she accepted. He wrote her on February 10, 1975, confirming the appointment. Commenting on it, he said "Diane Lund will bring many perspectives to the Judicial Nominating Commission. She has distinguished herself in three very different types of practice – in public interest law, in a major Boston law firm and now as a professor at Harvard Law School. This varied experience augurs well for both the Commission and the people of the Commonwealth."*

The JNC would be large – eleven members – each one appointed to represent a different constituency. Raymond Kenney, a highly respected trial lawyer, became chair of the JNC – despite his never having met Dukakis – as the nominee of the Massachusetts

---

* *Lexington Minute-Man*, February 29, 1975.

Bar Association of which he'd been president. Diane, who Dukakis had known not only from law school but from her later public and academic service, was chosen both because he trusted her judgment and because she would be a voice for the women's bar. Other women were also appointed, including Frieda Garcia, executive director of Allianza Hispana, to represent the Hispanic community; and Julia Kaufman, chair of the Legislative Action Committee of the Massachusetts Council for Public Justice (a committee on which Diane also served). Both women looked to Diane for guidance in this unfamiliar territory. Rudolph Pierce, a lawyer and board member of the Roxbury Multi-service Center, later a Superior Court judge, represented the black community. Richard Milstein, a towering figure in Continuing Legal Education for members of the bar, represented Western Massachusetts.

The JNC was sworn in on February 13, 1975:

Judicial Screening Panel Set – Dukakis Turns On Nomination Spigot*

Five lawyers and six laymen from diverse backgrounds have been chosen by Gov. Michael S. Dukakis to assist him in selecting judges and court clerks. The eleven-member bipartisan Judicial Nominating Commission, sworn in Thursday, includes seven men and four women. Appointment of the special panel was described by the Governor as "a first step in eliminating politics in courthouses....

Under terms of the January 3 gubernatorial executive order providing for the commission, Mr. Dukakis will fill all future judicial vacancies from lists of "well-qualified" potential nominees it recommends. As its first assignment the unpaid panel will focus on seeking out and screening prospects to be considered by the Governor for four existing or impending bench vacancies.

"....The public must be assured that judicial officers, appointed for near-lifetime tenure, are selected in a completely non-partisan manner," the Governor contends. "The only criterion for choosing judges and clerks must be merit." The Governor emphasized that it is the responsibility of its members "to ensure that politics or any suggestion of politics is removed once and for all from the process in judicial selection."

The offer of this public sector opportunity was not one Diane could have refused. It resonated with her in every aspect of her views concerning public service, the rights of the public and the interests of women to be considered for office on a level playing field with men.

---

* *Christian Science Monitor*, February 14, 1975.

The *Harvard Law Record* took note of the appointment in its issue of March 7, 1975:

> Lund feels that it is important to have considerations other than political considerations enter into the selection of judges and clerks "and to have the public believe this is the case. At the moment, we are developing our operating procedures and when they are finished, we will make them public," she said...
>
> Lund also feels that having a majority of the [commission] members coming from outside the legal system is a good thing. Courts, she feels, "are one of the significant points at which the community and the law intersect," and it is important to look not only at the ongoing development of the law but also at the effect of the courts on the community. Lay persons will be able to better take into account the latter, she added.

Apart from her friends, her Harvard colleagues took no note of the appointment. It was a local matter and had little to do with them.

The JNC had neither rules nor guidelines to follow and had to make its own. They met on nights and weekends to hammer out their procedures. There existed a similar nominating commission in Colorado and its chair came to Massachusetts to give guidance. Some things were established by Executive Order No.1. One was that in the case of district court judges and clerks – the persons who dispensed justice at the lowest level – there were to be public hearings in the communities in which they would serve so that the community could voice its views about various candidates.

On a theoretical level, this represented an admirable example of democracy at work. On a practical level, it slowed the process enormously and threatened to derail it. Had the first district court judicial nomination which the JNC had to deal with been typical, the process would have proved impossible.

Guy Volterra, the brother of an elected state representative to the legislature, had applied for the vacancy in the district court in Taunton. The possibility that he might be appointed set off vociferous opposition from his political opponents. The JNC held two public hearings in Taunton – far removed from Boston – concerning the vacancy. Hundreds of people came, both pro and con. Diane wrestled with ingrained skepticism concerning relatives of elected officials seeking to become judges, but she overcame her skepticism in favor of the candidate who was most qualified by education, temperament and experience to serve the community. That person, she concluded, and the JNC concurred, was Guy Volterra. Dukakis appointed him and he became an outstanding judge.

The JNC met as a committee of the whole. There were no subcommittees – everyone did everything, making telephone calls to persons who recommended candidates, sharing their information with the entire body, and interviewing. In the first two years of its existence, JNC meetings were held every Monday evening in Boston and other evenings in communities outside of Boston. More than 500 applicants were interviewed for positions on the judiciary and in the court clerks' offices. Diane participated in all the interviews. According to Ray Kenney, she had both a marvelous intellect and a way of putting everyone at their ease when discussing candidates. She wasn't an advocate for women, as such, but she made certain that every woman candidate was given equal consideration. *

It was difficult to find women candidates for the judiciary for the same reasons it was difficult to recruit women to a law-school faculty: there were few women trial lawyers (experience in the courtroom was one of the criteria specified by Dukakis) and their candidacy was subjected to sex-biased scrutiny. Kenney recalls to this day that he once made the mistake of asking a woman candidate with young children how she was going to manage the care of her children. After she left, he received from Diane a quick and forceful seminar on sexism and employment discrimination. He never made a mistake like that again, either in the context of the JNC or in his firm's private law practice.

On the face of it, taking on this new task with its huge time commitment wasn't consistent with the decision Diane had made. The commission worked long hours. In the first twelve months, twelve judicial vacancies were filled, including that of the Chief Justice of the Supreme Judicial Court. The issue, however, wasn't that simple. The JNC was precisely the kind of public service that was important and to which she could contribute in a meaningful way. She couldn't let the opportunity pass by. She was seeing and serving the legal profession from a new perspective, one that was unique and to which a woman could be a pivotal force. While her decision regarding Harvard had made her decision to accept the JNC appointment and work easier, she had to accept the fact that this new commitment would take its toll on the time she had available for our family.

That toll would sometimes be poignant. The spring of 1975, in Ted's first year playing Little League baseball, Diane and I saw a few games, but a very few, and rarely on weekdays. The games were played on various Little League fields throughout Lexington. Nearly every other player had one or another parent present at the games, and parents would transport their kids to and from the faraway games. Ted had to get there by himself, riding his bicycle. One afternoon, his bike had a flat on the way to the game and he had to walk his bike the last mile. It was late when the game was over and he was worried about getting home – and resentful about the fact that his friends' mothers seemed to be able to get to their son's games while his didn't. How was he to get home? A teammate's mother became aware of the problem, loaded both Ted and his bike into her station wagon and brought him home.

_____

* Ray Kenney interview, January 2005.

Rescue wasn't the same as his parents being there and Ted wasn't convinced of our family-comes-first plan. We tried to avoid other events like this, but inevitably there were others. There were bugs in the system that needed to be worked out.

April came, and with it Lexington's Patriot's Day celebration of the nation's bicentennial. Revolution and freedom from oppression was the theme, a theme which Lexington members of N.O.W. extended to encompass women's struggle for recognition and equality. A powerful symbol of that struggle was the march of women strikers out of the Lowell woolen mills a century earlier, singing as they walked out:

> As we come marching, marching, in the beauty of the day,
> A million darkened kitchens, a thousand mill lofts gray,
> Are touched with all the radiance that a sudden sun discloses,
> For the people hear us singing … bread and roses, bread and roses.

They would sing the song again, Diane and Kristin among them, arms and fists upraised. The other song they sang along the parade route had as its chorus:

> Oh life is a toil and life is a trouble,
> Beauty will fade and riches will flee,
> Pleasures they dwindle and prices they double,
> Nothing is as I would wish it to be.

Both songs held echoes for Diane.

We fulfilled the first part of our family promise when we flew to Mexico City in the first week of July and then to California for a lengthy visit with grandparents, cousins, Noreen and Carl. Mexico was as interesting and exciting as we'd hoped. For the first

---

Riding the subway in Mexico City was itself an adventure, in more ways than one. All our children were blond, a miracle to riders who wanted to touch their amazing hair. There were anatomical touchings as well, and so we rode in a cluster, back to back. Later, after Diane had used her high-school Spanish to get directions to the "El Directo" bus to the pyramids at Teotihuacan , we found ourselves on a local, rattle-trap bus with natives, ranging from Indians in brightly colored shawls to merchants carrying their produce, to peasant farmers. One was transporting a crate of chickens on the roof of the bus. It was fun. No one on board could speak English, Diane used her Spanish some more, all the passengers laughed a great deal, and as we neared the pyramids everyone pointed them out to us and made sure we got off at the right stop.

time our children were exposed to another culture. Wide-eyed, they drank it in as we rode the subways and buses and trooped around Mexico City. We saw pyramids and castles and the Temple of Quetzalcoatl, and Mexican pilgrims on their knees moving across a vast stone-cobbled courtyard toward the cathedral built to commemorate the local sighting of the Virgin – and we bargained with vendors in marketplace stalls for their goods. Diane described the entire trip, including California, as "an unbelievable jaunt to Mexico City, Mexico's archeological ruins and 19th century European castles, then on to Los Angeles, Big Sur, Carmel, San Francisco, Boron and Sequoia National Park. We loved all of it. Being in academic life makes for nice summers."

In truth, what made for this nice summer was the *absence* of academic life and its demands. Diane and our children arrived back in Boston in late July and a week later we were all at the island. It was a cherished summer, but very unlike the prior year.*

Reality returned with a vengeance in September.

Between teaching, the Admissions and Appointments committees, and the JNC, we reprised many of the stresses of the previous three years. While Diane's schedule was no less harried, there was a difference: she wasn't having to cope with an unwanted ambition.

It wasn't an easy time for feminists. Ratification of the Equal Rights Amendment was facing increasingly stiff resistance at the state level. In late fall, Ruth Bader Ginsburg, who had appeared and testified at numerous legislative hearings, commented on the opposition's success:

> Ginsburg, a Columbia Law School professor, cited the cause of rising resistance to ERA as "deep-seated fear."
>
> She recalled that one of her first contacts with such fears occurred in 1971 when she was teaching a gender discrimination course at Harvard Law School (the first sex-discrimination course offered here). After one class, a young man came up to Ginsburg and said, "It's not just equal pay you want. You really want to change everything, don't you?"
>
> In addition to facing public opposition to ERA, Ginsburg is vying against a more invidious danger: claims that the 5th and 14th amendments, the "due process" amendments, provide adequate tools for the judiciary to strike down discriminatory legislation and practices. She believes such interpretations can only be achieved by painfully stretching the plain meaning of the 14th amendment. "It was not designed with women in mind," and the Supreme Court knows this, Ginsburg said.†

* August was marred by the death of my mother, who we both loved very much.
† Her comments, reported in the *Harvard Law Record*, confronted the suggestions of the eminent Professor Freund five years earlier that women should follow the precise route Ginsburg termed an "invidious danger."

The momentum generated by what Diane had done would continue. Two hundred and eleven women were admitted in her last year on the Admissions Committee. Had they all accepted, they would have represented 40% of the class of 1979. One-third of them – more women than had even been admitted in prior years – declined, decisions that reflected both new-found confidence and a reluctance to attend a law school, however elite, whose faculty was nearly entirely male.

In admissions practice, the old-boy men's college network had been breached, and equal consideration, regardless of sex, was being given to applicants, but the faculty appointment process was another matter. The admissions pattern would continue, thanks in no small part to the September 1975 appointment of Patricia Lydon as Assistant Dean for Admissions and Placement.

That fall Diane notified Sacks and Frank Michelman, another member of the Appointments Committee, of her decision not to seek tenure. Sacks was dismayed, and concerned about repercussions. While he'd been supportive of Diane from the time she first came to Harvard, the nature and extent of the burden he'd asked her to carry for women – and that she'd carried for four years – couldn't easily be shifted. No other women had been invited to join the regular faculty. He was relieved, however, that she wanted to continue teaching both the family law course and the professional responsibility course. Her presence and her influence would continue.

On February 5, 1976, Michelman sent a memorandum "to Tenured Professors":

> At the Faculty Meeting to be held on February 18, 1976, the Appointments Committee will recommend that Assistant Professor Diane Lund be appointed Lecturer on Law for two years beginning July 1, 1976. Faculty members may obtain additional information about this recommendation from any member of the committee.

Diane attended the faculty meeting, but withdrew when the recommendation was considered:

> The Dean called on Mr. Michelman to present the recommendations of the Appointments Committee with respect to Diane Lund. He reported that Ms. Lund had decided that she could not combine teaching, scholarship, practice and her family and had concluded that she wished to increase her practice and abandon scholarly work. She had asked therefore to be considered for a part-time lectureship in the expectation that she would teach one or two courses a year. It was unanimously
>
> **VOTED**: That the Faculty of Law recommends to the President and Fellows that Diane Lund be appointed Lecturer on Law for a period of two years commencing July 1, 1976.

On a Saturday evening a week later, Diane was driving me to Emerson Hospital because of severe chest pains occasioned by a difficult meeting with clients on a *pro bono* case arising out of an unauthorized and noisy teen-age party which Lexington's police had broken up using police dogs, handcuffs and nightsticks. She was at my bedside for several days and batteries of tests, until it was determined I'd had a severe hiatal hernia event, not a heart attack. It was a scare that prompted still more conversations, this time about my workload, not hers.

That same week, Susan Estrich was elected president of the *Harvard Law Review*, the first woman to be accorded the honor.*

As the academic year drew to a close, Sacks invited us to a small cocktail party and made a point of spending time in conversation with Diane. He spoke about his own career, his tenure as dean, soon to be over, and his plans for the future. "I've concluded," he said, "that the demands of a professional life have natural cycles. I seem to run on an eight-year cycle. Then I need something new, some new challenge, to engage my attention. It's a mistake to continue to do the same thing for too long. Life becomes unsatisfactory."

Sacks wasn't speaking only of himself, and the conversation wasn't accidental. He was reinforcing for Diane the legitimacy of her decision, and it was a conversation she would come back to in the following years.

On the day after her last class in May, Diane's decision paid another dividend, one important to us, extraordinary for our children and a challenge for the Lexington school system. In March, we had advised the schools – not asking their permission – that we'd be taking our children away for three weeks, leaving on May 8 to Norway so they could learn about their heritage, meet their relatives and witness the Independence Day celebration on May 17th, and then on to England. We hoped the schools would understand. The response we received was enthusiastic.

Diane – to the dismay of my Norwegian relatives – had reserved rooms in an inexpensive Oslo hotel near the waterfront favored by visiting sailors whose ships were in port. We wanted to be on our own as much as possible, to walk through Oslo and ride its trams and its ferries. The sailors had other things in mind for themselves. Our kids were old enough to understand, and we got along well with the exuberant sailors.

We rode the ferry to Oslo's Viking museum to see the magnificent Oseberg and Gokstad ships, enormously long, sleek and seaworthy. One could understand how both lightning raids and long sea voyages were possible. We took the tram to the Folke-Museum, an assemblage of traditional farmhouses and outbuildings and a 500-year-old stave-church. We walked to the Frogner Park, with its signature obelisk and bridge lined with Vigeland's muscular sculptures depicting the joys and struggles of life.

---

*   HLR, February 27, 1976.

For the first time in many years Diane bounced as we walked hand in hand, our children running on ahead. We lazed in the sunshine and watched them play Frisbee.

We drove to a farm whose manor house, built by a great-uncle in 1860, was still in the family, owned by a cousin who was seeing to its restoration. We heard family stories, including that my widowed great-grandfather had taken up with his housekeeper, and my grandmother had been born out of wedlock. The parallel with Diane's own grandmother didn't go unnoticed. The five of us worked on clearing and weeding land and gardens on the farm.

A grand family party with cousins of all ages took place in Oslo. Diane had never met so many of my relatives in one place at one time and what she found were the kinds of relationships and feelings she'd experienced growing up in her own extended family. She felt quite at home as the younger and the older cousins, first cousins, first cousins once removed and second cousins, our children included, all competed in wheelbarrow races in which cousins drove the wheelbarrows with other cousins in them and the object was as much to keep the wheelbarrows from tipping over as it was to win. It was a joyous day, a month from midsummer, and the sun stayed high in the sky, motionless until well toward midnight.

May 17 was brilliant and sunny, perfect for the Independence Day parade. Yet another cousin had reserved seats for us in stands next to the castle. King Olav, Crown Prince Harald, their wives and their children, stood gamely on the castle balcony and waved and saluted as the multitude of bands and flags and uniformed schoolchildren trooped by. They were followed by a madcap parade of the "Russ," the soon-to-be high-school graduates. The pageantry was splendid, so impressive, said Diane with a smile, to make her reconsider whether she could be a monarchist.

An early-morning train carried us up over the high plateau of Norway, where snow beside the track was still piled up in meters, past ski huts and skiers trekking in the snowfields. The ride down to Bergen from that wintry plateau was spectacular. We plummeted alongside cliffs and through tunnels, following an ever-widening river fed by snow-melt waterfalls, and watched winter turn into spring before our eyes. In the snowfields the birch trees had barely begun to bud. As we lost altitude, the buds swelled, leaves came out, flowers popped up and we were surrounded by springtime green on all sides. The river became a torrent of whitewater leaping over rocks, down falls, through rapids and overflowing its banks in the valley. As Bergen came into view in bright sunshine, we looked behind us at a backdrop of snow-capped mountains.

It was a trip Diane called enchanted, unlike any she'd ever experienced, ending in a city which had no choice but to face the sea because of the steep surrounding mountains. If the mountains had but shivered, it seemed, Bergen itself would have been shrugged off into the sea. That night, having arrived late, we found still open a waterfront restaurant which served excellent salmon, and where a few Bergensers had collected to play guitars and sing. The next night, another cousin took us to a performance of the Fana Folklorica, a gathering which featured traditional food and dancing. I was invited to participate in the folk-dancing and could not refuse, much to Diane's amusement as my face turned red.

While everyone was careful to speak English to her and to the kids, Diane had heard a great deal of Norwegian, a language she called musical, but of which she didn't understand a word. When we arrived in London, it was a relief to be in a place where – if she listened closely – she could understand what was being said. She and the kids were no longer dependent on me to translate. We walked from Big Ben to Buckingham Palace to Westminster Abbey to Trafalgar Square. We saw Henry VIII's gigantic suit of armor and the statues of Eros and Admiral Nelson. We took the river boat to Windsor Castle. One afternoon, leaving the kids on their own, Diane and I even went to the Old Bailey and had a busman's holiday watching bewigged and powdered barristers trying their cases before elaborately bewigged judges. Both men and women barristers were required to wear the powdered white wigs that their predecessors had worn in court for centuries. An interesting custom, Diane thought, but how absurd! Why should women have to pretend to be men? Not unlike other attitudes she'd encountered.

After driving through the Cotswolds, it was time to go home again and time for Diane to begin to plan for a very different professional life, one in which her teaching at Harvard would be peripheral, not central. Freed from her other law school responsibilities at last, she could enjoy teaching for itself and focus on the students who responded to her. She and Regie, teaching the family law course together, brought humor and perspective to the classroom and received enthusiastic reviews from their students.

There was yin and yang to her changed status. She was no longer a member of the regular faculty. Just as she had cast off her non-teaching ties to the school, the school and its faculty cast off their ties to her. The women who came after her to the faculty knew her only in passing, a lecturer they all liked. They had no knowledge and little awareness of what she'd done to prepare the way for them in Harvard's hostile environment, and it was still a hard road.

Meanwhile, the professional responsibility course that she'd originated – once only a curiosity in the regular curriculum – became mainstream as both the legal profession and the public became aware of the need to educate lawyers-to-be regarding the ethical standards of their profession and their broader public responsibilities. The course became mandatory in law-school curriculums, not only at Harvard but throughout the country.

Seven years later, in the spring of 1983, Diane was at the height of her career within the legal profession. She had served since 1979 as a member of the Massachusetts Board of Bar Overseers, the organization charged with enforcing lawyers' ethical and professional obligations in Massachusetts, and had been appointed its chair in 1983, the first woman to serve in that capacity. She was one of the profession's most knowledgeable members in the entire country on the subject of professional responsibility. Unimpressed by those credentials – which were, after all, not academic – Harvard advised her that since the course had become a required part of the curriculum, it would be taught, beginning in the fall, by a regular member of the faculty, not by a lecturer.

Having lost the appointment to teach the course she had introduced, and which was important to her and to the profession, she wrote Dean Vorenberg (Sacks' successor) in the winter of 1984 to question whether, given her lack of exposure to students through the professional responsibility course, the enrollment in her family law course was sufficient justification for her to continue as a lecturer. Her letter was never acknowledged, nor was she ever advised she wouldn't be reappointed. That news came to her when the law school's fall 1984 catalogue came out and her family law course wasn't listed.

She received no recognition, nor letter or word of praise or commendation for her contributions to Harvard Law School at a critical time in its history, when it needed her. The honor of having had the opportunity was to be her only reward. It was a bitter pill and she determined to pretend not to notice the slight, but I know she did. She had moved on, she thought, and whatever Harvard did or didn't do was no longer important to her. That was history, and a remote history, at that. She had created a different and worthwhile career, one that served not only women and not only her clients, but the legal profession as a whole. Still, it stung.

TENURED WOMEN PROFESSORS ON THE HARVARD LAW SCHOOL FACULTY

Unlike the impact she'd had on the admission of women law students, Diane's legacy with respect to women on the faculty was not as she would have wanted it. No woman had been tenured by the time she herself had withdrawn from the tenure track. What then, was her legacy? She had shown that a woman could gain the respect and confidence of both students and faculty and could succeed as a teacher. The way in which students responded to her style of teaching demonstrated that to succeed, a woman did not have to teach like a man. The aggressive and denigrating teaching approach of the *enfants terrible* of *The Paper Chase* and *One L* was on the wane. She'd demonstrated that a cooperative problem-solving approach to teaching law stood as great a chance of success as the old ways. After her time, it was not only women who approached the teaching of law differently, but men as well.

In principle, then, she'd established that women deserved a place on the faculty, and she'd helped set in motion the process by which they'd be chosen and invited. It was no longer a question of "if" but rather a question of "when" and "who." That question itself wouldn't be easily answered because many men on the faculty were still openly hostile to the concept of hiring and tenuring women. It is a paradox that Diane was so warmly liked by the faculty, some going so far as to say she unquestionably would have been granted tenure, and yet women following after Diane continued to find the road rough and treacherous. Each has had to make her own way and each has her own story to tell. A few of those stories from the late 1970s are worth recounting, if only to show that the battle for women law professors was far from over when Diane withdrew from the field. Indeed it's far from over even now.

Mary Ann Glendon.

Mary Ann Glendon and Diane had much in common in their experiences and outlooks on the uses of the law.* Both were raised in families of modest means and both were influenced throughout their lives by the teachings of the churches they and their families attended. They were about the same age, each had graduated from university at nineteen and entered law school the following fall, graduating in 1961. Glendon was one of four women in her law-school class. Both Mary Ann and Diane had pushed through their early schooling and then college in three years.† Each had done well in law school and been elected to *Law Review*. And both had experienced similar discriminatory experiences in the hiring process.

Glendon had a two-year fellowship in Europe where she worked in Brussels for the European Common Market (the forerunner to the European Union). She then returned to New York City to interview with major law firms. At Cravath, Swain & Moore she was told they wouldn't hire her, despite her outstanding record, because they "couldn't bring her to a meeting with Tom Watson of IBM any more than [they] could bring a Jew." White & Case said they didn't even hire female *secretaries*. All the New York firms turned her down. She couldn't get a job.

Discouraged, she returned to Chicago where Professor Soia Mentshikoff took her under her wing and explained the facts of life for a woman in the legal profession: among other things, she had to dress right if she expected to be hired. Mentshikoff sent her to Peck & Peck where she was outfitted with sensible but refined-looking clothes including a girdle, something she'd never worn ("It doesn't matter. Wives wear girdles. When you interview, you have to look the way their wives look."), gloves, hat and high heels. Glendon says she walked down the street from Peck & Peck looking

---

* Mary Ann Glendon oral history, December 9, 2003.
† In retrospect Glendon thinks that she was too young for the experience, that she didn't know what she wanted to do with her life and that the University of Chicago "hustled" people into graduate school. She had no real idea what lawyers did. There were none in her family – she'd worked as a journalist for the *Berkshire Eagle* in summers. She was inspired to apply to Chicago law school by a lecture on Plato given by a law-school professor.

at her reflection in store windows and wondering who *that* was – but it worked, and she was hired by Chicago's leading law firm, Mayer, Brown & Platt, where she became "the Ford man" (the designation of previous lawyers who had done Ford Motor Company's work).

Like Diane, Mary Ann Glendon was focused on using the law as a tool for social justice and social change. She pursued, *pro bono*, public defender, civil liberties and civil rights work on the side (including voter registration in Jackson, Mississippi) while at Mayer Platt. ("I think I was the first person who ever asked the managing partner for *pro bono* work. I think I was a bit of a trial for them.") Eventually the firm agreed it had a responsibility to do things for the public interest and that, in doing so, she would be getting "experience that's useful to us."

In 1968, she came to Boston College to teach at the invitation of the law school's Jesuit dean, Father Drinan, who was in the process of building a national law school and trying to attract highly qualified teachers for it. She was the only woman on the faculty but found the atmosphere "wonderfully welcoming." What she didn't have was a role model, and "to be a law professor in a school that has never had women law professors was a challenge." She achieved tenure there before being invited to visit at Harvard.

Teaching at Harvard – simply *being* there – was vastly different from her prior experiences at the University of Chicago and Boston College. Chicago, she thought, was gender-blind and color-blind. Many of the men who were students and who taught there had gone to co-ed schools with women at both the secondary and university levels, rather than to single-sex schools like those that predominated in the Northeast. The issue at Chicago was intellectual: it wasn't who you were and where you'd been.

She had anticipated that faculty would visit her Harvard classes to evaluate her teaching, and was surprised when they didn't appear until the very end of her visit. When they came at last, she felt under tremendous pressure. It was relieved somewhat by the presence of Diane and Elisabeth Owens, who she felt were there to be supportive. (It was, however, part of their responsibilities as members of the Appointments Committee to visit and observe classes to evaluate teaching ability.)

Glendon had an additional burden. She was staunchly Catholic and pro-life (well before that mellifluous phrase was invented to supplant "anti-abortion"), and was therefore viewed with suspicion by many activist women. Diane didn't allow politics to interfere with her evaluation: what was important was not whether she agreed with another woman's politics; what was important was women advancing in the profession, and Mary Ann, while she may have been part of a different political spectrum, already embodied in her career the achieving, hard-working woman. Diane was Glendon's advocate, and sorely disappointed when her advocacy failed.

Despite the downsides of her experience there, Glendon would have accepted an offer from Harvard if for no other reason than that she was ambitious and because the

Mary Ann Glendon's ambition extended beyond the academic world to the judiciary. In 1980 she was a candidate for appointment to the First Circuit Court of Appeals. A blue-ribbon selection panel was appointed. The panel consisted of sixteen people, including prominent academics such as Professor Paul Freund, all male and dressed in suits except for one member, Diane Lund. After the men had grilled Glendon, Diane's question was "What book have you read this past week?" The question reflected her view that judges, like teachers, shouldn't be one-dimensional, and carried with it an aura of good will and support designed to offset the law-school harshness and aggressiveness embodied in the men's questions. Glendon was up against tough competition. On November 13, 1980, President Carter nominated Stephen Breyer, then Chief Counsel to the United States Judiciary Committee and for thirteen years a professor at Harvard. Breyer was confirmed a month later.

Harvard credential would have opened important doors for her in the legal community and elsewhere.

But Glendon's Harvard story didn't end there. A prolific writer, commentator and lecturer during the following twelve years, she developed a national and international reputation in the field of human rights and as a leading lay voice in the Catholic Church.* As a result of her prominence and her publications, Harvard came to view her as an important asset for its faculty, and once more approached her. This time – to her considerable satisfaction – the offer included tenure, and she accepted, joining the faculty in 1986.

In the academic year following Glendon's visit in 1974-75, Harvard hired Sally Neely, the first woman assistant professor on the tenure track after Diane. Neely, a 1970 Stanford graduate, had clerked on the Ninth Circuit Court of Appeals and had been an associate in private practice at a prestigious firm, but she hadn't previously taught at any law school. Young, attractive and inexperienced, she joined the faculty in the fall of 1975, and had the temerity to teach what a later, distinguished woman law professor, Tamar Frankel, calls "men's courses" – Contracts and the Legal Problems of Limited Partnerships. Undermined and badly mistreated by the men in her contracts class of 150 students, her experience at Harvard was traumatic.

---

* Glendon, still teaching at Harvard today, became the first woman president of the Pontifical Academy of Social Sciences, which advises the Vatican on its most sensitive social issues, and is viewed as the highest ranking woman in the Catholic Church.

She was challenged unmercifully and cruelly by men who were unwilling to give her the respect and deference automatically given to male professors, no matter how inexperienced. They resented being taught by a woman, and made no bones about it. Openly comparing her credentials to those of older distinguished law professors, many of whom had clerked on the United States Supreme Court or for other prominent jurists, they found her credentials lacking. She wasn't a graduate of Harvard and had merely clerked on the Ninth Circuit for a judge no one knew. Rudely talking over her comments and questions as she conducted the class, they refused to permit her to control the classroom.[*]

After two years, Neely requested a leave of absence. At the end of that leave, she resigned her position and moved on to a successful private practice.[†]

The next woman to join the faculty, Elizabeth Bartholet, came in 1977. She would become the first woman hired on a traditional track who achieved tenure, but not without angst, anger and admirable strategy. Bartholet had graduated from Harvard in 1965 and had fashioned a remarkable career as an activist lawyer in the public sector. She, like Diane and Glendon, viewed the law as an instrument for social change, but there the similarities ended. She came from a privileged class, the daughter of an investment banker. In her twelve years of practice, she'd been both a courtroom lawyer and an administrator promoting social justice, and she was ambitious. She was, moreover, self-assured to the point of being cocky, and had no doubt whatever that she belonged on the Harvard faculty and would be offered tenure in due course. She, like her predecessors, learned she would have to cope with a different reality.

Bartholet had focused on doing good in her professional career, both before coming to law school and before coming back to teach in 1977. While at Radcliffe she'd contemplated a career as a social worker but concluded it wasn't intellectually exciting. The law, on the other hand, was not only intellectually challenging, but provided a path for women to become powerful in a people-oriented service field. That was how people, particularly women, understood the law then.

Bartholet had married before coming to the law school in 1962, and her admission was almost by happenstance because her husband had already been admitted and she wanted to join him. She received no familial support in her decision: women weren't *supposed* to go to law school and *ambition* was a bad thing. The social and family pressures on women not to be ambitious and instead to serve others was overwhelming. "Everybody in my life, my husband, his family and my family were telling me it was a terrible idea" to go to law school with him. They'd be in competition and she would

---

[*]   Larry Field interview, June 23, 2005.
[†]   She declined to give an oral history to Harvard Law School's historian and likewise declined a request for an interview in connection with this book.

"ruin my husband's career and life at law school by coming to law school." She would become a different person, a "hard-driving ambitious type" instead of the nice person she was. *She might even do better than him,* which would be devastating.*

She – like Diane – did do better than her husband and was selected to *Law Review* at the end of her first year. She learned after the fact that there had been a discussion among some of the professors about whether her grade should be adjusted downward in order to spare the two of them this agony. Her husband's family was upset that she was invited to join *Law Review* and was higher in the class than he was – but she *was* ambitious and wasn't going to let this opportunity pass. It was hard to absorb the guilt she felt about it. Even now she is bothered and offended by the conventional wisdom of the time, that her joining the *Law Review* was a dreadful thing.†

Being on *Law Review* served Bartholet well in a variety of ways helpful to her career. Gannett House (the *Law Review*'s office) was a place of refuge for her. Others on the *Law Review* were supportive and became lifelong friends. Both the writing experience and the credential itself were important in her professional life after law school. She made a point – subtly, she hopes – of letting the judges before whom she appeared in court know not only that she had gone to Harvard, but that she was on the *Law Review* there. It made a difference in the attention they paid to what she had to say and to her arguments.

Where it didn't make a difference was in job hunting for clerkships and for employment in prosecutors' offices in New York. She badly wanted a U.S. District Court clerkship because she saw her future as being in litigation, but she couldn't get an offer. She did manage to secure a clerkship with Judge Edgerton of the D.C. Circuit, who regularly employed women as his clerks. (He was virtually unique among judges of the time in doing so.) She later interviewed with both U.S. Attorney Morgenthau, and Suffolk County Attorney Hogan in New York: while each seemed intrigued at the idea of hiring a woman as a prosecutor – she felt she was being viewed as a different species and a possible experiment – neither one offered her a job.

Instead she followed the few paths open to women: she first worked on the staff of the District of Columbia Crime Commission, then in the D.C. Public Defenders office. After she and her husband moved to New York City, she worked for the NAACP Defense Fund (a rare white face in its offices), then went on to serve as Counsel to the Vera Institute of Justice, which she hoped would assist her in founding a new public-interest law firm. In 1973, with the assistance of both foundation funding and government funding, she founded the Legal Action Center, whose mission was to assist society's outcasts, people coming out of prison, people with arrest and conviction histories, with drug convictions. Its focus, as the major way in which to help this group,

---

*   Bartholet oral history; interview June 29, 2005.
†   Bartholet oral history; interview June 29, 2005.

was on breaking down barriers to employment. She ran the center until she came to teach at Harvard in 1977. Only twelve years out of law school, she'd already had an extraordinary career litigating important issues of the time, and founding, finding financial support for and managing a public-interest law firm that survived and thrived for more than thirty years.

From the outset, Bartholet was an outspoken advocate for the law school's devoting a significant amount of its teaching to what lawyers could accomplish in society to make the lot of oppressed people better – but what she found soon after she arrived was that there was virtually total disinterest among the faculty in her and what she'd accomplished and what she was advocating. She found herself isolated. There was no place at Harvard for an activist lawyer.

Bartholet had been out of the academic law-school environment for a long time working among and with other activist lawyers and thought of herself as highly successful, but she had no natural cohort at Harvard, no one her year, her age or with her experience. Oddly, it didn't occur to her that there might be a question in the future as to whether she would get tenure. The issue for her, she thought, was whether the transition was doable for her and whether she'd want to stay.

When Bartholet came up for tenure in 1981, she learned she was going to be turned down, ostensibly (she was told) because of inadequacies in her teaching abilities. She was outraged. She thought of herself as a great lawyer, a very bright person – and who were these people who felt they had a right to judge her? She had a strong sense of self and cared about the law for all the right reasons. She also understood from the history of women before her that women were firmly, routinely and discreetly pushed aside. And they were expected to depart quietly.

Betsy Bartholet had never been fired, and she wasn't *going* to be fired. She dug in and made it clear she was going to fight. Knowing Harvard's history of expecting women to meekly decide to seek their fortunes elsewhere, she mounted a campaign to have the decision postponed a year so that she could "demonstrate" how she had learned from the school's teaching techniques and had become a "better teacher" who was equal to the "standards of excellence" expected of her. She tugged at her forelock and asked the advice of senior professors on the faculty – especially those on the Appointments Committee – what she should do to become a better teacher – and she arranged to have the tenure committee's attendance at her classes the next year shadowed by professors of her choice.

Having shown the appropriate amount of deference and willingness to learn, and that she wasn't going to go quietly away, she created a situation where the law school didn't want to get into a public battle and where it had a face-saving way to get out of it. She was given another year, but it was clear that so long as she behaved herself during that year she'd become tenured. It wouldn't have happened but for her decision to put up a determined fight. She was the first woman assistant professor granted tenure. It was only afterwards that she felt she'd regained her First Amendment rights.*

In 1978 three women, Martha Field, Barbara Black and Sally Moore came to the law school in a single year. Others would follow, but the unique problems women had to confront because they were women didn't go away. One who had worked her heart out teaching during her first year at Harvard was devastated when she read her students' evaluations of her teaching and found that a significant number criticized her because she wore too much red in class. They were more intent on what she was wearing than on the quality of her teaching. Another woman was criticized for wearing black all the time. The equation and the mystery of the different ways in which men and women teachers are viewed is hard to articulate.

Except for Glendon, these women did not know Diane well, nor did she serve as an explicit role model for them. What, then, had she contributed to them, their efforts and their careers and the efforts, ambitions and careers of the other women who came after them? The question is complex for reasons having to do with the historical bias of the system toward women and with the nature of women themselves.

Women of the period gravitated to those sectors of the law that were of particular interest to women but that men considered "soft" and not worthy of serious attention. In teaching those aspects of the law and attracting students to her classes in them, Diane legitimized these aspects of the uses of the law and paved the way for other women to teach them. Glendon's concentration on the core concepts of family and woman's role within it, and Bartholet's teaching of legal concepts involved in adoption and in reproductive sciences would not have been considered acceptable in the Harvard curriculum had it not been for Diane's family law courses dealing with abortion rights and birth control and with discrimination against otherwise legally disadvantaged people. Prior to her teaching these courses and generating interest in them, they would not have been accepted as a routine part of the curriculum.

She introduced and made acceptable – at least in the eyes of the administration, if not in those of the faculty as a body – the teaching of legal problems and concepts that were important to women and to poor people. Through her advocacy on the Admissions Committee she helped ensure that the audience to whom these problems and concepts would be taught would be interested and receptive. She planted seeds in the academic sector that made uses of the law in the public sector to advance the

---

*   Bartholet is still angered by this period, how she was treated and forced to kowtow and become humble. Her tactic was reminiscent of the well-known *Ladies' Home Journal* cartoon feature of the 1940s and 50s – the "Watchbird" ("This is a Watchbird watching a [fill in description]; and this is a Watchbird watching you!"). In her view, once she made it clear she intended to fight, the law school decided it didn't want a fight, and therefore the decision in favor of tenure a year later was a foregone conclusion. Another view might be that her strategy of having a shadow committee following the tenure committee was brilliant.

interests of the disadvantaged and powerless as legitimate and important subjects for discussion. She empowered women law students to understand that these issues were an important part of the mainstream of the nation's developing body of law.

Courageously, she transformed decades of traditional study of lawyers' fiduciary responsibilities *away from* the accumulation and preservation of private wealth and *toward* lawyers' fiduciary responsibilities in a broader, public sense. She virtually invented the first serious studies of lawyers' professional responsibilities independent of their fiduciary responsibilities, studies which would become required parts of every law-school curriculum. She caused students and faculty to think in broader terms than those required for a "work-obsessed skill-bank for big firms."

Most important from Harvard's perspective, she helped restore Harvard's credibility among both women and government agencies at a critical time for the university.

What resulted from her efforts were steps in the right direction. The physical and emotional energy required was extraordinary and perhaps not commensurate with the advances which actually occurred during these four years. The advances themselves, however, were not made in sand and thus easily washed away. They remained there for all to see and for others to build on and move forward, while Diane herself moved on to another phase of her life.

[1]   In the last analysis, it may have been fortunate for the women's movement that Ginsburg wasn't offered tenure at Harvard. She would orchestrate a "carefully constructed litigation campaign" which ultimately led to the Supreme Court's accepting the view that sex, like race, was a suspect classification within the meaning of the 14th Amendment's equal protection clause. Indeed, Justice Blackmun, the author of *Roe v. Wade,* didn't view that decision as being based on women's rights, but rather as permitting physicians to exercise their best judgment in treating their patients. (He'd once been general counsel to the Mayo Clinic.) It wasn't until 1986 that Blackmun, writing for a 5 to 4 majority in *Thornburgh* (striking down anti-abortion regulations in Pennsylvania), adopted the view that a woman's decision whether or not to choose to have an abortion was a fundamental right with which neither legislatures nor courts should interfere. It's unlikely that this shift in focus on the Supreme Court would have occurred without the efforts of Ruth Bader Ginsburg. [Linda Greenhouse, "The Evolution of a Justice," *New York Times Magazine,* April 10, 2005.]

[2]   During her short tenure at Northeastern, Diane formed lasting bonds with many of her students, and they continued to look to her for advice and counsel long after she'd departed for Harvard. Among them were Catherine White and Margot Botsford, both of whom became judges of the Massachusetts Superior Court (and later, in the case of Botsford, of the Supreme Judicial Court). Catherine Farrell became General Counsel to the Massachusetts Water Resources Authority and the Massachusetts Department of Environmental Management, Jeanne Baker, an articulate and outspoken feminist, became counsel to Vermont's governor Madeleine Kunin.

[3]   My involvement in Harvard's faculty social events was leavened by occasional conversations with Larry Tribe, then thirty-two and perhaps the most brilliant member of the faculty. His interests were broader than Harvard and his own work and achievements. Also, happily, I struck up a friendship with the wife of a visiting professor from Stanford, Gerald Gunther. Gunther, a pre-eminent Constitutional scholar, the biographer of Judge Learned Hand, formerly a law clerk to Judge Hand and thereafter to Supreme Court Chief Justice Earl Warren, was forty-five and at the height of his career. He'd been at Stanford since 1962, and Harvard wanted to woo him away. She and I discussed subjects other than law. As the year wore on, she remarked dryly that they could hardly wait to return to Palo Alto, where his colleagues were real and the atmosphere not elitist.

[4]   Dukakis' predecessor, Frank Sargent, had employed a "kitchen cabinet" to assist him on judicial appointments. The group, which consisted of his counsel, William Young (later Chief Judge of the U.S. District Court), and a few prominent members of the bar and judiciary – Judge James Roy (a conservative known as "the hanging judge") and my partner Tom Burns among them – not only recommended appointments but actively recruited candidates for the Superior Court from the trial bar. The appointments to that court had been excellent. The trial bar could now try cases with confidence that the new judges who guided our juries knew what they were doing – but the kitchen cabinet was only consulted on Superior Court appointments. The local District Courts – the ground level at which the public met the judicial system – remained the province of political favors and who you knew. Sargent didn't address the political abuses of the appointment process at the community level and of clerks of court at all levels. His approach was idiosyncratic and hadn't been formalized. It was in no way binding on his successors.

CHAPTER EIGHT

MOVING ON

CHOOSING TO LEAVE HARVARD WAS DIFFICULT IN SOME respects, easy in others. Harvard had provided Diane with the opportunity and the means to influence its institutional attitude toward women law students and teachers, and she'd done that. However, the institution within whose confines she had been working was elitist, and not one with which she felt comfortable being identified. She wouldn't regret the choice she had made.

During the next ten years Diane had "productive, socially useful and forward-looking work to do" and "shared life on a daily basis with people I really care about." These years were, she would write later, "some of the happiest experiences of my life." It was a time when she continued to teach courses on family law and lawyers' professional responsibilities, an occupation she genuinely loved. As a member of the Massachusetts Board of Bar Overseers, she put to practical use her views on lawyers' obligations to their clients and to the public. Importantly, she also had a law practice in which her cases advanced the interests of women and children in domestic crises, especially children's interests. Most importantly, she felt no pressure to be anyone other than who she was.

Who she was, however, was complex. She was and continued to be a role model for women generally and women lawyers in particular. While she wouldn't abide sexual discrimination against herself, she nevertheless had to tolerate professional disappointments whose root cause was precisely that. There were triumphs as well. What made the disappointments tolerable during these years was the renewal of her family life and the solid foundation the law firm she and Regina Healy founded gave her.

Regie was a kindred spirit. On graduating from law school in June 1971, she was awarded a Reginald Heber Smith Fellowship, part of a national program intended to create coordinated public-interest law firms across the country to represent poor people's interests. Fellows – usually bright law-school graduates – received two weeks' training and then assisted in establishing local public-interest entities. The entity in Regie's case was the Cambridge Legal Assistance Office (CLAO) sponsored by Harvard and run on its behalf by a public-services attorney named John Cratsley. Cratsley also lectured at Harvard, and CLAO provided its students with one of their rare opportunities to do clinical work while still in law school.

After her first year at CLAO, a year Regie recalls as "heady," a time when it was still thought possible to save the world, she received an additional two-year fellowship. CLAO, meanwhile, morphed into Cambridge and Somerville Legal Services (CASLS), which operated independently of Harvard and without its support. While continuing to work at CASLS, she was appointed in 1973 as one of three commissioners of the newly-minted Massachusetts Commission Against Discrimination, where she sat as a hearing commissioner on individual cases and as a board member on their appeals. In theory the MCAD appointment was – like Diane's position at Harvard – a part-time job, but the task of establishing and running the first-ever governmental body charged with remedying discrimination in all its forms was daunting. Among other things, the MCAD had no rules or regulations to govern its proceedings and decisions, and the task of developing those regulations – like the task of developing regulations for Chapter 622 – was complex and time-consuming. For Regie it was a frenzied time.

It was frenzied not only because of the issues the MCAD faced, but because of other matters in which both Regie and Diane were involved. Although they had left the employ of MLRI in 1971, they didn't leave behind either the friendship they'd formed or the issues that had engaged them. In their various capacities at Northeastern and Harvard, and at CLAO, CASLS and the MCAD – and as individuals – they worked together on poverty law, women's issues, and employment discrimination. Regie and Diane consulted frequently on CASLS issues.[1] On their own time they worked to implement Chapter 622. One assignment in Diane's course on the legal status of women was to develop guidelines to combat gender discrimination in lending practices. She sent the end result to Regie and it was adopted in toto as an MCAD regulation.

They collaborated on another important step for women. As a state agency, the MCAD had the right to ask the attorney general for opinions regarding legal standards and requirements. Regie and Diane drafted an inquiry as to whether married women had to go to court to gain the right to resume using their original names. The attorney general's opinion stated that there was no need to go to court, and that women were free to use any name they wanted, so long as the use of the name was not in furtherance of a fraudulent or illegal scheme. Some years earlier, Regie herself had had to go to court to obtain permission to resume using her original name. A skeptical judge allowed her request only because her husband appeared in court and testified, under oath, that he had no objection.

Regie's decision to resume her original name had unexpected repercussions. My male chauvinist partner Tom Burns – an excellent trial lawyer in most respects – represented one of our firm's corporate clients in an appeal from an MCAD decision of Regie's that our client had discriminated against a female employee. The appeal was heard by Judge James Roy, the same judge who had served with Tom on Governor Sargent's kitchen cabinet on judicial appointments. The gist of Tom's argument was that Regie had an obvious bias favoring women: how else could one view a woman who had rejected her husband's name in favor of the one she was born with? Roy, a stalwart Episcopalian churchgoer, agreed, and reversed the decision.*

The stars were aligned for Diane and Regie in the spring of 1976, and they joined forces. Reg had determined to move on to private practice and had tentatively explored a space-sharing arrangement with another attorney, Nancy Gertner, who was developing a formidable reputation as a trial lawyer in the criminal defense practice. When she mentioned her plans, Diane argued that she shouldn't simply be sharing office space. She needed a law partner, and the only appropriate partner Diane could think of was herself. Both the timing and the practice made a perfect fit because Diane was leaving the regular faculty at Harvard, Reg intended to go into a domestic-relations practice that would concern the interests of women and children, and, since Diane would be continuing to lecture at Harvard, they could teach the family law course there together.

They needed a low-overhead operation because neither one had an established practice, and they wanted their office near the probate and superior courts in Cambridge because the practice they hoped to develop would focus on representing women and on employment discrimination in cases tried in those courts.

HEALY & LUND

The firm of Healy & Lund opened its offices in Cambridge on July 4, 1976, in five small rooms of a fourth-floor walk-up in a commercial building at 189 Cambridge Street. Their offices were three floors above the Esquire Bar & Grill and across the street from the Middlesex County Probate Court. Regie and Diane each chipped in $3000 to start the firm.

Healy & Lund began with two lawyers and two flex-time receptionist/assistants (Diane insisted the firm should provide part-time employment for mothers who had child care responsibilities). They had only one typewriter, but a great deal of carbon

---

* When I learned about it, I was appalled, both at what Tom had argued and what Roy had decided. Reg and I didn't know each other well in those days, and it took Diane's considerable persuasive powers to convince Regie that I had nothing to do with the case and hadn't suggested the argument. I was never certain she was entirely convinced.

paper. When they wanted to copy something, they went across the street to the courthouse to do it. In those days before computers and word processing, they did their own typing. The furniture was secondhand or acquired at auction. In the waiting area on the fourth-floor landing they placed an outdated Danish-modern couch that had been our first furniture purchase.

The probate courthouse across the street was where much of their work representing women and children in domestic strife would be done. Another block away was the Middlesex County Superior Courthouse. A block further to the east was the District Court where the city's petty crimes (and some not so petty) were prosecuted. The Probate Court was where emotions were laid bare, and this was the environment in which the two women would practice law.

My firm had moved its offices to the fourth floor of Boston's Old City Hall, a 19th-century porticoed building in the Greek style which had been gutted and redeveloped to provide modern office space, and was acclaimed as part of Boston's architectural heritage. On the ground and first floors, and (in warm weather) on its outdoor patio, was Maison Robert, the best French restaurant in Boston at a time when Boston's fine dining was beginning a renaissance. Diane wrote that the "difference" between our two firms was that "Erik's office is over Maison Robert while mine is over the Esquire Bar & Grill."

One-eighty-nine Cambridge Street was (and is) an unassuming brick building next door to the East Cambridge Fire House. The workday would be punctuated by bells and sirens as engines roared out of the firehouse on calls and on drills. The rigorous climb to their offices ensured that most of their clients would be hardy.

The Esquire, a lunchtime watering hole for locals, and for lawyers and their clients and witnesses who were engaged in trial at one of the courthouses, consisted of two adjoining rooms. One was a smoke-filled bar where blue-collar locals and unaccompanied lawyers congregated; the other was the grill where lawyers and their clients and witnesses came during the lunch recess and at the end of the trial day to sit in booths and talk privately under the cover of raucous popular music coming from stereo speakers in the corners of the room. The food, accompanied by a small salad, recently unfrozen cooked vegetables and mashed potatoes, came off the grill. It was a good idea to have some Pepto-Bismol along. The atmosphere favored long-timers who knew each other, whether as lawyers or habitués or both.

Their landlord, Manny Costa, both owned the building and operated the Esquire Bar & Grill with great pride. Manny was a Portuguese immigrant who'd worked hard to make a success for himself and his family in his new country, and he had a Southern European male's-eye view of the proper place of women in the world. He was tickled by the idea of a two-woman law firm in his own building, and he thought the presence of the firm added class. Happily from every respect, they liked each other. He took a paternal interest in them from the start.

The rent was $300 per month. Each year Diane and Regie would visit with Manny in one of the Esquire's booths and agree on what the rent would be for the next year. They would talk to him at length, telling poignant stories about their elderly clients and the difficulties their clients had making it up three flights of stairs without an elevator. Often, they said, they had to confer with them in an Esquire booth. While it was a sacrifice for them, given other available rental space, Regie would say (while Diane had difficulty keeping a straight face) they liked Manny a great deal and wanted to stay there anyway, despite the hardship to their clients. So long as they could afford the rent, of course. Manny was gentle and considerate throughout the negotiations, always smiled at their stories, was charmed by the attention and could scarcely bear to raise their rent at all over the next ten years.

Manny responded to their client concerns by renaming the Esquire Bar & Grill "The Barrister's Lounge," which added another touch of class to the building and to the meetings held in his restaurant booths. His clientele remained the same, ignoring the name change. In truth, there were many booth meetings, usually with Diane's loyal upper-class trusts and estates clients, who had stayed with her from her days at Herrick, Smith, or had since been referred to her by those clients or her Harvard colleagues. The "conference room" in which the clients found themselves may not have been quite what they anticipated, but Diane never lost a client on that account. Her clients undoubtedly dined out on the stories they had to tell.

They were not the only ones. Regie found it delectable that in the firm's early days – given the amount of *pro bono* and appointed work it undertook – the wealthy clientele whose fees kept the firm afloat rarely met with Diane in her office, but instead in the booths of the Esquire Bar & Grill. The two of them made house calls in their *pro bono* practice, including to a client who cooked for a well-to-do family on Beacon Hill. The meals she cooked for them, like the stories they garnered, were delicious, better, perhaps, than a fee.

To go out on their own with little more than academic and public-interest practice backgrounds required courage and commitment. They had no promise of clients then or that there ever would be any. "When we founded the firm," says Regie, "we were scared to death because neither of us had any experience at being in private practice. It was an article of faith for us that the domestic-relations practice needed our services and that we'd have clients. From where? That was the question for us." Diane, always optimistic, had no doubts. She believed that if they built the firm, clients would come because the firm was offering services and advice that were important to ordinary people. Their firm's principal objective was to see to it that women and children caught up in difficult domestic circumstances had adequate representation, and that they were dealt with fairly in the courts and treated fairly in the outcome of the disputes. The fees they might generate were secondary. No other firm in the Boston area had ever taken such an approach toward the resolution of domestic issues.

In the early years Diane and Regie did all their cases together. They interviewed together and went to court together. Diane was the brief writer and Regie the zealous advocate. It was a wonderful time. They enjoyed each other, liked what they were doing, and felt their clients were being well served – which they were. Comfortable together, they laughed a great deal as they worked out strategies and resolutions for their clients, and were truly happy in working on the practice they'd founded. They became not just professional partners and associates but close personal and social friends, with their families thrown into the mix. In off-hours they took extension courses together at Harvard, delving into Shakespeare and into the traditions and great works of opera. They viewed what they were doing, in its entirety, as being the balanced life which all women – and all persons – should live.

At the outset most of their cases were *pro bono*. They had to deal regularly with bombastic male lawyers who felt insulted at having to deal with women on the other side and who attempted to intimidate them in person and over the telephone. Diane and Regie were unmoved. On one occasion Diane told Reg to hang up on a lawyer who was shouting abuse at her over the phone. He was so loud that when Reg held the phone away from her ear he could be heard throughout the office. Diane, laughing at Reg's sour facial expression, mouthed the words, "Hang up! Hang up!" She did and refused to take his return call. They enjoyed his discomfiture, being unwilling, correctly, to take his posturing seriously.

They decided to donate 8% of their modest fees to charity. Naively they included a notice to that effect in their fee agreements, thinking their clients would approve. "Good for you!" they'd say, but that was not the reaction. Instead – despite the modest rates – the client reaction was that they were being overcharged. If any of their money was going to go to charity, they themselves should be the charity. Diane and Regie took the clause out of their fee agreement, continued to charge the same low rates, and afterwards did what they wanted to do with their earnings.

Diane was always sympathetic to where people were coming from, and could scarcely bring herself to refuse to help them. As a result, Healy & Lund took on more than their share of difficult cases and clients. Extraordinarily patient with others, Diane worked hard to understand what it was the clients needed and what she could achieve for them. And she worked hard for that result, even when the clients themselves, being unversed in the law, had unreasonable expectations and couldn't see the value of what she wanted to do for them.

One case that received notoriety concerned a woman who refused to move out of her home on the North Shore after having been ordered to do so by a judge. She was psychotic, and without a lawyer. Diane insisted to Reg that she needed representation, regardless of her psychological state or the merits of her position. Reg was dubious, but they volunteered and took the case on. Ultimately they were unsuccessful in vacating the order, and their client had to move. The client came away believing that she was not alone and that someone cared for her in this situation, but she was unable to accept the fact that she'd lost her case and had to leave her home. This was hard lawyering.

They were concerned about their clients in ways that most lawyers aren't, and their concern caused them on occasion to lend their clients money. One case involved a woman on welfare who'd been divorced years earlier from a penniless husband. He had become extremely successful at Polaroid, but refused to increase his minimal support payments. Diane loaned the woman the money she needed to pay her taxes. Eventually the husband lost the case and she was repaid.

Their cases involved a panoply of difficult issues having to do with the rights of parents vis-à-vis their children, with children's welfare and best interests, and with the Massachusetts Department of Social Services' often overreaching attempts to deprive the parents and the children of each other. Over the course of eight years, decisions in their cases set standards that still guide domestic-relations court judges in dealing with these issues.

In one case they represented the paternal grandparents of a minor child who'd been removed as custodial guardians by a probate judge in favor of the child's step-grandmother – even though both parents had assented to the grandparents' appointment. The parents had separated in 1969, before their daughter was born, and were divorced in 1974. Their other two children had resided with the grandparents since 1974, but the mother and her infant daughter had moved in with her father and stepmother in 1970. She and her second husband had obtained legal custody of her daughter in 1977 and her daughter lived with them until 1981, when she and her second husband separated. Her daughter resided with the step-grandmother for one month before the grandparents were appointed as custodial guardians. The child had had almost no contact with her siblings until 1981.

The probate judge found that the child wished to live with her step-grandmother and to visit her grandparents, and that she loved both families. He awarded custody to the step-grandmother.

The Appeals Court affirmed the decision, and the case was further appealed to the Supreme Judicial Court. Diane argued that further appellate review was required because the prior decision in the case was contrary to the statutory law and the developing judge-made law on parental rights. This position was vindicated by the Supreme Judicial Court's decision that while the step-grandmother could properly bring to the probate judge's attention "any facts which might render the approved guardians subject to removal," the judge was not free to vacate the grandparents' appointment without finding that they were unsuitable or unfit. If the child's parents were found to be fit, the judge was bound to grant custody to them or to honor their wishes as to custody. The interests of the child to be reared with her natural parents must take precedence. The probate judge's findings did not warrant a finding of unsuitability or unfitness.*

Based on the same judicial principles, Healy & Lund successfully brought a number of cases challenging DSS decisions on the ground that the evidence was insufficient to establish unfitness on the part of a mother or, in some instances, both parents. In one case the Supreme Judicial Court decided that the parental visitation rights of even a parent who had *voluntarily* relinquished her child to DSS could not be terminated without a current showing of unfitness.† DSS had to reconsider and amend what had often been its arbitrary approach to cases. Before this, its actions had gone unchallenged.

Many cases Diane and Regie took on represent landmarks in the legal history and legal precedents of Massachusetts, particularly as that history and those precedents concern women and children. One of their early cases, *Gardner v. Rothman*, first heard by Probate Judge Haskell Freedman, and then decided by the Supreme Judicial Court in 1976, concerned the rights of an out-of-wedlock mother to deny visitation rights to the father. The father had acknowledged his paternity and asked the court to grant him visitation rights. The mother had denied him visitation because he'd failed to provide financial support and because she feared emotional harm to herself and the child. She asserted that she had the "sole and complete right to the care and custody of the child," and, as there was no controlling Massachusetts precedent, cited British common law concerning "natural right to custody" (in Britain the mother has the right to custody and control) to support her case.

In her brief, Diane also argued that the father was not asserting a legal relationship with the child in which he had a "definite interest." In fact he had never been legally determined to be the father. It was a precondition, she wrote, that he obtain a declaration of paternity before he could pursue any alleged rights. Moreover, the status of an out-of-wedlock father is different. He doesn't have to support the child and the child has no right of inheritance. A custodial mother who is completely and properly caring for the child should be allowed the right to determine what is in the child's best interests.

It was a case of first impression for the Supreme Judicial Court, presenting an issue not previously decided. It was, moreover, the first case – as the Court noted during oral argument – in which two women lawyers had argued opposing propositions before the Court.‡ The Court's decision, written by Justice Robert Braucher, a former law professor and Harvard colleague of Diane's, held that while there is judicial power to grant visitation rights to the father of an illegitimate child, the guiding principle must be what is in the best interests of the child, a principle Diane had espoused. The case was remanded for the lower court's consideration, to settle the question whether in

---

* *Chaplin v. Freeman*, 388 Mass. 398 (1983).
† *Petition of the Department of Public Welfare to dispense with Consent to Adoption*, 1981 MA adv. Sheets 1157.
‡ Opposing Reg in the oral argument was another woman attorney, Gene Dahmen, a pioneer in her own right.

this case, as the mother contended, visitation by the father should rest entirely in her discretion. Diane and Reg were successful for their client in further proceedings. The judge decided, after trial, that the father would not be granted visitation.

In a number of cases, Diane and Regie represented women who were married to controlling and physically abusive husbands they were afraid of. One significantly successful case resulted in a comprehensive decision by Justice John Greaney of the Massachusetts Appeals Court, which clarified the process that probate court judges should follow in making custodial and financial rulings in connection with a divorce.* Their client, Marie Angelone, had had three episodes of serious depression, one in 1963 when she was on her own for the first time, one in 1974-75 when she was physically exhausted, and one in 1976 when the marriage was breaking up. However, the children had been living with her since 1976, and she was the stable figure in their lives. Her therapist testified that he didn't foresee future problems, and the guardian *ad litem* appointed by the trial court concluded that Marie should have physical custody. Her husband, he said, should only be allowed carefully scheduled visitation rights with "definite arrival and departure times" – and she and the children should remain in the family home. The judge ordered the husband to convey his interest in the family home to Marie and to pay $200 in weekly support, orders which were upheld on appeal against the husband's argument that she was an unfit mother because of her episodes of depression.

Unwilling to accept the outcome, the husband stalked his former wife and harassed her, showing up unannounced on her doorstep and telephoning at all hours. He wasn't deterred by the court's protective order or by the prospect of being held in contempt. Marie told Diane she could take it no longer and was going to disappear, taking the children with her, to Alaska. Diane was enormously conflicted, knowing she couldn't advise her client to scamper – but she didn't try to dissuade her. In a lengthy and sympathetic meeting, Diane told the client that if she did go to Alaska, it would be against her legal advice, she could no longer represent her, and she'd have to withdraw her appearance as a lawyer on her behalf. She asked Marie to write her after she arrived in Alaska to let her know she was all right. Marie left with the children, and Diane immediately withdrew her appearance, but she refused to disclose her knowledge of Marie's plans because their conversation came within the protection of the attorney-client privilege. Marie raised her children in Alaska and later returned to live with them elsewhere in the country. She and Diane corresponded from time to time and spoke on the telephone. They remained friends, and Diane never doubted that the outcome was just. Marie's husband did not learn their whereabouts.

Occasionally, Reg and Diane found humor and justice even in abusive-husband cases. One involved the then-treasurer of Norfolk County, an obese and physically

---

* *Angelone v. Angelone*, 9 Mass. App. Ct., 728 (1980).

violent man whose wife came to them to represent her in divorce proceedings. She was more interested in her freedom than in his money. She told them she thought her husband had been embezzling funds from public employees' retirement accounts and depositing them in an account in his name in a bank in Lowell. When they deposed him in their conference room, examining him at length about the source of the money in his bank accounts, he became visibly uncomfortable and began shifting from side to side in his chair, one of the cane-seated antique chairs Diane and I had acquired at auction. Suddenly it collapsed, and he found himself on the floor. (He wasn't injured – but I had to repair the chair.) Somehow the Norfolk County district attorney got wind of the case, subpoenaed the deposition transcript and brought criminal proceedings. He was convicted, and, ultimately, he died in jail.

Their representation of clients wasn't limited to women's and children's interests. One client who came to them was a janitor in a local medical school. He wanted to be identified as the father of out-of-wedlock twin daughters with a woman who was now a prostitute, and to obtain custody of his daughters. He talked to Diane and Regie at length about his life and ambitions, and convinced them that he was going to turn his life around. They were successful in representing him, and he succeeded both in obtaining custody and in his ambitions. While raising his daughters he obtained his high school diploma, went on to college on a scholarship, and then on to medical school, all as a single father. He became a practicing physician highly respected in the community, and his daughters were themselves a success story.

Healy & Lund took on cases no other lawyer would touch. Reaching the right result was often difficult. One client, a woman sent to them by a Cambridge city councilor (a Catholic who didn't want his name associated with the case), was taking care of a retarded daughter who had become pregnant. She wanted her daughter to have an abortion, but she refused. The client said it was difficult enough at her age to have to take care of her daughter; she couldn't also take care of her daughter's child – and her daughter was incapable of taking care of the child herself. They agreed to represent the mother in a guardianship proceeding to give her the power to compel her daughter to have the abortion. Diane insisted the daughter should be separately represented and notified the American Civil Liberties Union about the case. It appointed a fiery advocate, Diane's former student Jeanne Baker (a proponent of choice), to contest the case. She argued vigorously that the daughter had the capacity and had the right to choose. The case was rendered moot when the daughter's sister told her she should have an abortion, and she did, during the trial. Diane and Regie taught this case as part of their family law course at Harvard.

The firm doubled in size, adding two lawyers. The first was the improbable addition in 1979 of John Adams Fiske, a Yale graduate with an impeccable Yankee pedigree on both sides of his family. The firm's name changed to Healy, Lund &

Fiske. They were joined later by Philip Woodbury, who came to them after a legal-services career.

John had spent the early years of his Boston practice with Choate, Hall & Stewart (for a time sharing an office with me), and then ten years in public practice, first as First Assistant Corporation Counsel to the City of Boston under Mayor Kevin White, then as Executive Secretary to the Supreme Judicial Court. He came back into

The staff of Healy, Lund and Fiske, l. to r.: Diane, Philip Woodbury, Regie, Laurie Udell and John Fiske.

private practice believing – correctly and presciently – that domestic-relations clients were outraged both by delays in resolving their cases and by the inordinate size of their own lawyers' legal fees in resolving marital and domestic issues. Mediation rather than litigation, he believed, was the wave of the future. Mediation – the use of third-party lawyers not affiliated with either side to assist in resolving the parties' issues – was beginning to be used in domestic relations practice but was still a novel concept in legal practice generally. Diane and Regie had thought about offering mediation services, but when each of them tried it, they found they didn't enjoy it. A process by which the domestic warring parties reached agreement without regard to the fairness of the resolution or the best interests of the children wasn't something they felt comfortable with.

Looking for an appropriate place to establish his mediation practice, John had spoken to several probate judges who recommended he should talk to Diane and Reg. He had a sunny disposition and they liked him immediately. While they personally had reservations about mediation (Reg was, and always would be, an advocate), their practice had grown to the point where they needed another lawyer to help out. John could fill that role while pursuing the development of a mediation practice – and he could contribute to the overhead. The arrangement was made, and they both came to regard him with a great deal of affection. He would go on to become the dean of domestic-relations mediators in the Boston area well before mediation became the process du jour in every aspect of litigation, and well before mediation became big business for the mediation firms that sprang up later.

When John first joined them, the firm occupied only half of Manny's fourth floor. To accommodate him, Diane and Reg had to share an office for a time – shades of their days at the Massachusetts Law Reform Institute. Then, when the lawyers who occupied the other half of the fourth floor fortuitously decided to move, Healy, Lund & Fiske was able to take over the remainder of the floor. They hired a contractor to create a more substantial entry and waiting area, and to incorporate the rest of the fourth floor into their space. More furniture was added from auctions and the firm still has its offices there today.

In representing one side or the other in divorce proceedings, Diane's concerns and sympathies lay less with the warring parents and more with their children. Her interests coincided with those expressed by Probate Judge Edward Ginsberg, who believed that the children involved in a divorce should have a separate voice and separate representation in the cases before him. Only if that were the case, he felt, could he be satisfied that the "best interests of the children" – the legal standard he was bound to apply – would be adequately represented. His approach was innovative, the first of its kind in Massachusetts, and it created a different and novel kind of legal practice for Healy & Lund.

Ginsberg respected Diane and Reg because of the way they dealt with cases before him. They appeared in his court as a team, an unusual team because Reg was a zealous advocate while Diane's approach was not adversarial. She looked at the entire picture, and her advocacy focused on what she believed was best for all the parties. He watched them (as he watched all lawyers who appeared before him) to get a sense of how competent they were and how they dealt with their cases. Most lawyers in his court simply schlepped through many of their cases. Not Diane and Regie. They always prepared well for every case and did it well, no matter the economics involved, down to the smallest case. They did what lawyers are supposed to do. It was impressive to see.*

An extraordinary and difficult case involved a custody battle against DSS for a client with a young baby. The mother had been briefly institutionalized, but Healy & Lund had succeeded in regaining custody of her newborn baby from DSS – a victory that was no small feat in itself. Ten weeks later, at the end of April, they received a late-afternoon call from the mother, from a phone booth in a Howard Johnson's in Lowell. She told them she'd decided to hitchhike with the baby to California. Reg would have been inclined to advise the mother that she shouldn't do that and inform her of the consequences if she did, and then let events take their course. Not Diane. Even though it was our daughter Kristin's birthday, her immediate reaction was that they couldn't abandon the baby to the mother when she was plainly having a psychotic episode. "We have to go get the baby!" She talked to the mother, told her they were on their way and asked her to wait.

They drove to the Howard Johnson's and persuaded the mother that she needed to commit herself again. They then drove mother and baby to a mental health center where Regie took the mother in to arrange for a commitment while Diane stayed in

---

*   A judge, says Ginsberg, wants the job done well because lawyers doing their job well help the judge do his job. Doing the job well before a judge is the way to get appointments. For a good judge, appointments aren't a political question. They're based on merit and what the judge sees particular lawyers can bring to the case to help him do his own job.

the car for two hours with a wailing ten-week-old baby who was hungry and needed his diapers changed. After the mother's commitment, they drove the baby to Beth Israel Hospital looking for temporary help until the baby could be turned over to DSS the next day. Beth Israel gave them diapers and a bottle of formula, but refused to take the baby because its policy was not to take in infants more than ten weeks old. They drove on to Children's Hospital, which agreed to take the baby overnight and to call DSS the next day.

One of their signal achievements was that the day the mother was released from her commitment, they succeeded in regaining custody of the baby for her from DSS. The mother had no further episodes, and the baby was brought up by his mother in a normal fashion.

Ginsberg began appointing Diane and Reg to represent children and to advocate their interests. As their office was directly across the street from his court, it was convenient to call them when he wanted to appoint an attorney to represent children. They came every time they were called.

Diane, he felt, was perfect for the job because it was clear that children trusted her and would talk to her about things they wouldn't discuss with anyone else. She threw herself into the effort, spent time with the children, interviewed their teachers and guidance counselors and, in cases where they already had professional help, spoke with their psychiatrists. The result would be a detailed, reasoned report of her findings and recommendations to Judge Ginsberg. She had a talent for flushing out the relevant information and then writing straightforward, uncomplicated reports. She had, says Ginsberg, a "wonderful command" of the English language and "wrote beautifully" in a clear, simple style. And she really cared about children. *

Judge Ginsberg's colleagues on the bench thought his approach was unnecessary. One said, "We don't need that – the judges represent the children!" Ginsberg felt differently. The parents' interests and the children's interests weren't the same, and the information parents gave during divorce proceedings wasn't reliable because it reflected each parent's interests. Since the judge is required to make decisions based on what is in the best interests of the children, he felt that the children needed a lawyer to represent them so the judge could get as much information as possible for the purpose of making that decision.*

---

* Edward Ginsberg interview, November 15, 2005.

---

* She was not (in Ginsberg's words) a "causist." Whatever her own feelings, she put them aside. She understood there were competing interests and gave weight to all of them. She analyzed the situation and came up with a clear and well-reasoned analysis for her recommendations. She had an extraordinary combination of talents, the rare exception who worked with both her head and her heart. She had no ego involvement in her cases. It was rare, Ginsberg says, for anyone as talented as she was not to have an ego that interfered with the job.

A memorable case involved the children of two psychiatrists who were using their young children as pawns in their marital war. Both sides were represented by prominent members of the bar. Appointed to represent the children, a son and a daughter, Diane came away from her interviews with them appalled at the callousness both parents showed toward their well-being. She agonized over what recommendations to make, but finally concluded that joint custody would only result in further harm to them as each parent used them against the other. Joint custody was the usual order of the day, but not in this case. Ginsberg awarded sole legal custody to one parent only, the wife, ordered the husband to release all interest in the marital home to her and cut back his visitation to two weeks in the summer. The traumatized husband appealed.

On appeal, Ginsberg's order was upheld. The Court said the case was controlled by the earlier Angelone case, and that in deciding custody matters the overriding concern must be the best interests of the children and their general welfare. The Court said it was a difficult proposition to maintain that there should be an award of joint custody in a divorce traumatized by personal and emotional conflict – and noted Ginsberg's determination that an award of joint custody in this case would be an "invitation to continued warfare and conflict."*

In another battle with DSS, Diane was appointed guardian *ad litem* for a severely disturbed, apparently autistic, six-year-old. In the absence of a biological relative to care for her, she was living in an institution for the retarded, a setting clearly damaging to her. The issue was whether she could be deinstitutionalized and placed in foster care, which, after investigation, Diane recommended. Her responsibility then evolved into ensuring that state agencies provided appropriate services for the child and to monitor the mental health, social services and educational components of the child's program. She filed reports with the court on fifteen separate occasions documenting what turned out to be a success story for the child. Due in part to her monitoring, the child was raised by dedicated and loving foster parents and attended a private day school where she made excellent progress.

Not all the cases had happy endings. One custody case involved the adolescent children of a marriage between an indigent and long-suffering mother and a gangster father who'd moved to New York where, it seemed, he had access to a great deal of money, little of which he was willing to pay – or had been ordered to pay – to the mother for her support. Proving the amount of his income or its sources to improve her position was impossible for obvious reasons. The father, who had visitation rights, was seeking full custody. During his visitation periods, he would send a limousine to pick up the children. He treated them royally when they were with him, something the mother couldn't do. The children adored their father.

Diane, believing both parents should be involved in raising their children,

---

*   *Rolde v. Rolde*, 12 Mass. App Ct. 398 (1981).

recommended an order which would have required the children to bridge the gap with their mother. The children opted to follow the money. Judge Ginsberg went along with their wishes and awarded physical custody to the father, although his order specified that the parents would have joint legal custody and the mother would have visitation rights. Immediately after the judge's decision, the children climbed into their father's limousine and drove off to New York while their mother and Diane, helpless, stood and watched from curbside.

Over time, Ginsberg began to deviate from the idealistic principles which had led him to appoint Diane to represent children. More and more, his priorities became to resolve divorce cases through agreement of the parties as to the terms of their divorce, regardless of her reports and recommendations as to the best interests of the children. He became primarily interested in one thing – having the couples before him settle their differences without a trial (which would have forced him to make decisions he believed they should make for themselves) – and that often meant sacrificing the interests of the children as Diane saw them. That was hard for her, and it became harder. Given the judge's caseload and pressures to expedite the cases he had, his changed approach is understandable, but Diane found she couldn't accept outcomes for children based on expediency.

Representing clients and representing children in the divorce court is difficult and emotionally draining work in the best of circumstances. On top of this, to see her work cast aside was too much. Diane visited Ginsberg in his chambers in the spring of 1985 and told him she wasn't going to do this any more. "The system," she said, "is destructive, and I'm not sure I'm doing anything to help the children."* She told him she was going to work with children in a context where she knew she was helping them. She needed something tangible. She was going to give up the law, volunteer doing day care and become involved in the education of young children. This would be hands-on work whose result did not depend on the behavior of other people. She'd be able to see the results herself, right away.

"What a loss!" thought Ginsberg. The court needed people with her training, her experience and her intellect. It was a shame. She had never shown signs of burn-out or even irritation or frustration in his courtroom. What was it that ate her up inside? He thought about trying to talk her out of it, but it was clear she wasn't there for that purpose, and to do so would demean the decisions she'd made.†

---

* It was typical of Diane that she would confront problems directly, but not assign blame to anyone. She had a great deal of respect for Ginsberg and believed he should be given an explanation for her decision to withdraw. Her explanation was accurate, if incomplete. In Ginsberg's memory of the conversation, it was the behavior of warring parents who used their children in their war without regard to the effect on them that had gotten to her. For someone as principled as Diane, he knew, this kind of behavior was incomprehensible.

† Ginsberg interview, November 15, 2005.

The family at home in Lexington, 1985: Kristin, myself, Ted, Diane and Ben.

What Ginsberg didn't understand was that what drove Diane had little to do with the structure within which she was working, or with financial reward, or with the stature and reputation she could gain personally within that structure with the people who controlled it. What drove her was whether the end result of her work was worthwhile for the persons whose interests she represented. At MLRI, she was intent on advancing the interests of women and poor people. At Harvard she'd been the face of women's interests in admissions and in academics. In private practice, while she continued to represent women's interests in fair outcomes in their divorce cases, her focus had shifted to what she could do for children. Ginsberg's original concept had given her the opportunity she needed. His retreat to expediency made her efforts irrelevant. And there was nothing she could do about it.

But this wasn't the whole of it. Other events also contributed to her decision.

OTHER EVENTS AND OTHER CHALLENGES

The two years between the spring of 1983 and the spring of 1985 were important personally and professionally. After Kristin graduated from high school in June 1983 and entered Middlebury, we were alone together in an empty nest for the first time in twenty-two years. Ted was a junior at Bowdoin and Ben was at Oxford, soon to enter Harvard Law School. With two of my partners I had left Burns & Levinson in 1980, taking seven lawyers with us to form Posternak, Blankstein & Lund, and the new firm was growing rapidly as its practice was burgeoning. I was spending more and more time at my new firm and in court in what seemed an unending series of trials.

Diane was at the summit of her professional career in 1983, but that was soon to change. With those changes, and with all three of our children preparing for independent lives, she took time to think back over the previous twenty-five years and to look ahead to what she wanted to do in the next twenty-five. In June 1985 she wrote that it was "crazy to keep rushing along through life this way…. I'm not clearly doing good in the world and I want to spend more time doing that."* She had decided to do something other than the practice of law. Exactly what she'd do wasn't clear, but her decision was.

Apart from her law practice and lecturing and the close attention she'd paid to our children during their teenage years, Diane had continued to serve the public good in a variety of capacities. She had represented N.O.W. in litigation attempting to enjoin the Knights of Columbus from distributing anti-ERA material just prior to an election on the grounds that it hadn't registered as a "political committee."† In 1980 she'd become a board member, and later president, of the Council for Public Justice. And beginning in early 1978 she'd served as a member of the Board of Bar Overseers, the governing body for Massachusetts lawyers, whose members were appointed by the Supreme Judicial Court.

The Council for Public Justice was a nonprofit organization of volunteers whose purpose was to bring the Massachusetts court system into the twentieth century. Courts needed to be made more accessible to everyone; judges should be chosen on merit; district court judges should be required to serve full-time rather than be allowed to practice law part-time; sentencing in criminal cases needed guidelines to ensure uniform treatment of defendants regardless of their skin color or social or financial status. These were some of the issues addressed by the Council.‡

Although the Council was important to her, Diane's service on the Board of Bar Overseers was at the core of her public work. She was an advocate for transparency with respect to the Board's work and its decisions regarding lawyers' ethical transgressions so that the public would be well-informed and would understand that the profession was conscientiously policing itself. While the leading publication for lawyers, the *Massachusetts Lawyers Weekly*, had published disbarment decisions, it didn't publish censures and public reprimands. Diane argued not only that the BBO should persuade *Lawyers Weekly* to publish the facts and outcomes of more minor disciplinary actions, but that the BBO's decisions should be widely available so that lawyers would have

---

* June 10, 1985, letter to her mother.

† The superior court judge who heard the arguments, Vincent Brogna, asked in disbelief, "You mean if the Sons of Italy did something like this, you'd call them a 'political committee'?" and shook his head on receiving an affirmative reply. Needless to say, the Knights of Columbus weren't enjoined.

‡ Ironically, the CPJ expired in the mid-1990s, not because its issues had been resolved, but for lack of funds and lack of volunteers. As women came back into the workplace alongside men, the numbers of volunteers diminished, and the organization didn't have enough people to make the continuation of its work possible.

precedent to look to and rely on in the conduct of their practices. Eventually the Board decided to publish its decisions in bound volumes which would be available to the public and to lawyers for that purpose.

Julia Kauffman, a prominent activist volunteer who served with Diane on the Judicial Nominating Commission, on the Council, and as a lay member of the Board of Bar Overseers, had many conversations with her concerning one's obligations to do service to the community. The concept of service to others, she says, was "the essence of Diane," and her efforts in service of that ideal inspired those serving with her.*

She had a gift for teaching others without lecturing to them, and she was particularly helpful to the two lay members of the BBO, Curtis Prout and Julia. Each member of the BBO served, in turn, as a hearing officer to hear evidence in cases charging lawyers with ethical violations. They then wrote up the cases and made recommendations for decisions for the consideration of the entire board. When Julia's and Curtis' turns came, they were concerned that they were out of their element and might write something that would demonstrate their lack of experience. They asked Diane if she'd read over their work and comment on it so that they wouldn't embarrass themselves. She said immediately she would. She came to the hearings, listened to the testimony, talked through the issues with them, and then commented on their reports before they were submitted. †

Between her work on the Board and her lectures on professional responsibility and on family law at Harvard, Diane often missed dinner at home twice a week or more. Even though we'd brought our family life back into focus, some of her priorities remained firmly affixed to being of service to others outside the family. The Board was a place where she was making a real difference.

While she wasn't one to jump in and try to take over a meeting, she had no hesitation in speaking out when it came to doing things that were right and best for the system. In the context of the BBO, she was considerate of other people's opinions and careful to take them into consideration when she spoke. She wasn't shy about expressing herself, but she waited her turn before she spoke her piece, often raising pertinent questions no one else had considered. She wasn't aggressive. Her approach was gentle and nonjudgmental.

Experience, she believed, was important in serving on the BBO and, absent unusual circumstances, Board members should serve more than one three-year term. In 1981 when the Supreme Judicial Court decided Board members should *not* be reappointed, she objected. When the Board was unwilling to take a position on the subject, she took it on herself to do so. She sent the following memo on July 27, 1981, to the other members of the Board:

---

*   Julia Kauffman interview, November 15, 2005.
†   Ibid.

I am sending this memo around to remind everyone that the Supreme Judicial Court has taken the position that no Board member who has served a full term should be reappointed. I think at least some of you agree with me that this policy should be changed. It is my feeling that because of the start-up time needed before one becomes a fully effective member of the Board, the limitation to three years robs us of Board members just at the time when they are most valuable in terms of providing continuity and perspective, as well as creative thinking with respect to future directions for the Board.

I am writing to the Chief Justice urging reconsideration of the policy and I hope others will do likewise.

The policy was reconsidered, and it wasn't the last time she would make her views known to the Chief Justice.

By September 1982, she had served two terms as vice-chair of the BBO. By custom and practice, the vice-chair was appointed chair for the following year. Diane was the first woman vice-chair and in her case the custom wasn't followed. John Brooks, a distinguished and eminent member of the bar who'd served as chair already was reappointed. The message was clear and she understood it, but she also respected John Brooks. She admired him a great deal for his commitment to public service and would do nothing to embarrass him or the Board. Nor would she meekly bow her head and let it go. What she did do was to make it clear, privately, to Chief Justice Edward Hennessey that she wouldn't stand for sexist treatment of this sort, and it needed to be remedied. A pragmatic man, he understood, without being told, that there would be consequences if it weren't.

On October 26, 1983, nearly two months after her second term had nominally expired (no successor had been appointed) Hennessey wrote to her:

The Justices are very pleased to appoint you as Chairperson of the Board of Bar Overseers for the remainder of your present term on the Board, expiring August 31, 1984. This is about the best way that the Justices could express their appreciation for your splendid and loyal service to the Board, the court and the public. Please accept my thanks and congratulations.

Not knowing the details of what had occurred, Sandra Lynch, another member of the Board who was already familiar with the onerous responsibilities of its members, particularly its chair, asked her why she would want to serve still another year, even if as chair. Diane replied, "Because no woman has been Chair of the Board of Bar Overseers."

Both the succession principle and the issue of sexism, with which she'd been dealing her entire professional life in all its contexts, were on the table and Diane had made it plain, firmly and convincingly, what needed to be done. The sexism issue never became public and the Supreme Judicial Court was praised for its liberal open-mindedness in a time when that quality was rare in considering the status of women. Diane herself never crowed, not even in a letter to her mother two weeks later:

> My job as chairperson of the Board of Bar Overseers means I'm the head of the appointed and unpaid group in charge of disciplining unethical and dishonest lawyers. We're the ones who investigate complaints and recommend suspension or disbarment when it turns out there has been wrongdoing. And there's quite a lot if it. It's a twelve-person group, appointed by the judges of the state's highest court. I've earned my position. As you might guess, I'm the first woman to hold it. It's one of those positions that goes to "distinguished members of the bar" and I seem to have been around long enough now that I fit into that category.

She'd succeeded in remedying one snub, but she still had Harvard's snub to deal with that year. When Harvard advised her she could no longer teach its professional responsibility course, she had contacted Northeastern's Dean Michael Meltsner, who had loyally asked her over the years if she might be available to teach a course there. She said she was available and would like to teach a professional responsibility course in the spring of 1984. Her offer was accepted immediately, and she began teaching at Northeastern again, starting in March.

In the meantime, another opportunity came her way.

This opportunity came *sotto voce*. Diane was working at a small desk in the reference-book stacks of the Harvard International Law Library, preparing to teach a class, when she heard a familiar voice saying, "Diane, what are you doing here? You should be on the Appeals Court!" The voice belonged to Governor Michael Dukakis, who was roaming through the stacks before a speaking engagement at the law school. "Don't you think I have enough to do?" she laughed. He stopped for a few minutes' conversation before heading off to his talk, but his remark stayed with Diane. Not long afterwards, when an Appeals Court vacancy came before the governor's Judicial Nominating Commission, she received a message from a mutual friend that the governor hoped she'd apply.

This was no casual message: if she applied, she'd be appointed. She was torn. On the one hand, she wanted the appointment – it would be a logical conclusion to the public-service career she'd pursued; and she could bring a great deal of knowledge and practical and academic experience to bear on important appellate decisions in Massachusetts. At issue on the other side of the equation were the professional life she'd built with Regie, and the family life we'd been building for eight years, a life based on freedom from fixed dates of employment and freedom to explore those things we wanted to do when we wanted to do them. We had borrowed to buy a ski condominium on Sugarloaf Mountain in 1977, and had spent two weeks there each winter – Christmas week and school vacation week – with children and friends; we had a month on the island each summer; and with our children in college or graduated, we were beginning to talk about traveling.

The personal considerations weren't minor. They defined the way we had come to live our life and how we wanted to continue to live it. In the balance, however, the personal considerations may have weighed less than her attachment to 189 Cambridge Street and the professional life and firm she and Regie had built. The thought of leaving what they'd created to go off on her own – even if into the judiciary – was troublesome, and the issue wasn't easily resolved. We would be able to resolve the personal issues – we'd adjust, as we always had – but the professional issues were agonizing. Regie encouraged her to apply ("Of course, you should! John and I will manage…."), but Diane knew the prospect was more difficult for Reg than she let on. In the end she had to internalize the conflicts and reach a decision by herself.

As had been the case with Harvard, she decided the opportunity to continue to serve the goals she'd set for herself was too great to be ignored, and she couldn't let it go by. She made her peace with Regie, and with me. Her growing disillusionment with the effectiveness of her role in the representation of children in Ginsberg's court played an important role in the process, but the key question for her was what she could accomplish in this new role. There was still much work she could do that would benefit others. She decided to go for it.

The timing couldn't have been more propitious. She was Chair of the Board of Bar Overseers. She had originated and taught lawyers' professional responsibility courses for ten years and was also still teaching a family law course at Harvard. She was responsible (together with Regie) for significant appellate decisions. The field in which she had concentrated her private practice was an important one. She received an enthusiastic recommendation from Ginsberg, a highly respected judge who'd observed and applauded her work in court in that field. And the governor who would make the appointment had always held her in high regard. Having made the decision, having applied, and having interviewed with the Judicial Nominating Commission, she was excited and expectant.

Her response to the application questionnaire listed eight significant cases in which she'd been counsel, and included the following statement concerning what qualified a candidate to serve on an appellate court:

> The attribute of an appellate judge to which I would give the most weight is breadth: a general familiarity with the world derived from a variety of experiences, and the capacity to learn from them. I think this gives an individual a foundation for confident and balanced judgment. In my own case I believe my range of experience has given me this kind of breadth.
>
> I would give almost as much weight to demonstrated interest in the law and

the functioning of the legal system. An appellate judge has to remain interested in his or her day-to-day job of deciding legal questions. He or she needs to be sensitive to and concerned about the shaping of the law that occurs through the process of appellate decisions. I would rate myself high on this characteristic as well.

Additional attributes with which I would be concerned would be integrity, intelligence, objectivity, the ability to work hard, and collegiality. Again I would rate myself high on these.

Retired Justice Benjamin Kaplan possesses many of the qualities I think a good appellate judge should possess. He has an incisive mind, writes to the point and with style, is immensely well-read and has a strong background in the law. In addition I think he is a practical and humane man with very few preconceptions.

A funny thing happened on her way to the Appeals Court: the Judicial Nominating Commission whose task it was to send to the governor the names of three qualified candidates didn't include Diane's name among the three.

"What I thought was going to be really important didn't happen – no judgeship for me," she wrote her mother. She was told by one source that there "seemed to be an issue of conflict between the Governor and the Nominating Commission, with me caught in the middle." In one way or another, the governor's office had made it known to the Commission that he wished Diane's name to be one of the three sent up to him. The Commission resented his interference in a process in which he'd said he would never interfere. "I'm disappointed but not devastated," wrote Diane, "and there may be another chance some day."

There wouldn't be another chance. But there would be consequences from the process she'd gone through to reach her decision to apply. Having decided that she was willing to separate from her partnership with Regie, she now knew that she no longer wanted to continue in the private practice of law. She and Regie would teach together for another year at Harvard, and then at both Northeastern and Boston University law schools, and their friendship would be undiminished, but the process she'd begun of withdrawing from Healy, Lund & Fiske was in her mind irrevocable.

At the BBO's 1984 end-of-year dinner, she was honored and presented with a plaque:

> Diane Lund
> Chairperson
>
> In recognition of efficient and dedicated service to the bar and to the public as a member of the Board of Bar Overseers of the Commonwealth of Massachusetts,
>
> And in the promotion and maintenance of the highest standards of ethical conduct within the legal profession.
>
> March 31, 1978 – August 31, 1984

More important than the plaque was the letter she received from another member of the Board, Margot Botsford, who had once been Diane's student and who, two decades later, would become a Justice of the Massachusetts Supreme Judicial Court:

> [I'm writing] to tell you what a wonderful job you did as Chairman. With gentle humor combined with a strong sense of direction, you continually managed to move a group with divergent viewpoints and some strong personalities into agreement, or at least a resolution. It was impressive to observe, as was your wonderful command of prior Board actions. Most impressive, however, was your commitment to the job…. [W]hat I saw in you was someone who [devoted] enormous amounts of time working on Board matters and [who had] a total grasp and control of the Board's operations. I miss you as the chairman but I'm sure you're glad to have some time to yourself.

Time to herself, however, was not what Diane had in mind.

---

[1] CASLS continued in existence for more than twenty years, until the federal government's support for legal services became so tied to burdensome conditions (e.g., no class action cases, no immigration cases) that the various legal-services programs around Massachusetts consolidated under a single Boston-based umbrella that rejected federal aid. Other entities were set up to do federally-approved (and funded) individual cases.

Meryl and George, c. 1978.

In front of our first house in Lexington, c. 1966.

A formal family potrait when the children were teenagers.

Ted, Kristin and Ben on Nantucket, c. 1992.

Kristin's graduation from Harvard Law School, 1992.

Cycling in Bordeaux with Joyce and Charles Muckenfuss, 1993.

CHAPTER NINE

TRANSITIONS

LIFE WAS CHANGING FOR DIANE AS SHE NEARED FIFTY. SOME things were beyond her reach, others seemed temptingly close, and she was restlessly looking for new ways to serve the public good. Her accomplishments as a law professor and role model in the legal profession were behind her. She knew she would not become a judge. Although her representation of children in the probate courts had reached a dead end, her professional focus on their best interests had not. It was shifting away from the law, however, and toward education, specifically toward the long-term importance of teaching preschool inner-city children to read. Her own children were out of the house, either out in the world or well on their way. She was planning to withdraw from law practice and put her talents to uses that were better pursued in other ways. And while she would find a variety of new challenges awaiting her, perhaps an overriding consideration in her thinking and planning was how we and our close friends should spend the next fifty years.

It was a unique time for us. Diane and I were soon to be alone with each other again. Our friends were in much the same stage in life. Merely growing older and doing the same personal and professional things we'd always done was, to her, an unattractive alternative. She had in mind a collective life in which we'd all continue to be useful and productive, but in different ways than had been the case in our separate lives to date.

A major impediment – and Diane saw it clearly – was that I'd become immersed in the success of my law firm, which had grown by then to forty lawyers and showed no sign of tailing off. That needed to be one of the first orders of business. She wrote Kristin in the fall of 1985:

I've adjusted my career plan after finally getting Erik to talk about it. He's really fallen into a not good habit, which perhaps I'm in too, of thinking that my life when I'm not physically with him is something in which he doesn't have to interest himself – so I always have the feeling I'm boring him or taking up his valuable time if I want to talk about what's going on with me. There are all these subtle things that happen in relationships that have nothing to do with attachment or love – it's more what's expedient and also connects to self-concern or self-interest.

Gently, she worked at moving me out of the monoculture of my law firm into activities the two of us could do together. We began taking week-long bicycling trips and long-distance hikes in other parts of the world, making friendships with people who had nothing to do with law practice and who offered us very different perspectives on the world. When Kristin finished her junior year at Oxford, we flew to England to celebrate with her and her friends, and then spent ten days entirely on our own hiking along the Cotswold Trail, calling ahead each night to a bed & breakfast in the next town. We had time to ourselves again, time to reflect and to dream without the pressures we'd had in our daily lives for decades. The freedom was astonishing, as were our treks. Over the course of the next ten years we hiked across the girth of England coast-to-coast, down the Offa's Dike path at the border with Wales, and in the Loire and Dordogne Valleys, and bicycled in California, New England, Pennsylvania, the Outer Hebrides, France and the South Island of New Zealand.

Never one to dwell on the past, Diane envisioned the remainder of our lives as closer, more personal and, significantly, something we should share with others. Building on the Danish concept of co-housing (about which much had been written), she conceived of our forming an elders commune in which we and our friends would return to the land, work the land itself, have other productive occupations and live and work together, sharing the fruits of our efforts and the pleasure of companionship. The co-housing

Having navigated Bowdoin summa cum laude in 1983, Ben graduated from Harvard Law School in 1987 and began his legal career with a firm in Portland, Maine. After a somewhat checkered Bowdoin career, Ted graduated fourth in his class at Boston University Law School in 1990. Following her junior year abroad at Oxford, where she was invited to row crew on the [Oxford varsity] Blue Team, Kristin graduated from Middlebury in 1987 summa cum laude, Phi Beta Kappa, and went on to Harvard Law School. She became the first daughter of a woman graduate to also graduate from the law school. Diane and I had reason to be proud of all three of our children.

concept wasn't novel, but Diane's vision of friends gathering together in a collective in their later years was. While co-housing projects existed in the U.S., an elders co-housing project would be unique.*

Recognizing that such a radical concept would require a great deal of explanation and persuasion if it were to be realized in the long term, she began the process early. In the winter of 1986 she first wrote the group of friends she hoped would join us in what she was calling the "Orchard Collective":

> This is about an adventure. I thought it might be a good idea to set down the philosophical and the practical thinking that has led me to suggest that we band together....
>
> [Here is] the adventure I am proposing to the rest of you. We all have led rather matter-of-fact lives. We are now approaching the time when we have options, if we're willing to consider them. I'd like to do some different things with the next fifty or so years that I have. I particularly would like to avoid becoming more and more trapped by material possessions and the compulsion to have them (now that I have this computer, my life is complete). I would also like to be involved in seasonal activity – with growing something. This stems from a sense that I've never led a life that is related to or governed by natural patterns, and I would dearly like to try it out.
>
> Then I think I would dearly enjoy the opportunity to work at something with Erik; we haven't had much of a chance to do that so far.
>
> There is a lot more I could say, naturally, but I'll get on to the practical concept. This was just intended to make you stop and think a moment about what you would like to have happen in the next fifty years....
>
> The residential concept is that a certain number of compatible people should acquire housing in close proximity to each other so that we can share both facilities and responsibilities....
>
> The "Orchard" name reflects my original concept of what we were going to do once we were all settled in our happy little houses – a potentially satisfying occupation that might produce enough income to sustain us on a reasonable level.... Other ideas have been raised. Running an inn is an obvious one... There is the option of raising animals as well as crops....

The initial response from our friends was bemused but encouraging. They were, they said, open to the idea. Besides, it was an excuse to get together. A number of us drove to Connecticut to look at a winery for sale, a trip which made it clear to Diane

---

* Twenty years later, in February 2006, the *New York Times* would describe a similar concept in California as the first of its kind in the U.S.

that no one in the group would consider an immediate life change. "No one is prepared to march off behind me into the wilderness right this minute (except possibly Regie, if Bob would come too)…. My own personal timetable has been four or five years, when we're all approaching the magic age of 55 or more. Remember that part of my idea is to have the time to engage in satisfying work with people I care about. That's an experience I would like to have out of life…."

Cajoling and persuading over the next seven years, she moved her concept forward to its infrastructure stage. Knowing Diane, she might well have succeeded in bringing it to fruition, and changing all our lives entirely.

In the interim, she was pursuing thoughts of a new and different professional career. Her experience working with children through Judge Ginsberg's appointments led her to consider how else she could influence educating children of poor people to read at an early age, and to find out whether that would help lift them out of poverty and into the mainstream of American culture and business. She had observed empirically the importance of reading ability to self-esteem and independence, observations that coincided with her own childhood experience. She knew for a fact that her own ability to read and comprehend abstract ideas at an early age had opened opportunities for her not readily available to other children, and had given her advantages many others hadn't had.

She believed she'd found the key to a better life for the children of inner-city families, and she intended to put that knowledge into practical use. It was time for her to see if she could give something of importance to these children. And she decided to go about it in ways that were outside her experience as a lawyer.

In September 1985, Diane began volunteering at an urban day care center that served primarily Hispanic and Asian children in the industrial city of Lowell. She read to them out loud, interested them in books and then taught them how to learn to read. They responded to her, began learning, and wanted more. Their reactions reinforced her views and sent her home energized and enthusiastic about the future. She began taking teachers' education courses at Wheelock College.

The center's administrator, knowing Diane's background, was uncomfortable using her in such a low-level position. Not knowing quite what to do, he offered to promote her to a desk job. She politely declined and explained what she'd begun and what she hoped to do. A paper written at Wheelock in May 1987, "Intellectual Expansion in the Reformation," reflected her views of the importance of teaching reading skills and the uses to which those skills could be put:

> Perhaps more important to western intellectual development is the role which written language plays in the development of abstract thought. It has been hypothesized that our ability to produce and understand language which is abstract, argumentative and unrelated to the circumstances in which it is

comprehended is totally dependent on our ability to read and write; absent the skills of literacy, humans remain context-bound in their thinking...

The increased production of printed material brought books and reading to many more people and they acquired both new ideas and an enhanced capacity for abstract thought. The particular ideas they were acquiring were in large part religious ones since the leaders of the Reformation were prolific and effective writers and the defenders of the Catholic faith used the written word with equal zeal. It is the Protestant writings which are of concern here, however, for in them could be found the encouragement of independent inquiry and intellectual independence which are the precursors of modern thought....

The Anabaptists, as the radicals were loosely called, were persecuted ferociously for their religious beliefs and ultimately only a few isolated gatherings of them remained. Much of the fresh thinking they introduced, however, has survived, notably in the secular doctrines of Unitarianism and in the New World constitutional doctrines of separation of Church and State.... The broader legacy of the Reformation has persisted. The spirit of independent and critical inquiry, fostered by processes which bring enlightenment to great numbers of people, is a heritage which has continued to thrive in our society and has served us well....

While continuing to volunteer in Lowell, she enrolled in the fall of 1987 as a special student in the Harvard Graduate School of Education. ("I've become interested in what can be done with very young children with reading to maximize their chances of later success. Harvard has a very good program and research going on in the general area of reading. So my plan is to investigate it this year and then enroll full-time next year [assuming they'll admit me] to get a master's degree and become a specialist in this area. Then I could do consulting and program design with day care centers."*)

Diane and Regie continued to teach at Northeastern and Boston University law schools into 1988, but given the shift in her focus, she felt it was time to stop.† That fall she was admitted into a master's program in reading and language at Harvard. Her thesis, entitled "Episodic Structure and Storybooks Preferred by Children," concerned "the significance of stories as a means of gaining insight into cognitive processes." In June she received her Master of Arts in Education at Harvard's commencement exercises, with her family in attendance.

Day care centers had been springing up around Massachusetts with the help of federal funding, some of it targeted precisely toward reading programs. As a consultant

---

* September 19, 1987 letter to her mother.
† "Diane felt if she wasn't actively practicing family law, she couldn't teach a family law practice course. This was a sad time for both of us because we'd had a lot of success with our joint teaching. The student evaluations we received were uniformly excellent and the law schools wanted us to continue." (Healy interview, 2005.)

working with urban day care centers she believed she could promote her conviction that early reading to children in the 3- to 6-year-old age group was critically important for their development. She could at the same time read and teach reading to inner-city kids personally, something she'd found enormously satisfying. She was ready to move into the future.

But shortly after graduation, federal funding dried up. Despite months of looking into other options, she could find no other sources of funds for what she wanted to do. Ultimately she concluded she had no choice but to abandon the plan and her ambition to give disadvantaged children a head start in their lives. This setback was harder to accept than the lost judgeship. Although she hated to admit it, even to herself, there had been an element of ego involvement in the latter, something she'd found uncomfortable. Her dreams and hopes for influencing the course of inner-city day care centers had no similar aspect and was consistent with the selfless pledges she'd made when she threw her faggots into the bonfire at the Presbyterian retreat, many, many years earlier.

What to do now? Diane needed other challenges, and had already accepted one, when she became a member of Bowdoin College's Board of Overseers in 1985. In that volunteer capacity at a former men's college still in the throes of its co-ed transition, she believed she could effectively advocate women's interests and influence policy, and she had. Ultimately she would undertake a massive and time-consuming task for Bowdoin, but that task would not come her way for some years. In the meantime, as her day care ambitions slipped away she wanted to find regular gainful employment.

In March 1990, she learned that Dan Klubock, who'd been Bar Counsel to the Board of Bar Overseers during Diane's tenure, had been appointed a district court judge, and the board was soliciting applications. Experienced and well-qualified, Diane applied ("The Bar Counsel is hired by the BBO, the Board that I was on for six years and chairperson of for about two years…. I know a great deal about the job…."), but her application was rejected: she was too old, they thought, and inexperienced in running a large office and besides, the board felt they needed new blood. Another disappointment, but she was undeterred.

That fall, when Scott Harshbarger was elected Massachusetts Attorney General, she applied to become an assistant attorney general in the Charities Division, and was hired. Her task would be to ride herd on 25,000 Massachusetts charities to see to it that the funds they collected and administered were being used for charitable purposes and not for personal gain. She was enormously pleased, both because of the nature of the job and because the position would give her the strong focus she'd been missing for two years.

"My first week at work was a strenuous one," she wrote. "I've set myself a vigorous new regime…. The work is interesting and the people as nice as I thought they'd be…. Right now I'm concentrating on charitable fundraising, keeping an eye on the people and organizations to ensure that they are legitimate and doing what they should be doing with their money."

It was a challenging task. Charities (which pay no taxes) are a motley lot. A number of them had objectives that had become obsolete and no longer qualified as charitable. Their charters needed to be amended. Others had been set up by families in the Yankee establishment as a sinecure for family members who needed a job and a source of income, and had been hired to run them at handsome salaries. Diane became an expert in the field, to the dismay of several charities who found themselves having to scramble to reorder their priorities in order to retain tax-free status, or to reduce salaries they were paying to a level commensurate with the resources being managed and the work being performed.

She remained in this job until May 1993, and her experience there meshed nicely with the enormous project she later undertook at Bowdoin regarding the use of its various endowed funds.

CHAPTER TEN

BOWDOIN COLLEGE OVERSEER

I N THE WINTER OF 1985, PAUL BROUNTAS, A FRIEND FROM LAW
school, one of Boston's leading corporate attorneys and president of Bowdoin
College's Board of Overseers, asked Diane to become a member of the board.
After existing as a men's college for 150 years, Bowdoin had barely a decade's experience
as a coeducational institution. Its uneasy makeover was yet an ongoing process to which
there was considerable deep-seated antipathy, not only among many of its alumni but
on its governing boards as well.

Brountas believed it was important for the college not only to have women on its
governing boards, but to have distinguished women with experience and an established
track record in business or the professions, women who would contribute substantively
and who would be listened to in board meetings. He was looking for a woman who
would consider Overseer to be a working position, not just an honorary one. He'd
known Diane in law school and her academic record there* and had followed her
professional career. Believing she fit the profile perfectly, he proposed she be appointed.†

---

* He knew among other things that she'd been invited to join the *Harvard Law Review* but had
turned down the invitation, a decision he describes as "one of the boldest moves I ever saw." (Brountas
interview, November 1, 2005.)

† The process of bringing women onto Bowdoin's governing boards had begun before Diane was
recruited. Rosalyne Bernstein, a well-known Portland, Maine, attorney served eight years as an overseer
beginning in the 1970s and later sixteen years as a trustee. Her experience was much like Diane's at
Harvard. ("Because I was the only woman, I was overwhelmed with committee assignments…. I felt it
was very important to show that I would not be a token, but would be a full participant in the work of
the board.") Author and Holocaust survivor Judith Isaacson, a human rights and women's rights advocate, became an overseer in 1984. Alumnae Deborah Swiss, Elizabeth Woodcock and Laurie Hawkes
became overseers in 1983, 1985 and 1986 respectively.

When it reviewed her qualifications – a practicing lawyer who'd concentrated in the trusts and estates field, who was a moving force in the passage of important social legislation, who'd led the way for women in the teaching profession and who'd served in high-level public positions – the board readily agreed.

This was a critical time in the history of Bowdoin's governing boards, one requiring experienced judgment and a perspective on women's issues, and Brountas felt Diane was someone who could provide exactly that perspective. He foresaw and described to Diane significant problems that still needed to be dealt with in Bowdoin's transition to a co-ed institution. The only social organizations on campus were fraternities, and although they had begun admitting women to their membership locally, this fact was hidden from their national headquarters. The "nationals" were important to a large segment of the alumni, many of them generous donors. Although an increasing percentage of the student body was female, the college had serious problems recruiting women for the faculty. Thorny issues lay ahead.

He described the history of Bowdoin's becoming co-ed. The 1970s committee charged with considering the possibility had begun its work by taking a straw poll among the overseers and trustees. The outcome, visceral and emotional, was never in doubt: opposition was unanimous.* What would happen to the words and singing of Bowdoin's rousing alma mater, "Rise Sons of Bowdoin!"?

The committee's chair, William Curtis Pierce, was undeterred by the straw poll. He believed the college's survival in modern times depended on its becoming co-ed, and the issue should not be decided by a popularity poll. The question, he posited, required considerable additional study and the committee would continue its work. He and his committee members, one of them Brountas, set about the difficult task of persuading board members to set aside personal feelings and consider the merits objectively from the perspective of Bowdoin's long-term interests. A year later the tide had turned and the decision to admit women was made, however grudgingly.

While the decision was irreversible, its wisdom was still being questioned by the alumni, and more than a few male members of the governing boards questioned what possible contribution women on its boards could make to the governance of Bowdoin College. None of its too-young alumnae yet commanded the respect needed to influence the board's decisions. Far better, perhaps, to have stereotypical overseers who regarded the position as a reward for loyalty (or for the money they'd made, a goodly portion of which, it was hoped, would be given to the college), and not one that involved heavy lifting. They looked forward to being on campus the four times a year that the Overseers met, when they could renew old acquaintances.

Diane believed she could fulfill the role Brountas envisioned and accepted the

---

*   Brountas interview, November 1, 2005.

invitation. In her ten years on the board she would more than justify his judgment and expectations. She was instrumental in causing the college to accord completely equal status to women. Her advocacy resulted in cutting-edge decisions to establish, staff and fund a preschool children's center for children of faculty, staff and others in the community. She single-handedly caused the college to recognize and honor legitimate restrictions in the terms of its endowed funds, and enabled it to bring its record-keeping concerning the availability and use of the income generated by those funds into the twenty-first century. Each of these efforts built on the experience of the career she'd forged, and on the beliefs and ideals that had guided it. Now she would apply them in a new and different context.

THE CHILDREN'S CENTER

Soon after she joined the board, Diane began to pursue an objective that combined her views on the importance of early education of children and the need to add women professors to the all-male faculty. She believed and advocated that the college should found and finance a day care center for preschool children on campus, a project which dovetailed nicely with the college's efforts to recruit women for its faculty. The existence of a college-sponsored day care center, she argued, would resonate with women whether or not they had young children. It would cause them to view Bowdoin in a favorable light at a critical time.

It wasn't enough merely to integrate the student body if the faculty were not also integrated. It wouldn't be easy to attract qualified women to the faculty of a college located in Brunswick, Maine, one of the remoter parts of New England. The pool of women academics was still small, and those the college deemed qualified were likely to be young. Statistically those young women were more apt to be married and to have preschool children. Bowdoin would need to be able to assure them it regarded their family life as important and that their preschool children would have available to them a high-quality early childhood program. Unless the college could do that, it would lose out in recruiting top-drawer women candidates. The existence of the day care center Diane envisioned would enable Bowdoin to place women faculty members on a par with its men.

If the college didn't create a day care center, she argued, and if as a result it failed to attract qualified women to its faculty, women students would perceive that barriers existed to their own ambitions and that they'd have to settle for something less. The existence of a college-sponsored day care center would make it clear to students, as well as faculty, that women were welcome in academia at Bowdoin, and Bowdoin intended to remove barriers to their enjoying equal status to their male peers. These lessons would have consequences, not only to the college, but to the careers the students themselves would pursue.

Methodically, politely and firmly, Diane pressed the administration. She'd seen firsthand the importance to working mothers of a day care center in which their preschool children had the opportunity to begin learning, reading and creating at the earliest opportunity. Her observations and conclusions concerning the children had been confirmed in her studies at Wheelock and Harvard.

It was an uphill task because the connection between the existence of a day care center and recruitment was not immediately obvious, either to the administration or to other members of the governing boards. There were several reasons for antipathy, some of them visceral. For a college or university to found and finance an on-campus day care center was expensive, and unprecedented at the time. The cost and ongoing subsidy of such a center was not part of any Bowdoin long-range plan.

To undertake this project would strain the resources of an institution already struggling with its finances, but the opposition she faced wasn't wholly financial. What she was proposing wasn't traditional. Why should Bowdoin consider such privileged treatment for women when it didn't offer the same to men? Wasn't this a form of reverse discrimination?

Diane responded that the children's center would offer the same opportunities to fathers as well as to mothers, and that this was particularly important to men as more and more married women were entering and wishing to stay in the workforce. The existence of the center, then, would help Bowdoin in its recruiting of male faculty members as well as women.

Why should Bowdoin found and fund such a center when no other college or university had done anything similar? Bowdoin, Diane said, should recognize changing needs in our society and should be a leader, not a follower, in responding to them. Its standing in the academic community would be enhanced by an attitude reflecting its intention to be on the cutting edge.

In 1988, the Bowdoin College Children's Center was founded in a modest house retrofitted for the purpose, which the college had purchased on South Street, two blocks from the campus proper. Its opportunities were open to children of members of the faculty and the staff of the college and, to the extent of space available, of other parents in the Brunswick community. Initially it had a staff of two and a population of twelve three- to five-year-olds. It was only a beginning, but an instant success.

Diane wasn't content to accept its modest beginning as sufficient for what she'd envisaged. She continued to press the administration and the governing boards, and to support the center financially herself. In the fall of 1990, the program expanded into a second building acquired by the college on South Street, and included children from three months to three years of age as well as three to five years old. In May 1990, before the expanded program opened, Diane received a letter from Bowdoin President Roy Greason:

Dear Diane,

I am writing simply to express my special thanks for your support of the Child Care Center. As a result of the gifts that you have given and also the support which we have received from the Margaret Milliken Hatch Charitable Trust, we are going to be able to enlarge the facility, as I know you realize from the last meeting of the Governing Boards. The nice result is that we will be able to take care of more children with less subsidy, a kind of double victory.

Thank you so much for helping to make it all possible.

Sincerely,

A. LeRoy Greason

On May 6, 2003, Bowdoin dedicated a state-of-the-art architect-designed facility one street closer to the campus. By then, the center's staff of seventeen provided day care to forty-one children. (Three years later, the enrollment had increased to fifty-eight children, and there was a waiting list.) While the center has long been recognized as one of the premier childcare centers of any college or university in the country, it now has a physical facility that matches its standing.

The importance of the center is reflected in comments by two faculty women at the time of the 2003 dedication. The existence of an exceptional children's center on campus, said one, was a major factor in her decision to join the faculty because it "told me that this community had something very special about it, that the college valued faculty as parents as well as professors, and that I would be able to have a family and be a professional" at Bowdoin. The other said simply that "having my daughter on campus with me has been an immeasurable benefit of working at this college."*

_____

* *Bowdoin News*, "New Children's Center Opens its Doors," posted January 16, 2003.

Inside and to the left of the new building's front door is a plaque that reads:

> Diane Theis Lund
> Whose dedication to and support of the
> Children's Center
> helped make it possible.

BOWDOIN'S FRATERNITY SYSTEM

Next came another key issue for Bowdoin which Brountas had foreseen, as the problems associated with the historical social dominance of the fraternities came to a head. Many of the problems Bowdoin faced initially in integrating women – and the source of much alumni discontent – arose because the early social structure of the college had been built entirely around fraternities. Ninety-five percent or more of its alumni – notably its most *affluent* alumni – were fraternity men in whose memories the fraternity system was ingrained. Moreover, regardless of the social merits of that system, the college had depended on it because each fraternity undertook to feed its own members, relieving the college of all but a small portion of the burden. More than 40% of the college's students lived in fraternity houses rather than in dormitories.

As class sizes had increased in the 1960s and as women were admitted in the 1970s, the practical importance of fraternities to the college began to diminish. New dormitories had to be built and more and more of the burden to provide dining facilities began to shift to the college. Fraternities still hadn't become an anachronism because the college didn't succeed in replacing the social function of fraternities on campus. They remained the hub of weekend social activities and their parties were usually open to all (sometimes with publicly disastrous consequences).

During the 1950s, Zeta Psi (which happened to be my fraternity) had had a unique initiation ceremony that made its members instantly recognizable to each other. Somewhat like cattle, we were branded on the arm with the Greek letters of the fraternity by means of a red-hot branding iron. (Happily for us, cattle were branded on a different part of their anatomy). The practice had ceased by the time women became members of the local chapter.

When Bowdoin decided to admit women, the administration made it clear, informally, that it expected fraternities – despite the meaning of the word – to invite women to join them. Seeing the handwriting on the wall, many began to comply, some enthusiastically.* Purely local fraternities had an easier time of it than chapters of national fraternities, whose bylaws limited membership to men. Most chapters resorted to subterfuge: when they sent the names of their new pledges to national fraternity headquarters, they omitted each pledge's first name and used only first initials. "Don't ask, don't tell" didn't originate with President Clinton's administration. But it seems unlikely that any national fraternity headquarters was taken in by the ruse.†

Inevitably there would be a backlash because no matter how the problem was papered over, women were not being fully integrated into campus life. Although they

---

*   Sometimes more enthusiastically than was entirely comfortable for parents, as when Diane and I learned that our son Ted's fraternity-house roommate was a young woman classmate.
†   Racial and ethnic discrimination in national fraternity bylaws was an ongoing issue for Bowdoin's fraternity system for decades, especially in the period following World War II, when bylaws had explicit exclusions for blacks and Jews. One chapter had been expelled from its national in the late 1940s when it admitted a black to membership. It chose to become a local, unaffiliated fraternity.

were officers in Bowdoin chapters they couldn't participate in the national organization. Their very identity as women had to be concealed. Women on campus began rejecting the subterfuge and demanding equal status. Some men took their all-male fraternities off-campus and some women began organizing off-campus sororities. Bowdoin refused to recognize any of the off-campus organizations because they discriminated on grounds of sex. Alumni whose fraternities had gone off-campus transferred what had previously been annual gifts to the college to support their fraternities instead. Pressure was being put on local chapters to expel women and some of the men who believed the national affiliation was important, even if only as a cachet, began to demand that the women be expelled, on threat of the men breaking away and taking the national affiliation with them.

It was at best an anomalous situation. Bowdoin's informal policy that women should be totally integrated into all aspects of college life had been stopped far short of that goal. The chapters confronted the college. Diane argued there could be no turning back, nor was any compromise acceptable: it was time to adopt the policy formally and to require local fraternity chapters to reject outright any requirements of their national organization that discriminated against women, and to require single-sex fraternities or sororities to disband. Despite a storm of protest from alumni, as well as from segments of the student body, the college's governing boards formally adopted the policy.

On September 29, 1991, the *New York Times* reported the decision in a story which included the following:

> Some Alpha Delta Phi members say the new requirement is unfair because the fraternity had given the women in its local chapter equal standing for fifteen years, as opposed to "technically co-ed" fraternities…. [Others voiced different views, however, e.g.:] "Bowdoin is a forward-thinking organization in essentially forcing the process along," said a 1983 graduate, Benjamin Lund, a Portland-based attorney who is president of Bowdoin's Alpha Delta Phi alumni group.

Diane was pleased and proud when she read Ben's remarks, and still more pleased by the fact that Bowdoin had taken a position that was important to all women, everywhere.

Bowdoin's fraternity system was eventually abolished and replaced by a nondiscriminatory house system that continued to house a substantial number of the undergraduates. The new system was largely based in the former fraternity houses, and over time, the divisiveness engendered by the elimination of the fraternity system dissipated.

The Endowed Funds

Diane's advocacy for women and for the Children's Center may have given her the greatest personal satisfaction of the work she did for Bowdoin, but the work she did beginning in 1992 to analyze the terms of Bowdoin's vast array of endowed funds, and to computerize its records concerning them, was an equally significant contribution. The college was working its way out of a financial morass. The supposed balanced budget reflected in its past years' financial statements was a fiction. Although the problems ran considerably deeper and were more complex, much of the blame for the college's inability to balance its budget could be attributed to its failure to properly account for, identify and deal with restrictions on the use of its endowed funds.

Had the college been required to contract for the task for which Diane volunteered, the cost would have been prohibitive. It wasn't a labor of love she undertook, but one born of exigency. Hundreds of thousands of dollars given to endow once-charitable purposes were lying fallow because of the college's failure to deal with their restrictions and to free those endowed funds from those restrictions. And because it was ignoring the restrictions, the issues weren't identified and brought to the attention of the Overseers until after Bowdoin had a new president.

In the fall of 1990, Bowdoin inaugurated Robert H. Edwards, a Harvard-educated lawyer who had gone into college administration rather than the practice of law after graduation. He'd previously been president of Carlton College in Minnesota, a small college much like Bowdoin, and had later headed the Aga Khan's international school system headquartered in Paris, where Edwards and his wife had lived before coming to Bowdoin. He was astute and knowledgeable in financial matters – and appalled at the unexpected financial picture that confronted him after he took the reins at Bowdoin.

In the course of the due diligence he'd done before accepting Bowdoin's offer, he had been told that while there were a "few" financial problems, the college had a balanced budget and an excellent endowment. The precise nature and extent of the financial problems weren't disclosed, and indeed their full extent was probably known only to the college's treasurer (its chief financial officer) and its auditors, Coopers & Lybrand, and not to the governing boards. In fact, in business terms, the College was no longer a going concern. It hadn't balanced its budget for years except through using suspect means to dip into endowment in order to make up deficits.*

At the beginning of these years of financial legerdemain, Bowdoin's endowment had been the equal of its affluent rival, Williams College. While Williams had fully invested its endowment, Bowdoin had been engaged in out-of-control deficit spending. It had used the endowment like an undifferentiated fish pond, dipping into it for whatever was

---

* The origins and history of this situation are discussed in the Appendix entitled "Bowdoin's Financial Problems."

needed, in some years to the extent of 10% of its total endowment – more than double the rate of inflation for the time. Having been spent down, Bowdoin's endowment now trailed far behind Williams.*

Diane had been a member of Bowdoin's audit committee since the fall of 1987 (and would become its chair in 1993). As she listened to the treasurer's convoluted descriptions of the problems that required the college to draw on endowment to cover shortfalls, she learned that much of the blame that he assigned as causes arose from restrictions in the endowed funds themselves:

> A discussion ensued concerning the steps which must be taken to expend income from more of the College's closely restricted funds. It was noted the Administration is currently working on this. An effort is being made to change the terms of certain funds whose restrictions no longer provide the College with the ability to spend earned income in a manner which would support current program needs…. Of course the Administration realizes its fiduciary responsibility in interpreting the terms as stated by the donors. (Audit Committee minutes, December 14, 1988.)

* * *

> [The treasurer] prefaced the meeting by stating the financial statements are not yet satisfactorily completed. Specifically, additional work is needed on the current unrestricted fund balance [and] the transfer entries made during fiscal year 1989…. (Audit Committee minutes, October 16, 1989.)

* * *

> [The administration's budget director] provided the Committee with a description of the mechanics of distributing income to the participating funds. He noted restrictions often limit a fund's ability to expend income. Additionally there are funds in which the use of income is left to the discretion of the fund manager (and may not be expended in the year it is distributed to the fund)…. (Audit Committee minutes, February 16, 1990.)

Many of the deeds of gift for the college's polyglot of endowed funds reflected an intent that they be used for particular, specified purposes, and contained explicit restrictions concerning their use. A systematic study of the restricted endowment funds hadn't been done, nor had there been any effort to coordinate and centralize the decision-making process about their use. Absent appropriate controls, use of the endowed funds had resulted in multiple breaches of the college's fiduciary responsibilities.

Bowdoin's apparent inability to use the income from some of the restricted endowment funds represented one of the problem areas. The persons administering

---

* Kent Chabotar interview, December 14, 2005.

those funds believed they were hamstrung by the restrictions. No one had studied what could and should be done to free up those funds for more general use beyond the letter of the restrictions. As a result, hundreds of thousands of dollars which could have been made available for the college's use were not being expended. As trustee of these funds, the college had an obligation not to allow those funds to lie fallow, and to seek court approval for alternative uses. *

This was hardly the sole problem. By treating the college's investments as an undifferentiated whole and by using its appreciation to cover budget deficits, the college was treating appreciation attributable to the restricted endowed funds as if it were available for general purposes. It was not, because this hadn't been the donors' intent.

A related problem was that those responsible for the expenditure of income from restricted endowment funds had simply ignored the restrictions and used the funds for general purposes without regard to the restrictions. The latter practice occurred particularly in awarding scholarships and student loans where the college's guiding criteria appeared to be need rather than the intentions of the donors. Notable beneficiaries were members of Bowdoin's nationally ranked hockey team.

The task of analyzing and sorting out these issues should have fallen to the treasurer's office, but that office was both woefully understaffed and simply didn't have the capacity, much less the understanding of the college's legal obligations, to undertake the task. And the cost for the college to engage its outside attorneys to perform this work would have been something it couldn't easily have afforded, given its financial situation.

From her professional experience and work for the Charities Division of the Massachusetts Attorney General's Department, Diane understood both the financial consequences to which this conduct had exposed the college and that remedial work needed to be done, *now*. Keenly aware of the financial bind and the cost involved to contract for the work, she volunteered to do the work herself at no cost to the College. She would personally review the terms of all the college's endowed funds, whether for professorial chairs, department needs or student scholarships and loans, and determine what needed to be done for the college to fulfill its fiduciary responsibilities, and, at the same time, to free up income from endowed funds for the college's use. The college's treasurer – the principal source of the problem – didn't take her up on her offer – but his successor, Kent Chabotar, did.

Recruited by Edwards, Chabotar became Bowdoin's new Chief Financial Officer in late 1991. He'd been at Harvard Business School teaching the finance segments

---

* The classic legal term for this process, "cy pres," reflects the law's intent that when a donor has exhibited a general charitable intent, the gift should not fail merely because the purpose specified has ceased to exist. Rather the funds will be applied to purposes "near to" or as close as possible to the intent of the donor, as determined by a court.

of summer executive programs since 1982 ("Come practice what you're teaching," Edwards had said). He would be effective in putting theory into practice at Bowdoin, not only because he had Edwards's confidence, but because, as an academic himself, he was accepted by the faculty. Within three years, Edwards and Chabotar would bring the operating budget into balance, but not without cost to the expectations of the faculty and staff who'd been lulled into complaisance. Instead of a 10%-plus drawdown on endowment, the drawdown decreased to 4 1/2 to 5%, which was consistent with inflation. The financial difference contributed in a major way to Bowdoin's survival as a premier small liberal arts college.

The nature of the problems the college faced was quickly brought home to Chabotar not long after he came on the scene, when he received a message from the basement-housed accounting department that there was a problem with the financial records of the Hawthorne-Longfellow Library/Museum. The librarian had reported that the endowment funds for the library/museum appeared to be $3 million off from what she thought they were. Investigation disclosed that in order to cover the operating deficit for the library/museum, money had been taken out of endowment funds never intended for that purpose (e.g., money earned by a fund established for the purpose of "purchasing American art").

Chabotar looked closely into the broader question of how other endowment funds had been treated and found that the problem the librarian had reported was endemic. Bowdoin's endowed funds had been invested together as if they were essentially a mutual fund, with the financial results treated as a common pool. Each individual fund was credited with a proportionate amount of the investment returns – and each was debited with expenditures made for general purposes of the college without regard to the funds' restrictions – and without disclosure to the governing boards. The information caused an uproar. The money would have to be put back.*

Bowdoin had over two thousand endowed funds whose creation stretched well back into the 1800s. The donors had usually had specific intentions for their use spelled out in writing in their deeds of gift. In the absence of a catch-all clause which would allow the funds to be used for other purposes, the college had fiduciary obligations to honor the donors' intent. Certain of the restrictions could no longer legally be enforced, e.g., racial or ethnic restrictions. In other cases the intent of the donors could no longer be carried out because the college's curriculum no longer included those purposes. In either circumstance, the college wasn't free to use the funds for general purposes without court authorization. The language contained in the deeds of gift needed to be reviewed and interpreted in light of current circumstances, and recommendations needed to be made as to how the college should proceed with respect to each of the individual funds.

---

* Ultimately, when all the dust settled, over eight million dollars was returned and credited to the funds from which they had been debited.

In a letter to Edwards and Chabotar, Diane said she would develop a computer program to analyze the endowed funds and input the necessary information from each fund's deed of gift. The college would then have at its fingertips the information it desperately needed to determine what funds could be used for unrestricted purposes and what the restricted purposes were for which other funds could be used. As to the restrictions, she'd specify the uses to which the funds could be put, identify those restrictions which were unenforceable or obsolete and recommend steps the college's outside attorneys should take to obtain court approval for the restrictions to be removed or for the funds to be used for purposes that were legitimately related to those restrictions.

Her offer was gratefully accepted.*

First the individual endowment funds had to be reconstructed, and a separate folder created for each which included all the key terms of the gift or trust in question and any restrictions upon its use. A computer software program had to be developed to establish exactly what the money in each of the endowed funds could or couldn't be used for, information which would then inform the budget planners what they actually had available to them, for what purposes and from what sources. Then those folders for funds that contained limitations or restrictions would have to be set aside for further review and decisions on how to deal with them.

These were the tasks Diane undertook.

With the raw data in hand, Chabotar and the college's outside attorney, Peter Webster, met with Diane and discussed with her how best to make the data available and useful to the college. A tiny overheated office in the basement of Bowdoin's Hawthorne-Longfellow Library was set aside for her. She then arranged to take a three-month leave from the Charities Division during the summer of 1992. She thought that by working three days a week in the office set aside for her, surrounded by cartons of files, she could accomplish the task. The critical aspects of the work would be accomplished in that period, but she vastly underestimated the time required to input the information from the individual deeds of gift. Continuing to work at the task on a part-time basis, she was still in the final stages of it two years later.

Honoring the donors' intent was critical. She began reviewing each one of the college's files reflecting the terms of its various endowed funds to analyze and develop her interpretations of how the terms of the gifts could be construed. She developed a computerized protocol designed to set out for each fund its pertinent terms and the purposes for which its income could be used in order to honor the donor's intent. As

---

* There were over 220 funds which up to that point had been administered *ad hoc* without any significant controls over how the monies attributable to each fund were spent. Given her background in the administration of charitable funds, Diane's offer was a godsend. (Interview with Bowdoin's outside counsel, Peter Webster, December 15, 2005.)

to those whose intent could no longer be honored, whether by reason of obsolescence or changes in the law, she recommended to the college and its outside attorneys how to proceed. As she made her way through the boxes, she called for more file folders.

She spent much of the summer of 1992 in that tiny basement room going through stacks of green folders, reviewing their contents, determining their origins, and parsing the terms of each fund. She reviewed over 700 special-purpose funds, created categorizations for them, developed the protocol for inputting information into the computer and then worked on inputting the information itself.

She was about to become chair of the audit committee, and Chabotar visited her frequently to discuss the issues that would come before the committee, and to see how the project was coming along. Diane would be "hunched over her computer working on data entry. She always had a smile and a wave no matter how late the hour."

Having developed a form and the protocol, she had by August (she wrote) "completed the review and entry of the professorships, the lectureships and the special-purpose funds. I'll finish all the others, except scholarships, by Labor Day. I'll need to develop a second form for the scholarship data, and it seems to me only sensible to coordinate with the financial aid people so my work will be useful to them. I'm hoping that Kent will pull together a meeting at which this can be discussed. Barring unforeseen developments, I'd expect to be able to do the scholarship fund review next summer."*

She had identified a number of issues with respect to "those funds to which a legal opinion is needed and for which court action seems desirable." She prepared a "full written report" which included these recommendations:

> (a) A review of those funds for which court action ought to be considered. Those which appear to have unused income should receive attention first.
>
> (b) A review of those funds which we may want to "clean up" either through court action or by conforming the college practices to the directives in the instrument. These include some where the college is deviating from the exact terms and some which appear to contain inappropriate restrictions (which the College may not be heeding).... [In the case of the loan funds] an overall evaluation of their administration might prove useful.
>
> (c) Matters relating to the future administration of the funds:
>
>> a. Should there be individual protocols for the funds? I think it would be desirable to have each fund folder contain a written statement as to who is authorized to spend the fund income and for what.
>>
>> b. With respect to the professorships and lectureships, it looks as if some articulated policy decisions would be helpful.... I think it would be desirable to have a uniform policy concerning the use of excess income in those cases

---

*   August 4, 1992, progress report to Chabotar and Webster.

in which the salary and benefits of the chairholder do not exhaust the annual income. There appears to be quite a lot of unspent income in these funds.

c. There are a number of funds in which there is a planned accumulation of income. Unless the income is transferred to principal each year (and it is not in some cases) it appears that the fund will not be credited with the income earned by the accumulated income. I think this poses some problems which should be discussed.

The memo attached the detailed six-page protocol she had developed for the recording of endowment fund information.*

What Diane had done was extraordinary, and had combined all her training and her instincts to honor the intentions of those who'd given money to serve legitimate public interests of the time and, at the same time, to have those intentions looked at in modern terms, in order to apply historical charitable intent to what was now possible in the context of their intent. What she was doing was to serve the public good in ways consistent with her early training and with the guiding principles of Bowdoin College.

The confluence was, as with an earlier time in her career, serendipitous.

---

* August 4, 1992, progress report to Chabotar and Webster.

CHAPTER ELEVEN

HARDSCRABBLE FARM: THE LAST GREAT ADVENTURE

I N THE MEANTIME, THE ORCHARD COLLECTIVE HAD ACQUIRED a new name as the group continued to look at possible sites. One site was the Homewood Inn in Yarmouth, Maine, a sprawling mid-1900s resort complex with fifteen buildings and a $3.2 million price tag, too complex and too expensive for what seemed possible. Diane reported on the spring 1989 visit and what she now called "'Hardscrabble Farm' – the current name [she said] for a future community of compatible people who would like to share some responsibility for each other and to engage in possibly profitable enterprises while living in a setting in which some facilities can be shared." She began pressing for expressions of general interest: "Please let me hear definitely by May 1."*

In November, Diane revisited the concept in considerable detail in a letter to the group:

> Casual conversations, spurts of activity and interest aroused by specific properties, and more disciplined communications have all occurred during the past year. It seems like the right time to take stock of all of it and see what we have.
>
> What are the various goals people have for Hardscrabble?
>
> My original prospectus described it as an adventure, and proposed that we all band together for communal living and a communal money-making enterprise, with the dedicated lawyers, writers and other career-minded people among us remaining free to pursue their own occupations (within the geographical limitations of our new location). The concept was one of simplifying lives,

---

* April 9, 1989, letter to the group.

developing self-sufficiency, opting out (to some extent) of our greed-driven economy and actually having fun during what is probably going to be our last fifty years (Regie disassociates herself from that last statement).

No one is prepared to take such radical steps – at least not yet. And there are some differing ideas about what the features of Hardscrabble should be. The list below is a start at articulating these on a very basic level: Hardscrabble should provide:

(1) a rational arrangement for accommodating common needs in a reasonably economical fashion. While all of us need private space, there are space needs that could sensibly be shared.

(2) built-in opportunities to share both income-producing and recreational activities among compatible people (but not too many of them).

(3) back-up for dealing with life's problems, e.g., supervision of property during absences, help in emergencies, pet feedings, etc.

(4) the stimulus of differing people with differing interests and different things going on in their lives joined together by physical circumstances so that a fair amount of interchange is inevitable.

To me, the key to this is the possibility of income-producing activity as an integral part of the plan; otherwise, we're not talking about anything other than a retirement community, and that's rather dull.

Very few of us are willing to make any full-time or even part-time commitment to an active enterprise at the moment. This suggests that if we are to do anything now, the following alternatives are the feasible ones:

(1) setting up an organizational structure and a timetable;

(2) acquiring raw land with the expectation we will develop something on it in the future;

(3) or looking for a developed piece of property with some income potential, e.g., a farm, a B&B. The farm concept has not been met with wild enthusiasm; the inn/B&B seems to spark some interest. It has the potential for flexibility, for the possibility of communal living and if there were some acreage with it, the possibility of individual housing and perhaps some apple trees….

Diane and Bob had collected and read materials about co-housing developments, mostly in the Scandinavian countries, with a few in the United States. The concept envisioned a cluster of small houses individually owned around a larger communal house where the residents would gather for meals and social occasions. The co-housing members would pool their resources and their labor, and look after each other in many important ways. Needless to say, the literature spoke of the many problems that arise in a capitalistic society from the theory of a commune confronting reality. An elders commune such as Diane had in mind had never been tried. She had no doubt that it would work and that the problems and issues could be overcome.

The proposed location of Hardscrabble Farm continued to be speculative. On one occasion it became a different problem than Diane had bargained for, when we unexpectedly found ourselves in a scene out of the movie *Deliverance*. We had driven to a coastal waterfront property in Harpswell, not far from Brunswick, in a beaten-up jalopy owned by the broker, a former hippie still sporting lank blond hair down to his shoulders. A graveled right of way led from the road down to the property, but our broker somehow missed a right turn and we ended up at a well-maintained clearing, turnaround and anchorage, one which, it seemed to me, was likely being used for other important, if not licit, purposes. Suddenly our way out was blocked by two large pickup trucks with rifles racked in their rear windows and driven by large and threatening male members of the family that lived at the head of the gravel road. Strangers were not wanted, and especially not hippies. It was a surreal encounter. After they grudgingly moved their pickups to let our car squeeze by, we decided it might be wise to look elsewhere.

In February 1992, the hunt grew serious as Bob, Regie, Diane and I were looking at a sixty-four-acre saltwater farm not far from Brunswick. The land sloped down from a farmhouse and barn high on a hillside to a pier jutting out into one of Maine's fjords. The anchorage was protected by an island close offshore. The salt air was invigorating. ("This is the first time," noted Diane, "that Erik has indicated any interest in moving to a different environment, so I don't want to be negative about this prospect….") I was enthused; she was quietly dubious. We had looked at a lot of prospects by now, and this was so far the best of the lot.*

A different broker mentioned a property on the Kennebec River in Woolwich ("beautiful, but isolated"). We didn't have time to go see it, then, but Diane was warming to the idea that we could find a place in Maine. She would be contemplating this prospect as she spent her summer days that year in the basement office at Bowdoin defining and sorting out the incredibly complex issues regarding the college's handling of endowed funds.

On Columbus Day weekend in 1992, Hardscrabble Farm became, suddenly, a reality when our daughter Kristin and I went to see the property on the Kennebec River in Woolwich, across the river and upstream from Bath, and just below Swan Island. Except for its isolated location on the east bank of the Kennebec twelve miles north of Route 1, it was a perfect match for Diane's vision.

We saw an eighteenth century farmhouse and barn a hundred yards back from the riverbank on a hundred acres of fertile farmland and woods which had once been pasture for the dairy cow herds that had been housed in the barn until the 1960s. The farmhouse had a sweeping view across once-cultivated fields to woods now blazing

---

* With some misgivings, we nevertheless made an offer on the property in September 1992. Fortunately, as it turned out, the offer was turned down.

The Ames farmhouse as it appeared in the 1930s.

with the elegant reds, oranges and yellows of fall ascending the hillside on the far side. The farmhouse, little-changed since the 1780s when it had been built, consisted of two smaller side-by-side houses that had been joined. One was a four-room colonial, the other a cape with eight tiny rooms,* and there was an ell reaching back from the colonial toward a woodshed and privy in the ell and a stable at right angles at its far end. The parlor and the kitchen (which still boasted an ancient woodstove) were in the ell just behind the colonial. Everything was run-down, but structurally both the

One of Diane's many plans for our future was that we would become murder mystery authors and she had stayed home the weekend Kristin and I saw the Woolwich property to work with Regie on one.

We (all of us collectively) worked on one murder mystery concerning principals of the Board of Bar Overseers and lawyers brought before it for discipline. Another had as its opening scene a floating corpse in the grand pool at Graceland, Elvis Presley's abode. This book had to be abandoned when Elvis's estate (which controlled all references to Graceland) refused to grant permission.

---

* The cape, we learned, had been used in winter as a dormitory to house seasonal workers in the booming ice trade of the late 1800s. One of the giant icehouses that lined the Kennebec River had been built on the point of land into the river that marked one of the property's boundaries.

farmhouse and the barn were in good shape.

Diane and I drove back to see it together two weeks later. "The Woolwich farm is absolutely beautiful," she wrote. "It looks as if it belongs in a picture book.... If we carry out our master plan, we'd set up all the space inside for community use and build small efficient homes, probably connected to each other and the main building by covered walkways.... I'd gut the ell and make a living room, kitchen etc.... Other people are likely to have different ideas of course. It's the planning of it and the thinking about it that are so much fun...."

The negotiations were also fun, if a bit weird. The owner, whose ambition had been to make a ton of money by developing the property into a hundred house lots, had instead run into a ton of

> The farm had been owned by the Ames family for nearly two hundred years, until it was sold in the late 1950s when none of the sons wanted to take on the grueling work of farming. Roberta Ames, daughter of George Ames, the last family farmer, told me that in the 1938 flood, the farmhouse (which sits on a knoll) was isolated on an island and the only way the family could leave was by rowboat.

unforeseen problems having to do with local zoning, public road access and wetland protection. (A swampy watercourse runs from the river through the property north to south at the boundary of the fields and wooded hillside, and the fields themselves are in the floodplain.) Worst of all, he had overpaid for the property and was deeply in debt to a Portland bank which had itself gone under and was now in the hands of the FDIC. The owner, whose asking price was less than what he'd paid for it, had no equity left in the property and didn't care how much a buyer paid, so long as the FDIC accepted the amount in full discharge of his debt.

Rather than negotiate with *us*, he was negotiating *on our behalf* with the FDIC. We offered substantially less than his asking price and he urged the FDIC to accept. Finally he reported that with a slight nudge upward, the FDIC would allow him to sell to us and had agreed to discharge his debt. The transaction would close in late January.

Diane wrote the group:

> If you're a Hardscrabble fence-sitter, as some of you are, do not at this time try to figure out if you are really going to do this. Instead, go with the flow and participate in all the planning processes – which are likely to be almost as much fun as actually doing it. Our first process is for everyone to identify what he or she would like to have in the common living space and in the outdoors. A questionnaire will appear in the near future, but in the meantime, think about it.

The questionnaire went out at the end of December. The subjects included communal organization, outdoor needs, outdoor facilities and planning, arrangement of physical facilities, location of principal communal facilities, aesthetic amenities, indoor needs and possible occupations. Twelve people answered, expressing their preferences. Diane now had a viable co-housing group. She turned her thinking to what occupations we could pursue. A bookstore in Bath was one possibility. Another, perhaps more practical, was to write, edit and publish a newspaper for Maine lawyers. Although none of us had ever been engaged in such a venture, she was confident – since all four of us, Diane, Bob, Regie and I, were lawyers – it would be no problem. (But we would probably need to take and pass the Maine bar examination the next July.)

Diane's year-end letter to family and friends was filled with optimism:

> On the brink of new possibilities, we're feeling very adventurous – and very nervous. Most important we're waiting to become the proud co-owners of a 114-acre farm on the banks of the Kennebec River. It's a lovely place with fields and woodland and an eighteenth century farmhouse which needs work. This is our second-time-around life plan in which we're hoping to collect a compatible group of over-fifties who'd like to share some aspects of daily living and some – enough – remunerative activities, which we refer to as the "Hardscrabble Farm Enterprise." I have definitely decided that my career as an 8 a.m. – 6:30 p.m. bureaucrat [in the Charities Division] is going to end on May 31, 1993. I was going to finish out the fiscal year (June 30), which would sort of connect with my 55th birthday, but we're going biking in France in June, so it seems to make sense to clear out my desk before I go. I may stay on in a volunteer capacity, working a couple of days a week, but in control of my own time.

In mid-January Diane was on a week-long family visit to California when my Maine-based brother, Jon, alerted me to an ad offering to sell all rights to the *Maine Lawyers Review*, a monthly legal magazine which was moribund, having not published for months, together with its associated hardware of antiquated computers and printers. Its principal value was the name and its advertising list. Jon and I met in Portland with the broker and the seller and made a deal for astonishingly short money. The purchase and sale agreement was signed January 18th and I had it in hand to surprise Diane when she stepped off the plane in Boston two days later. Excited, she wrote her mother that her plans had changed:

> While I was en route, Erik and Jon bought the Maine Lawyers newspaper, so now we've got that. We're really committed to this new life plan of ours. Regie and Bob are going to be half-owners with us.
>
> The bottom line is I'm giving my notice today to the Attorney General's office, telling them I'm leaving at the end of March. This is a little scary. I'm intending to continue to spend time there on a volunteer basis but I'm going to need at least a week each month to put out the newspaper.

Our plan was to publish a newspaper whose format mimicked a successful lawyers' newspaper in Massachusetts, *Lawyer's Weekly*. Unlike *Lawyer's Weekly,* however *Maine Lawyers Review* would come out to its subscribers every other week, with a quarterly issue going to all members of the bar regardless whether they were subscribers. The front page would have news stories, some describing and commenting on decisions important to the bar, others dealing with topics of interest which weren't reflected in the decided cases. Inside pages would feature calendars and gossip, interviews with judges and clerks, and articles written by well-known members of the bar on topics of general or particular interest. The articles, we hoped, would be contributed free on the theory that the exposure would be good for the lawyers writing them. I suggested we should have a cartoon in each issue. Advertising, of course, would be the key to financial stability.

We were aware of another lawyers' publication in Maine, published out of her home by Deborah Firestone, a non-practicing member of the Maine bar. Her publication contained summaries of current published decisions in the trial courts of Maine (but not its appellate courts). This was an important source of income for her and her family and Diane was concerned that we would put her out of business. I wrote Deborah a letter at the end of January explaining our plans and proposing a merger. Three weeks later it was done, and in theory the new *Maine Lawyers Review* was ready to be launched. Diane described how we would all work together, and in what locations, until the Woolwich office was ready:

> The three of us [Diane, Bob and Deborah] should have equal tasks and responsibilities. This model does not allow for Erik's participation....* Diane and Bob will work in the office over the garage in Brookline and Deborah will work in Portland. She'll prepare the Superior Court digests and send them to Brookline by modem. We need to hire a part-time advertising manager. Bob and I will go to Maine every other week and stay over one night, do interviews, make local contacts, spend time with Deborah and the ad person and deliver the copy. We'll put out four free issues in May and June. The first subscription issue will be in July.

There were hurdles and glitches yet to be overcome, but Issue No. 1 of the *Maine Lawyers Review* – published to all members of the Maine bar – appeared in their mailboxes hot off the presses early in the first week of May 1993. It had been written, edited, put together, pasted up and published out of a motel room on the second floor of a rock-bottom inexpensive Days Inn in South Portland where we – Diane,

---

* My participation would be as an emergency fill-in on writing, editing and paste-up to help see to it that the paper went out on deadline.

Bob, Deborah, Regie and I – had collected the prior owner's obsolete hardware, much of which simply didn't work at all, and some of our own. Regie and I shuttled between South Portland and our law practices in Boston, ferrying our own laptops and other stopgap electronic equipment. The finished paste-up product was placed in a flat cardboard box and delivered to the U.S. Post Office at 4:55 p.m. Friday night, five minutes before it closed, for shipment to the printer, the *Ellsworth American* in Ellsworth, Maine.

Driving together from Boston, Regie and I arrived afterwards, drove into the inner court of the Days Inn and saw our spouses and Deborah sitting exhausted in folding chairs on the second-floor balcony of the motel, celebrating with a bottle of champagne, fists raised high in the air. They'd done it. *Maine Lawyers Review* was on its way! ("An exciting time, the most fun in years!" Diane wrote.)

Fortunately, little by little, its way would become less frenetic and more sophisticated, but putting out each issue would be an adventure for the next year and a half. Then, beginning in September 1994, we were able for the first time to publish *Maine Lawyers Review* out of a second-floor office in what had once been the stable at the farm in Woolwich. And that, of course, had been Diane's plan.

In the interim, much had happened at Hardscrabble Farm. We had engaged like-minded architects Steven and Wiebke Theodore (who lived in an energy-efficient house they'd designed and built in the neighboring town of Dresden) to work with us in the restoration and rebuilding of the farmhouse, ell and stable. They were enthusiastic about our plans.

To help us decide how to proceed in dealing with a house more than two hundred years old, we went through it in March with an expert in historical construction and restoration. Bob – an antiquarian at heart – described the event in a March 1993 report he prepared afterwards for the group:

> We began in the part of the house just inside the side door. This part of the ell, with the kitchen right behind it is arguably the oldest part of the house. There was a large center chimney long since removed behind where the mantle in the living room now is. It would have served both the living room (parlor) and the kitchen for heating and cooking. There is an ancient door leading into the shed.
>
> The shed is framed in traditional ways – post and beam – above two bays. The shed is quite old, although not as old as the kitchen/parlor portions of the ell. At the end of the shed, the connected privy and large shed are of 19th C. vintage. The stairs from the parlor into the basement are among the oldest intact 18th C. features of the house. They were constructed without nails, and because they were built well and rested on stones, have survived without deterioration.
>
> There are two small rooms in the basement which were dug by hand. Their

floor today consists of bricks taken down from the original 18th C. chimney when it was rebuilt. The door between them originally hung by leather hinges. To the left of the door is a four-inch-diameter hole closed with a wooden flap to permit the family cat or cats access to the rodents. Food would have been stored in the basement because it was cool. The large (five-foot-diameter) arch in the ancient chimney base in the basement is reminiscent of the double arches in the Pownalborough Courthouse.

The first-floor bedroom has wide boards original to the house. The horizontal wainscoting is original to the house, as is the ceiling which has distinct evidence of 18th C. lathing which is accordioned from boards. The main entrance and stairwell are original to the house and are 18th C. The stairway is entirely original. The roof framing was constructed largely without nails and with the use of large pegs at the roof peak where the two long beams are joined.

Bob had developed a fondness for the buildings and an appreciation of their historical significance. His attention to detail and instinct toward preservation were clearly a force to be reckoned with as we decided what work we would do with the buildings. In a memo to the group that same month, Diane was more pragmatic:

In addition to the housing on the site, we'd like to use the site for these purposes: (a) wildflower meadow seen from the windows; (b) at least one drift of daffodils; (c) a planned, low-maintenance flower garden; (d) four-season vegetable gardening with a goal of raising enough to furnish a lot of what the residents need; (e) a small apple orchard; (f) raspberries, blackberries and boysenberries; (g) walking paths; (h) river view and access to a mooring; (i) leasing land for farming by others (this is important for us, to see the agricultural land put to use).

Existing buildings: (a) we have no particular attachment to the interior of the cape; but we would (b) preserve the architectural integrity of the federal; (c) maintain the appearance of the western side of the house, including windows appropriate for the period of the house; (d) provide light and airiness on the inside, including nooks and crannies; and (e) rebuild the ell entirely.

Our master plan ideas: co-housing for six no-child households with the farmhouse complex serving as the center for common activities; a second cluster of six households, preferably with children and with its own common center, not too distant from the farmhouse. Common use of the barn and the major link being the outside activities.

Time frame: we would like to have phase one living space ready in 18 months, which would mean renovating existing space to provide residences for two households plus an office for the newspaper; phase two: six separate units related to the farmhouse; we are not committed at this time to a second six-unit cluster which would be inhabited by strangers.

The stable would actually be physically moved off-site while the basement was being built, then returned, to be gutted inside and rebuilt. The wasps that had made their home in the wood walls for decades were only minimally disturbed and would continue to appear every late winter and spring.

We had tenants in the house, three Navy pilots stationed at the Brunswick Naval Air Station, who were into guns and deer hunting, for which the farm was prime territory. We promised them they could remain in the house until the fall. Then construction would begin. In the meantime we and our architects had to develop plans for the work and hire a contractor.

Over the spring and summer there were several meetings with the architects at the farm in which the entire group participated. In the end, the basic plan Diane had outlined would be followed: the exterior footprint of the cape, the colonial, the ell and the stable would be preserved; the cape would be gutted and its eight tiny rooms converted into three, with the third being a loft looking out over half the first floor through two-story-high windows toward the river; the original four rooms of the two-story colonial would be restored; the ell would be torn down and rebuilt entirely to become a spacious communal living room and kitchen over a new full basement; and the stable would become a dining room, television room and laundry, its upstairs to be guest quarters and an office for the *Maine Lawyers Review.*

By midsummer our contractor, Joe Caputo, was on board and ready to begin construction in the fall. Joe was a craftsman who enjoyed a challenge, but he'd never done a job like this one before (and was heard to say afterward that he'd never do one like it again!).

Meanwhile, every two weeks like clockwork, the *Maine Lawyers Review* miraculously appeared in a timely fashion. Part was produced in an office in Deborah's converted garage in Portland; the remainder was written, edited and pasted up in the second-floor office of Reg and Bob's garage in Brookline, Massachusetts, where the four of us (Deborah sent her work there electronically) would labor late into Friday evenings, then drive the finished product for shipment to Ellsworth to the Federal Express office at Logan International Airport before it closed at 10 p.m. It may not have been efficient but it was, as Diane said, an exciting time.

In her year-end letter in December 1993, she wrote:

    1993 has been even more adventurous than we anticipated. We've had a year we'll definitely remember. Once our offer on the farm in Woolwich was accepted, suddenly there we were, more or less committed to establishing a new way of life in the boondocks. I'm not sure any one of us really believed it was going to happen.

Even more surprising, we acquired a dormant publication for Maine lawyers. While I was gone in California, my trusty spouse and his devil-may-care brother Jon up and bought it! We decided we shouldn't waste any time in starting to publish it again. Our first issue came out at the end of April and we've been publishing every two weeks ever since. I never thought I'd become a newspaper editor at the age of fifty-five.

This year as I turn fifty-six it seems likely I'll launch myself on my farming career as well. Construction is coming along on the Hardscrabble project. Regie thinks she might like to run for the Maine legislature! We all took the bar exam at the end of July. We're now anticipating that 1994 will see me holding down the fort in Maine more or less with everybody else dividing their time and doing a lot of faxing and e-mailing.

Apart from the excitement of building a new life and a new career, Diane had continued to spend two or more days a week at Bowdoin on the endowed funds project, which was taking longer than she'd anticipated – but she intended to see it through. That had been her commitment. She identified still another problem, which was how to "use the income from endowed chair funds during periods in which there [was] no appropriate senior faculty member to be the holder of the chair." She suggested that "a junior, non-tenured faculty member could be named without contravening the usual terms of these gifts." This raised another question: that of "appearing to honor someone who does not yet have the necessary academic stature for the honor." She consulted with both the dean for academic affairs, Charles Beitz, and with Peter Webster, who would have the final say on the legal questions. Ultimately the problem was resolved so that the college could make maximum use of the funds set aside for endowed chairs.

The computer protocol she developed became the template for the procedure Bowdoin would follow with respect to every new endowed fund. The recommendations she made – which the college adopted – regarding standard language to be included in all future endowed funds ensured that the college would not again be stymied in the use of the funds because of obligations to honor a donor's intent which had become obsolete. Each deed of gift would be required to include what became known as the "Lund language," a savings clause that would enable the college, without having to go to court, to make use of endowed funds where the donor's intent had, for one or another reason, failed. The "Lund language" provided:

> If in future years altered circumstances make it impractical to use this Fund for the above stated purposes, the College, by vote of its Governing Boards, may use the principal and/or income of the Fund for such other purpose or purposes

as in the opinion of the Governing Boards will then most nearly fulfill the wishes of the donor.

In the meantime she had become chair of the audit committee, itself a daunting task not many trustees or overseers were anxious to take on. She and Kent Chabotar were in frequent contact. By the fall and winter of 1993-94, that ship was back on course and the minutes of audit committee meetings had taken on a markedly more professional tone. The college's books for the fiscal year ending June 30, 1993, closed two weeks earlier than in prior years. By March 1994, the last meeting Diane attended, the theme of the college auditor's management letter "differed from those of recent years. In fiscal year 1989 and fiscal year 1990 the institution was experiencing significant deficits and the focus of the letters was financial equilibrium. [A]ggressive management by the administration has brought the deficit under control."*

Construction in Woolwich had begun on schedule in the prior fall. We took frequent weekend trips to see to its progress and to allow Diane to continue her work at Bowdoin. Diane and Bob drove to Maine every two weeks to interview judges for the paper and to work with Deborah. It was a busy time and Diane was looking toward the future with anticipation:

> On Wednesday I went to the Brookline office and worked on the paper all day. It was a little chilly but I managed all right. Then I was back there on Thursday and Friday as well and Bob was there those two days. We needed to get the paper done by Friday night so that I could go to my Bowdoin meeting on Saturday. The Bowdoin meeting went until early afternoon. Erik spent the time talking to Roberta Ames, one of the last of the original family who owned and lived in what is now Hardscrabble Farm. He's compiling information about the house...."†

A disquieting note came into Diane's correspondence as winter turned into early spring: "I've been really sleepy all week – either I'm fighting off some kind of minor bug or it's spring fever. Erik says he thinks he's fighting something off, so we both may be." (April 18, 1994, letter.) Diane had never been someone who complained about personal discomfort. Her theory had always been that sooner or later it would go away. To this point it had. Would that she'd been right again this time.

Ten days later her dream was shattered. I'd driven her, doubled over in pain from intestinal blockage, to the emergency room at Lahey Clinic. After a day of testing with no firm diagnosis, but with colon cancer suspected, she was operated on. The surgeon

---

*   March 4, 1994 audit committee minutes.
†   February 1994 letter.

had asked me to wait in Diane's hospital room rather than the general waiting room. I remember the stricken look on his face as he came in the door, but very little of our conversation. They'd found the cancer high up in the colon, it had metastasized and spread to her lymph nodes – and he was very, very sorry. There was no hope of cure. How long did she have to live? A year to eighteen months at best.

Our children had all been in the waiting room, together with our neighbor, Nancy Kocher, one of Diane's closest friends for the past twenty-five years. They came into the hospital room to join me after the surgeon had left. I remember seeing their faces and that Nancy left us alone after seeing mine, but nothing else.

The bravest person among us that awful day was Diane. Once she'd returned from the recovery room, she learned of the surgeon's findings, diagnosis and prognosis from me. She accepted the news calmly but in disbelief.

It was several days before she was able to come home to Lexington. She was still extremely weak and unable to eat any regular food. In the interim we'd frantically but methodically searched the Internet and contacted every medical connection we had to find out where Diane should go for a definitive second opinion and advice concerning alternative treatments. The answer was Sloan-Kettering in New York. A woman oncologist there was reckoned the top of her profession. She could see us promptly, within the week. Diane was barely ambulatory but she, Kristin and I, carrying Diane's X-rays from Lahey, boarded the shuttle, stayed overnight and went to Sloan-Kettering.

The oncologist was thorough, understanding and kind, but her opinion was the same one we'd already heard. There were no cures. There were a few experimental programs in other parts of the United States hoping to find a cure, or at least a course of treatment that would prolong life, but no encouraging results had come out of those programs. She was doubtful whether Diane would be accepted into one of them because of the advanced stage of her cancer, but if she were to be accepted, there were severe drawbacks to the programs which we should consider. One was that we would have to move to the program's location; another was that the chemicals being administered to people in the programs caused severe discomfort, illness and pain. She gave us the contact information and said she'd help if Diane decided she wanted to be admitted to one of the programs.

We talked over the possibilities. None of this seemed real. How could someone so vibrant and so healthy her entire life be faced with a death sentence? But there it was, and it had to be dealt with. Typically, Diane confronted it. She rejected the alternative of experimental treatment programs. She was relatively free from pain now and wanted no more of it. More important she'd been promised that it was likely she would be able, before too long, to resume a nearly normal life for most of the time that remained to her. We were going to go ahead, she said, and we were going to have fun, just as we always had. Whatever happened, we'd do it together. And so we did.

We returned to Boston and to the Dana Farber Cancer Institute, where Diane had been referred for chemotherapy. Before beginning the course of chemotherapy, the Dana Farber oncologist who would be in charge of Diane reviewed her records independently and concurred in Lahey's findings.

Diane's chemotherapy at Dana Farber began in May 1994, a week before the spring meetings of Bowdoin's governing boards. The treatments took time and she asked if she could use a telephone while they were going on. She needed to discuss with Kent Chabotar the agenda for the audit committee meeting and ask him to convey her views on the subjects that would come before the committee. She wasn't prepared by any means to resign her position as its chair. Besides, the endowment funds project had yet to be completed.

Nor did Diane intend to abandon our plans for our new home in Woolwich, which would be ready for us in September.

The weeks of May and June were long and trying times. Still very weak, she fretted about inactivity and being house-bound in Lexington. She insisted on beginning work again on the newspaper, which had been held together in her absence by a combination of Bob, Regie, Deborah, me, and son Ben, who pitched in. Never one to wish for things for herself, Diane had talked wistfully of the comfort of a classic Eames chair and of being outside in the garden. Kristin and I found where Eames chairs were sold, bought one and presented it with the promise that on nice days we'd move it and her into the garden where, under a sun hat, she could do her work. She picked up strength and interest but still was unable to eat regular food.

We looked to the future, and to Hardscrabble Farm.

We had talked about wanting to have a small seaworthy lobster boat which we could anchor in the river opposite the farm and use for ocean fishing trips and cruising on the river itself. Poring over ads for used boats, we inspected several before finding exactly what we wanted in Portsmouth, NH, owned by a lobsterman who had decided to get out of the business. We took a test cruise out into the far reaches of the harbor, then made a deal. A week later Diane and I drove to Portsmouth to meet my nephew Will, an experienced ocean sailor who'd volunteered to come down from Portland to help me ferry the boat north to the Kennebec River.

Diane drove back to Lexington alone, having shrugged off my concerns, not just about the return trip, but her drive north to the island with Bob a couple of days later.

Will and I checked the gauges, started the engine and set out northward in impenetrable fog. We were sure of our ability to navigate with the help of the Loran on board – until at one point we found ourselves passing the same-numbered navigation buoy twice. Going into Cape Porpoise, we found ourselves on the verge of going aground, when, fortuitously, a local fishing boat came by, and we tucked ourselves in behind it.

Avoiding other misadventures, we found our way to Will's home on the water off

Cape Elizabeth. My brother Jon arrived the next morning in bright sunshine in time to help motor the boat up the coast, then up the Kennebec River past the farm in Woolwich and all the way to Hallowell, where Jon lived, and where Diane and Bob met me on their way to the island. She christened our prized lobster boat *The Venerable*, and the next day we took a celebratory cruise on her. Another friend and I drove it south on the river to Woolwich and anchored it outside the farm. Diane met us there and we drove back to the island.

What seemed a miracle happened over the July 4th weekend. Traditionally, together with our children, we had always hosted an expansive July 4th weekend party at the island for friends and relatives, with all available beds filled up. We thought the tradition should continue but Diane didn't want to burden the party. When Jon invited us to stay in the master bedroom of their camp on a neighboring part of the island – where they promised a low-key celebration with a couple of their friends – we were pleased to accept.

Jon steamed lobsters and grilled hot dogs. When Diane smelled the hot dogs, she grew hungry and insisted on having one. And then two. From that day on, she went back to a regular diet, and we resumed a life which – apart from the ongoing chemotherapy – was almost as normal for us as it once had been.

Somehow a dark cloud had lifted. For the rest of the summer we commuted between Boston and the island. We swam in the mornings, canoed, kayaked, took the sun and spent time with our friends and our children and their friends. Diane drove to Brunswick by herself to work on the endowed funds project. We drove together to Portland, where we met Bob and Reg at Deborah's office to work on the paper. Bob and Regie came on up to the island and we then drove 40 minutes south to kibbitz with Joe Caputo on the progress of the farmhouse reconstruction.

Toward the end of the summer, Diane decided it was unrealistic to think she could continue to fulfill her responsibilities as a Bowdoin overseer. On August 20, 1994, she wrote Brountas, president of the trustees, and Marvin Green, president of the overseers, a letter of resignation:

> Dear Paul and Marvin,
>
> It is with great regret that I have decided to resign from Bowdoin College's Board of Overseers. It seems clear that I will be continuing my cancer treatment for some time to come, and I do not think I will be left with the amount of time and energy to spend on Bowdoin's affairs which I feel is needed from a Board member.
>
> I hope, however, that I will be able to continue with the endowment funds project in the fall.
>
> Serving on the Board has been a constant pleasure for me, in terms of new friendships I have made, the insights I have acquired into the workings of the

College and the opportunity it has given me to make my contribution to the common good. I shall miss it – and all of you.

Marvin Green replied on September 7, 1994:

Dear Diane,

I have just received your letter of resignation from the Board of Overseers, a letter which must have been difficult to write. I accept it with much regret, but I know you have thought long and hard about the decision.

Your concern for Bowdoin and your commitment to its welfare have been manifested in many ways over many years. I can only express what I and many others feel – deep appreciation and sincere regret at losing you as a colleague. The College is in your debt for the work you have done straightening out the restricted endowment funds and it is wonderful news that you hope to continue on that project.

I trust there will be other opportunities for your colleagues to express their thanks and well wishes, but I wanted to take this opportunity to send you my thoughts.

With thanks and warm regards...

President Robert Edwards sent her a handwritten note on September 5, 1994:

Dear Diane,

The year has opened and the campus resounds again to the wonderful good humor and enthusiasm of the students. The College feels in very good shape and the first year looks very strong indeed—at least they all had smiles, firm handshakes and direct gazes when they signed in! It's been a good summer, with a mix of work and play; but we are delighted to begin again.

It was cruel, hard news to hear on our return that you had decided you must step down from the Boards. I have found you an invaluable source of reason and strength, and you have been an exceptional audit chair. And, heaven knows, the work that you have done to order our jungle of separate endowment funds has been absolutely indispensable.

We are all desolated by your illness. I'm dismayed and frustrated that there is nothing we can do or say to help or encourage a person who is confronting mortality. All we can do, I think, is admire the courage and clarity of mind with which you are taking decisions and hope that, when called, we shall do the same. And second, we pray that remission and cure – which do come to pass – will occur. This we most earnestly do.

We are going to miss your presence on the Boards a great deal. We shall not stop thinking about you and, if you are willing to accept emeritus status, we shall continue to send you policy papers and materials.

With our hopes and prayers, and warmest wishes...

Diane responded gratefully, accepting his offer, and took care to point out, tongue in cheek, that she should become an Overseer *Emerita* – not *Emeritus*. On October 4, 1994, the Governing Boards would vote: "that in recognition of devoted service to Bowdoin College, Diane T. Lund, elected an Overseer in 1985, be elected Overseer *Emerita*."

Two weeks earlier, in mid-September, the farmhouse was ready and we and Bob and Regie were ready to move in – and we did.

Bob and Regie's commitment was remarkable under the circumstances. In order to make the move they sold a vacation home they had owned (and loved) for many years in Wellfleet on Cape Cod. They arrived with a van-load of furniture in mid-September and settled in. Bob came to live in Woolwich every other week so that he and Diane (and Deborah and a fourth writer we'd hired) could do what was necessary to write and publish the newspaper. Regie spent more time than the rest of us in Boston in order to maintain her law practice. She drove up to join us on the weekends.

While in Woolwich, she and Diane planned a second enterprise, opening and running an antique shop in Damariscotta, a half-hour's drive away. An empty storefront was available, and they arranged to rent it, beginning in the summer of 1995.

While she was not in denial about her illness, Diane was determined not to give in or become depressed but rather to lead her life as normally as she could for as long as she could. There were surreal aspects to our life, given that it was running on two tracks, one of them finite.

She expected her time would be at least eighteen months, the maximum predicted. She wanted to celebrate the advent of the farm, our thirty-fifth wedding anniversary

The restored Hardscrabble Farm house, winter 1995.

and my sixtieth birthday with a grand party on Midsummer Night's Eve in June 1995. We hired a party coordinator to help Diane put it all together, including a caterer, a band that would play in the barn for dancing and miscellaneous other entertainment. She wanted her mother there for the party, and Noreen and Carl, anyone else from her family who could come, my Maine relatives, and all our friends. Putting together this extraordinary celebration helped carry Diane through much of the winter of 1994-95.

Our trips to Boston for chemotherapy were wearing, not just because of the chemotherapy but because of the travel itself. Each Monday for six weeks she had to go to Lahey. Then she had two weeks off, after which the same course would start up again. Some weeks – usually the off-weeks for the newspaper – we stayed in Lexington from Monday to Monday while I worked to keep my law practice going.* During the two-week hiatus we were at the farm doing those things Diane had always planned we would do. She worked on the newspaper with enthusiasm – and we invited a series of old friends to come visit, and to say their goodbyes.

John and Barbara Quarles came from Washington, DC, to help us plant hundreds of daffodil bulbs of different varieties in a long crescent extending in a "drift" from the driveway beside the farmhouse down to the river bank. John arrived with a flower bulb hole-borer which we could attach to an electric drill. With the drill and two lengths of extension cord, we managed to plant the daffodils in a day and a half.

Barbara and John Quarles visited in the fall of 1994. L. to r.: Bob Sloane, Barbara, myself and Diane, John Quarles and Regie Healy.

We piled into a canoe and paddled out to the anchored *Venerable.* We climbed aboard for a ten-mile upriver cruise past Swan Island and Richmond to the Pownalborough Courthouse.† Along the way an astounding four-foot-long sturgeon leaped clear out of the water in front of our boat.

Later we drove to the courthouse itself – once the only courthouse north of Portland and the tallest building (at four stories) north of Boston. John Adams had argued cases there before the Revolution. We toured Richmond, which was a center of White Russian settlement following the Russian Revolution. Diane was enormously pleased to be the tour guide through these artifacts of history.

---

* Something which wouldn't have been possible without partners who did whatever was necessary in my absence and sympathetic opponents who never objected to a series of trial continuances.
† The courthouse had, at various times, been a fort, a pub, an inn for travelers and the hub of commerce for the Kennebec Proprietors, owners of the British king's huge land grants in this part of Maine.

Our long-time bicycling companions, Charles and Joyce Muckenfuss, came to bicycle with us in the area south of Bath near Popham Beach and later in the Boothbay Harbor area. Diane's best friend from childhood, Donna Lawson, and her husband,

Diane, Alf and Ann Brandin and myself, winter 1995.

Art Wolff, came and stayed over Thanksgiving. Ann and Alf Brandin flew in from California for a few days' visit in February. Our neighbors and close friends in Lexington, David and Nancy Kocher, came whenever they could. Our children and their friends came for varying lengths of time, as did my brothers and their companions. Everyone brought food and cooked dinners in the warm atmosphere of the kitchen. The farmhouse always seemed full.

Bits and pieces of farmhouse furnishings kept arriving while Diane worked on a final punch-list for Joe Caputo. A large country dining table from an antique shop. The woodstove for the living room. A washing machine and dryer. My mother's old Howard upright piano on loan from Jon after he and I, Ben, Ted and one of Jon's sons loaded and transported it from Portland. Files, printers, computers and a fax machine for the *Maine Lawyers Review* office upstairs in the old stable. A giant television set and a satellite dish. A sleep-sofa which Regie coerced Crate & Barrel to produce from its Portland warehouse and load into our trailer late at night the day before Thanksgiving because we needed it to sleep guests.

At Thanksgiving we and Bob and Reg hosted thirty friends and relatives to feast on two turkeys at two tables in the spacious dining area we'd planned for the use of our co-housing companions. There was enough food to feed twice that many. All the bedrooms and sleeping lofts were full, as were spare rooms in relatives' homes and a couple of B&Bs in Bath.

Our upriver neighbors, who farmed and operated a farmstand in Bath, brought bushel baskets of vegetables for us and came down with a tractor to plow a section of field that we would plant for a cutting garden full of flowers. Bob dug and prepared raised beds where we would grow vegetables in an area that caught both morning and afternoon sun. Regie planted yellow raspberries. Bob and I planted a grove of dwarf apple trees and surrounded their tiny trunks with wire mesh to prevent their bark from being eaten by field mice.

Deer wandered into and through our fields, sometimes four or more at a time. A large porcupine lumbered at a good pace across the field from one wood to the other, looking like a small bear. Bob encountered an actual small black bear early one morning. The bear was more astonished than Bob and disappeared into the woods in a flash. Eagles soared and hunted over the farm and over the river. Turkey vultures came looking for carrion. Family groups of turkeys, old toms, young toms, hens and the current year's brood, sometimes as many as twenty all told, marched by in single file picking up food along the way, some of it seed spilled from our bird feeders.

A rare bluebird managed to find its way through a small opening into a screened porch upstairs in the stable. Diane and I found it, frightened and trying to escape. It cowered against a low corner of the screen as I managed to cup it gently in my hands, then carry it to an open window and set it free. Diane was thrilled and happy that we'd been able to save it, and, as we were walking away, gave a little bounce into the air the way she had done when we'd first known each other, and hugged me for it after we watched the bluebird fly away.

We saw a red fox methodically hunting, crisscrossing the fields and occasionally leaping up in the air and landing on its tiny prey – mostly field mice – pinning them under its paws. Foxes appeared often during the fall and the winter. On one occasion a pair of them made their way quickly upriver on the ice just beyond our riverbanks. Motionless, we watched them, one a red fox with a gloriously bushy tail, the other gray with spotty fur, probably suffering from the mange but keeping up with her consort on the snow-covered ice. They passed within twenty feet of us.

Our two families celebrated Christmas under a tall blue spruce in the communal living room. Regie cooked a goose with all the trimmings for dinner on Christmas Eve. My brothers came to celebrate Christmas and one brought lobster for Christmas dinner. Work began on the newspaper the next day while Ted drove a round trip with Diane to Lahey for chemotherapy.

Five weeks later Diane gleefully planned a surprise birthday party for Regie during which she would discover a large box sitting in the middle of the living room. When she lifted it up, Regie found her son, Burt, who'd flown in secretly from California. Everything worked to perfection.

In fact, the Hardscrabble Farm enterprise was working just as Diane had envisioned it, but that vision hadn't included the future we now contemplated, nor other family crises for which Diane was indispensable.

In January, we flew to California for a week because Diane's mother was moving out of the home where she'd lived for thirty years and into the guest room in Noreen and Carl's house an hour away. Diane knew that giving up her home and disposing of most of the belongings she'd accumulated over more than fifty years would be very difficult, and that Meryl needed her. Patiently, quietly and competently, Diane organized the move and supervised the rest of us as we emptied the contents of the house into a U-Haul trailer and drove it to a storage facility to be unloaded again. Diane's energy flagged in the process, but whenever anyone expressed concern, she brushed it aside.

We stayed with Carl and Noreen at the base of foothills on the outskirts of Palmdale with snow-capped mountains rising in the distance. We took long walks where the foothills begin to rise while Diane fretted out loud about the transition and Meryl's acceptance – after seventy years of independence – of the idea of living as a guest in her daughter's home. She had no doubt it was the right thing to do – she had, in fact, proposed it to both Meryl and Noreen, and had helped plan it – but she knew this would be the last thing she could do for her mother, and she hoped it would be right for her.

For all her years in California, Meryl had remained a flinty, independent midwesterner and rarely showed her emotions. Much of the same was true of Diane. Even so, when we prepared to drive back to the Los Angeles airport at the end of the visit, it was difficult for the two of them to say goodbye.

We had a great deal of snow on the ground in Woolwich that winter. Diane and I skied cross-country along a track that paralleled the river. Another track went up into wooded hills to an old town road abandoned sixty years before, but still open enough for skiing. The road, which had once been the main road through the area, took a sharp left-hand turn to head further into the hills and across the remains of a stone bridge over a stream. There was deep snow along the track that led to the old stone bridge, and even though I was breaking trail slowly, Diane was exhausted by the time we made our way back and down through our own woods road to our fields and across to the farmhouse. We would not ski that way again.

It was a cold winter. Diane herself was cold, colder than the weather warranted. We kept the woodstove going most of the day as she read or worked on the newspaper seated in the Eames chair drawn close to its warmth. Occasionally when Bob (or Ben, who was there helping out on the paper and usually cooking dinner) needed her, she would venture upstairs to the office to help resolve questions concerning the current issue of *Maine Lawyers Review*. Otherwise she was quiet and she read, just as she'd always loved to do, from the time she had first learned to read more than fifty years earlier, in a time and place very different from where she found herself now.

It was important to her that she finish the endowed funds project, but she wasn't quite able to do so. Toward the end of February, I drove Diane to Bowdoin so she could meet with Kent Chabotar and his staff to go over the work she'd done on the project over the past two and a half years, and to discuss how best to use her work in the future.

At their midwinter meetings in February, 1995, Bowdoin's governing boards formally adopted and issued a citation of the sort reserved for honorary degree recipients:

Diane Theis Lund

As an Overseer of Bowdoin College, your thoughtful consideration of complex issues and your willingness to take on projects that required not only clear thought and insight, but also great diligence and hard work, have been hallmarks of your dedicated and selfless service. President Edwards stated it well when he described you as "an invaluable source of reason and strength."

You have demonstrated generosity and support for Bowdoin in many important ways, but none we believe is so close to your heart as the establishment of the Erik and Diane Lund Children's Center Support Fund. You have marked your career with commitment to concerns of the family and rights of the child; your support of the Center affirms that commitment and makes a tremendous contribution to the quality of life for families in the Bowdoin community.

Your involvement as a member and chair of the Audit Committee has also been enormously important. Your systematic evaluation of Bowdoin's charitable gifts, grants and endowments has been an essential project; in involving yourself in this way, you have provided new order and confidence to the effective use of our resources. Your work has added a new term, "the Lund language," to our vocabularies. Your continued efforts to assist the accounting office in other ways are much valued.

As an Overseer of the College, you brought a unique perspective to the governing boards. Your experience as an attorney and as an educator, your advocacy to assure equal opportunities for women, your efforts on behalf of children and working families, and your involvement in broad issues within the legal profession are just a few of the ways in which your participation enriched our discussions and influenced our decisions.

Your service and dedication to Bowdoin are deeply appreciated. Your ideas and guidance have helped us to make a better college.

On behalf of the Governing Boards of Bowdoin College,

Paul P. Brountas   Marvin H. Green, Jr.
Chair, the President and Trustees   President, Overseers

Kent Chabotar delivered the citation personally, framed and featuring a photograph of a Children's Center staff member reading to three young children, to our new home on the Kennebec River, twenty-five minutes' drive from Bowdoin College.

The newspaper's largest issue ever – thirty-six pages – came out in mid-March, thanks to the work of its entire staff at the farm. Mud season came as the earth thawed at the end of March. Then April came, and with it the flocks of migrating birds returning to their summer quarters, most of which were far north of us. Some stayed, the bob-o-links, the brown-headed cowbirds, the robins, red-winged blackbirds, killdeer, doves, sparrows and chickadees. An occasional cardinal pair and the colorful evening grosbeaks and rufous-sided towhees soon moved on. Canada geese wheeled up the river in flocks, sounding like hounds baying on the hunt. As the ice in the river receded, bald eagles, turkey vultures and ospreys reappeared in the trees lining the riverbank, on the lookout for fish in the river.

Time passes more and more quickly as one grows older, and doubtless time passed quickly for us during our six months living on the farm in Woolwich, but in retrospect my memories of that time are not of days rushing to the end of Diane's life, but of days filled with life and its natural cycles, with enjoyment of each other and of the people we loved. My memory is of a *long* time. I have forgotten – blacked it out, probably – all the days we spent driving back and forth to Lexington for Diane's chemotherapy at Lahey, and the fact that Diane was limited to a diet of Ensure – cans to be purchased at the Bath CVS – from mid-January on. I remember this time as one in which Diane was content – and I think she was – even with increasing weariness and pain.

Despite wishes, despite the pleasure of enjoying and participating in life's natural cycles, despite our love, our time together was coming to an end.

In the first week of April, Diane was hospitalized at Lahey for two weeks. Other than controlling the pain there was nothing more they could do for her. They recommended that she stay there, but she wanted to return to the farm, and that was the decision we made. I arranged for hospice care in our home and for the rental of a big-wheeled wheelchair in which Diane could spend time enjoying the outdoors. Diane discharged herself from Lahey. Bundled in blankets in the reclined front seat of our car, with a prescribed supply of morphine and instructions on how much to use, we drove north to our home in mid-April.

Diane's sister and her husband arrived soon after. We took a few short walks outside, Diane's wheelchair bumping along over the uneven ground. We took turns wheeling it. Pictures were taken and then Noreen and Carl, crying, had to return to California. Bob and Regie were there for the duration. Family and friends began to gather and spend time with Diane. Whenever she had visitors, she rallied to stay awake and smile at them in appreciation for their coming. A wonderful hospice nurse came to help us, first only during the day and then ... when she judged her help was needed ... for two days of twenty-four-hour shifts.

On May 13, 1995, Diane died in her own home, where she had wanted to be.

When a memorial service was held in Lexington's modest Follen (Unitarian) Church, the outpouring of affection, love, sympathy and grief from people whose lives Diane had touched, so many lives in her lifetime, was extraordinary. Every pew was filled, and people stood crowded in the open area behind the pews. Ted managed to speak. I could not, but the minister, Louise Curtis, read what I wanted to say about the woman I loved.

For Diane

Diane was my love and my guiding light,
She was my guardian angel, my conscience, my wife, my best friend,
But she was never mine alone.

I shared her with many people, with many of you,
She knew when people needed her,
And she always responded to that need,
To our family, to her extended family that included so many of you,
To her students and her associates in everything she did.
She reached out to all of you and touched you all
In ways that made you love her,
Even as I loved her.

I could not begin to tell you the joy she brought to my life,
The things we did together that I never would have done alone,
Even in this last year, this last, wonderful year,
We were still building for the future.
She was full of plans and projects
She never gave up.

Whatever happens, she said, we are going to have fun – and we did.
We planted daffodils and we saw them spring up,
We watched the seasons pass, and celebrated them,
She never felt sorry for herself or angry at what was happening.
Sometimes, in sadness, she cried, and we cried with her,
But her concern in this year, as in all other years, was for others, not herself.

We were blessed with the chance to talk to each other
About things that, sadly, are often left unsaid,
And we did.
Diane died at home, at peace, surrounded by people who loved her
And who have cried for her and for ourselves.

I have been, and I am, the most fortunate of men.

Diane Theis Lund, 1938-1995

EPILOGUE

I have ended this biography of Diane as I began it, on a very personal note – and that is appropriate. Diane, however, would have said that there are lessons to be learned from her life, and the times in which she lived it, and these lessons should not be lost.

MANY DOORS WERE CLOSED TO WOMEN, EDUCATIONALLY, vocationally, academically and professionally when Diane received her degree from Harvard Law School in 1961. She and other women like her caused those doors to be opened. Diane played her role in this evolution in women's opportunities professionally and without fanfare, conscious always of the significance for women of what she was doing, and how she was doing it; hence the title of this work.

No one would question today the enormous impact the events described in this book have had for women, particularly equal educational opportunities and opening the trades to women. In the case of white-collar workers, however, core questions remain concerning the real value of this evolution because the evolution of women's roles has been accompanied by a pernicious evolution in the workplace – the 24/7 syndrome.

When Diane entered the legal profession, the expectation of Boston law firms was that their associates normally would bill between 1350 to 1450 hours to clients in the course of a year and that they and their families would have a life. We chose to practice law in Boston because of that expectation, even though it meant we'd earn less money than our peers who chose to work in New York or in Washington, where the seeds of the 24/7 model were already sprouting. It was a rational choice. Now that New York and Washington have become the norm, there has been a sea change in the way the legal profession is practiced, and those who decide to enter it no longer have that rational choice. The legal profession has become a business, not a profession.

Efficiency, productivity and greed have become the hallmarks of the generation of lawyers who control the work of their profession, just as is the case with executives who manage business corporations. Rainmaking lawyers are intent on making as much money as the principals of their corporate clients. In order to succeed in their ambitions, rainmakers began to work their associates far harder and for far longer hours. At the same time, their corporate clients, far from acceding to equality in wealth with their lawyers, have driven down the cost of legal work so that they are paying much less in real dollars today than they were for the same work product fifty years ago. The emphasis on and drive for cost-efficiency has driven down law firm margins and caused the rainmakers, in response, to work their associates even more hours, and to raise their hourly rates for that work to absurd levels.

This is not a humanistic, rational world.

Boston's leading law firms have abandoned the independence of which they were once proud, and have morphed into national law firms. An employed associate in those law firms can expect demands of 2400 hours billable to clients annually, or more. The demand for more and more billable hours has not been rejected by young male lawyers but has rather – for inexplicable reasons – been embraced. By god, if he can do that, I can do that! If he can do 2400 hours, I can do more! As they have matured in the profession and assumed positions of power, they have made the same demands of the associates who succeeded them. And so it goes. The cycle has been perpetuated.

What of women in this upheaval? Women first came in the newly opened doors saying – for good reason – we are as good as men and can do everything men can do. Then those who intended to have a life that included husband and children discovered that the opportunities which had been opened to them did not match the other aspects of their needs. Flex-time in the context of the new reality became essentially meaningless. Men were trapped because they were unwilling – or unable – to oppose the reality of inhumane expectations and working conditions that deprived them of a life outside their law firms. Women were trapped because they were in competition with the men.

As women have moved into the legal and corporate fields, areas which previously were fully occupied by men, no one has yet solved the problem of how women's important contributions to public, corporate and professional life can be achieved if they wish at the same time to have a family life with children. If men's career paths are taken as a model, women following those same career paths slip down the ladder of success unless they are single and without children. They have the capacity to do both roles, but our society hasn't succeeded in enabling them to accomplish both at the same time. If public and professional success for women depends on their being single and without children, then society is not receiving from women a very important aspect of what they have to offer.

In the commercial law world of private practice, women who have or want to have families are streaming away from the law firms. Private practice in the big firms presents an overwhelmingly bad situation for women, and the impact on them will continue to fall disparately, compared to men, so long as they are the principal caregiver and parent in a family. Women's lives are different; they have been socialized differently. If they are competing in the professional world and also have children, they feel universally that they are doing both jobs badly. Part-time work is not working: women are not gaining partnerships.

While the 24/7 syndrome can be viewed as something which has been imposed by people in power on those not in power as a means of generating greater wealth for themselves, the syndrome can also be viewed as a male defense mechanism to combat the intrusion of women into previously all-male fields. Because women who have or want children are torn, they will drop out of the competition, leaving the field to males and to women who are single and childless and intend to remain so. The behavior is not unlike the biological behavior of other species where one species develops new defenses against competing species – and it recalls the observation made by many women in interviews for this book, that they feel as if they are viewed as a different species.

These are issues which should be addressed by the profession as a whole, not just by women. Interestingly, women may be in a key position to force the profession to address these issues, at least as they pertain to women. As many able women lawyers have left the mega-firm track and turned to the less time-intensive in-house corporate practice with clients of the mega-firms, talented women are rising to the position of general counsel and other positions of power within these corporate clients. As they gain greater authority, they wield, and will come to wield, unique power with the mega-law firms because they are in a position to control the choice of law firms to handle their corporate legal affairs. As they become the objects of "beauty-contest" blandishments from the firms seeking their business, they can make it plain that the beauty contests are not to be all-male, that they intend to work with women in positions of authority within the firms and that they expect the firms to be family-friendly.

Perhaps they can alter the culture of law firms and force them to reevaluate the importance of women in maintaining the firms' practice. Otherwise an alternative that law firms might have to confront is that in-house corporate law groups will expand and corporate clients will make less use of outside counsel.

Law firms that have recognized the importance of retaining talented women lawyers who are willing to accept less compensation in exchange for a lesser burden have created the "income partner" category, a designation for lawyers who the firms wish to retain but are unwilling to accept as equity partners having a say in the governance and profit distributions of the firm. No good reason exists why a talented lawyer who is important to the firm's attracting and retaining clients should not also have a say in the firm's governance. It is a matter of leverage and negotiation. Women coming into positions of corporate power can exert that leverage from outside the firm and give women within it the power to negotiate satisfactory terms for their continuing in private practice.

So what was achieved by Diane and other women like her? They have enabled women to enjoy equal opportunities to compete with men vocationally, academically and professionally, even in the realm of athletics. Although with few exceptions women do not compete directly with men in sports because of men's greater size and strength, the requirement of equal expenditures for women's sports as for men's sports in public and private institutions has spawned an entire generation of women sports heroes as role models for others. Much as sport has opened the door for men who faced discrimination for other reasons in other fields, so has it opened the door for women.

Removing the barriers to equal consideration and equal opportunity for women was not a task easily achieved, but it has been achieved, at least in principle if not fully in practice. There is nevertheless a significant risk that what women achieved in the name of equality during the 1960s, '70s and '80s – and have sought to achieve permanently for our society – is now slipping away. It's worthwhile to remember the nature of law practice fifty years ago and the societal gains achieved by women since then. Those gains could not have been achieved without women like Diane who were willing to stand up against animosity and prejudice, to be role models for others and to lobby for and implement legislation that placed women on an equal footing with men.

Diane believed in a cooperative society, one that would define its goals and work together to achieve those goals. Professional competence, equality in education, concern for others, willingness to serve society's needs and the ability to lead a balanced life were key to her philosophy and the way she lived her life. If she were to look at how our culture has developed, she would be dismayed, and she would say to women everywhere that they should evaluate those developments and should pattern their own lives, not on the expectations of an oppressive society, but on the reasonable expectations women have for the lives they and their families should lead.

APPENDIX

BOWDOIN'S
FINANCIAL PROBLEMS

W HEN KENT CHABOTAR BECAME BOWDOIN'S CHIEF
Financial Officer in late 1991, the chaotic state of Bowdoin's finances was, as he later described it, "almost Kafka-esque."* There were essentially no financial controls in place, no financial systems. The college's in-house accountants, housed in the basement of the administration building, were number-crunchers, not financial people. Expenditures of income from the endowed funds weren't subject to centralized institutional control. Funds allocated to certain departments were being expended by those departments with no oversight. A crazy quilt of little financial fiefdoms had sprung up throughout the college. A few of those fiefdoms even existed within the college's governing boards, some of whose members believed – incorrectly – that their role was not limited to policy decisions and that they could and should make operational decisions concerning the expenditures of certain of the funds. There had been no effort to exert administrative institutional control over the expenditure of income from the endowed funds, and many of the expenditures bore little relationship either to the defined needs of the college or to the donors' intentions.

Bob Edwards's predecessor as Bowdoin's president, Roy Greason, had come into office in 1981 having to confront severe problems of a different kind. *His* predecessor, who'd been an amazingly unfortunate choice for the college, had succeeded in his brief tenure in severely alienating both the faculty and the alumni. Both mistrusted the administration, and one significant result was that alumni giving was down,

---

* Kent Chabotar interview, December 14, 2005.

273

dramatically. Roy Greason's overriding mission was to rebuild trust and confidence in an administration which, as President, he now personified.

Greason, a highly respected icon of the college who'd taught in its English Department for thirty years, was admirably equipped to step in and remedy the situation. He was trusted by both faculty and alumni, and it is no exaggeration to say that he and his wife Polly were beloved. He succeeded in bringing the alumni back into the fold and enthusiastically behind the college again – no small achievement. Faculty morale was high. Another significant achievement during the nine years of his tenure was that the college successfully completed a major-gifts capital campaign. The standing of the administration, just prior to Edwards's succession, was at its highest point in nearly forty years.

The college's financial affairs were another matter entirely. As he had had little day-to-day financial experience in his academic career, Greason relied on the college's treasurer and its auditors to see to it that the college followed a sound fiscal policy and that its financial statements fairly reflected the results of its operations. Unfortunately, he was misled by both.

The college's treasurer was likeable and persuasive in the presentations and explanations he gave to the governing boards and to the president – and companionable afterwards – but he wasn't well-equipped to deal with the complexities of the financial side of the college. His administration was fifty years behind the curve in contemporary college financial administration and he had no real understanding of modern financial analysis and controls. In fact, for all practical purposes, there were no modern financial controls in place at Bowdoin during his tenure.* He should have been replaced early on as annual operating deficits were mounting, but neither he nor the auditors flagged the seriousness of the situation or its causes to the administration or to the governing boards' audit committee when it met to consider the college's financial statements.

When the connection was made at audit committee meetings between the college's spending formula and the fact that excess use of appreciation in the college's investment portfolio would reduce the amount of the college's invested funds, inquiry was deflected by the treasurer's recitation of statistics and facially plausible explanations, e.g.:

> The Administration responded by highlighting components of the $1,431,000 shortfall…. $367,000 represents transfer of income to principal in keeping with the terms of the funds. $609,000 represents income added to principal due to the inability of the College to expend the income within the terms of the funds. The balance, $455,000, represents the difference between current year's yield and actual dollars spent. It was noted, however, that since the College

---

*   John Snow interview, January 20, 2006.

has adopted the Total Return Policy, use of appreciation to cover this type of shortfall is appropriate.*

Audit committee members had little information or experience on which to question the treasurer's explanations. That was the auditor's job. Even the full amount of the deficits weren't fairly disclosed, either to the audit committee or by the college's audited financial statements because of what was said to be "appropriate use" of endowment to cover the shortfalls.

Coopers & Lybrand were represented by a partner in its Boston office who was a Bowdoin alumnus. In approving the college's financial statements through its audit, Coopers glossed over the problems, which the financial statements themselves didn't disclose. Instead it issued so-called "management letters" which went to the treasurer's office and which, on close reading, were devastating and hair-raising. Given their contents, the auditing procedures Coopers followed in opining that the college's books had been prepared in accordance with GAAP (Generally Accepted Accounting Principles) and audited in accordance with GAAS (Generally Accepted Auditing Standards) were severely deficient. The issues should have been disclosed in the financial statements themselves, but they weren't.

The theory behind this conduct may have been that if the statements had shown the true state of the college's financial picture, Bowdoin would quickly have lost its high place in the national small-college firmament. The treasurer and Coopers & Lybrand evidently took it as their task to protect the college's standing, and so the full picture was concealed except for dire warnings in the management letters, warnings which went only to the treasurer and weren't reflected in the statements themselves or in any administration letters to the governing boards.†

It can be argued that the governing boards' audit committee, which consisted of trustees and overseers generally sophisticated in financial matters, should have become aware of the issues at an earlier date than they did, had they taken their fiduciary responsibilities seriously enough. They relied heavily, however, on the information and explanations provided by the treasurer's office and the auditors, and expected critical issues to be brought to their attention. This wasn't done. The committee was told, year after year when they were asked to vote to make up the deficit from the endowment, that although there were problems, the problems weren't unusual and were being solved – and *this* year would be the very last year.‡ It's also probably true that for some time they accepted what they were told uncritically and without the scrutiny they would

---

* December 14, 1988, audit committee minutes.
† Kent Chabotar interview, December 14, 2005.
‡ However at least one committee member, a former bank president, was concerned that the trustees and overseers were not fulfilling their fiduciary responsibilities. At the conclusion of his term, he did not seek to remain on the governing boards. (John Snow interview, January 20, 2006.)

have employed in similar circumstances in their own businesses and professions.

Bowdoin's financial difficulties began to become more apparent in 1989 and 1990. Six months after the close of the fiscal year in June 1989, the governing boards' audit committee was advised that the financial statements for fiscal 1989 were "not yet satisfactorily completed" and that there had been a shortfall covered by transfers from endowment.* In February 1990, after questions raised concerning those transfers weren't answered to the satisfaction of its members, the committee met in executive session to review the history of the Bowdoin/Coopers relationship.† The audit committee had become disenchanted with Coopers and at its meeting of May 25, 1990 decided "that the College's audit service ought to go out to bid, that Coopers should not be invited to participate [and that the College's attorney] should be consulted prior to informing Coopers about the termination of the relationship." (Memo summarizing events of the meeting.) Formal minutes of this meeting were not prepared "due to the sensitive nature of the discussion which took place."

Interestingly, Coopers was nevertheless able to retain the Bowdoin account by transferring the contract to its Portland office and transferring responsibility for the account to two new partners there.

---

* October 16, 1989, audit committee meeting minutes.
† Audit committee minutes, February 16,1990.

ACKNOWLEDGEMENTS

THIS BOOK HAS BEEN A LONG TIME IN THE MAKING. WHEN I first decided to write it, I didn't have any idea how long, but the more I learned about those parts of Diane's life of which I had not been a part, the more I wanted to know. I felt I wanted to speak to everyone who had known her well, from childhood on, so I wouldn't miss anything. And I wanted everyone to know what an extraordinary person she was.

My family, and especially my wife Sandy and my children, Ben, Ted and Kristin, have been patient and supportive throughout, and have offered helpful comments. Diane's family, and especially her sister Noreen Hunter, her cousin Valerie Sampson and her aunt Aldah Meyers, have contributed a great deal to this book, both by way of anecdotes and through commentary. Her closest friend, Regie Healy, and Regie's husband Bob Sloane, have assisted what I have written and critiqued it at numerous times. This book could not have been written without their support. Donna Wolff, Diane's friend since kindergarten, was essential to the process. At crunch time, when the book needed to be closed, final-edited and designed for publication, Genie Dailey, Susan Bourdon, Ann Abbott, Ruth Koury and Anne Meagher, my secretary/assistant of forty-five years, made it happen.

I was encouraged in this effort by every person I contacted, and every one of them willingly spent time with me and made clear to me what an enormous well of affection Diane had generated throughout her life. Others worked with me in the process of producing this book, and likewise encouraged me to do it. To talk about each one would take a great deal of space, and I'm not going to do that, but I want to list them and to acknowledge my gratitude for the time they spent with me in correspondence and conversation. They are: Alice Ballard, Elizabeth Bartholet, Rosalyne Bernstein, Hon. Margot Botsford, Ann and Alf Brandin, the late Clark Byse, Paul Brountas, Kent Chabotar, Hon. Cynthia Cohen, Norman Cohen, Dan Coquilette, Ann Colette, Betty Jo Davies, Joan Dolan, Hon. Raya Dreben, Hon. Fernande Duffly, Hon. Michael Dukakis, Zona Fairbanks, Michael Feldman, Larry Field, John Fiske, Hon. Edward Ginsberg, Mary Ann Glendon, Roy Greason, Elise Heinz, Louise Hornbeck Renne, Adria Goodkin Kaplan, Julia Kauffman, Ray Kenney, Charlotte Kaup Kleeman, David and Nancy Kocher, Rosalind Lazarus, Susan Lennox, Sue Borshell Leonard, Phil and Marcia Lieberman, Viola Berry Lund, Virginia Marx, Frank Michelman, Dick and Cindy Morehead, Elaine Morton, Jack Nessel, John and Barbara Quarles, Helen Rees, Bill Robinson, Allan Rodgers, Hon. Patti Saris, John Snow, Steve Subrin, Alice and Barry Swanson, Bill Torrey, Bill Tunney, Gretchen Vannice Tyler, Peter Webster, Hon. James Wexler, Peg Willey, and Mel Zarr.

If I have missed someone – and I hope I have not – the omission was not intentional. This has been an amazing experience for me, one I would not have missed, because of all the friendships I was able to renew and all the new ones I formed.

Thank you all.

Erik Lund
January 30, 2009